Long Cloud Ride

Also by Josie Dew

THE WIND IN MY WHEELS
Travel Tales from the Saddle

TRAVELS IN A STRANGE STATE
Cycling Across the USA

A RIDE IN THE NEON SUN
A Gaijin in Japan

THE SUN IN MY EYES
Two-Wheeling East

SLOW COAST HOME
A 5,000 Mile Cycle Journey Around the Shores of
England and Wales

SADDLED AT SEA
A 15,000-mile Journey to New Zealand by Russian Freighter

Long Cloud Ride

A Cycling Adventure
Across New Zealand

JOSIE DEW

Maps and drawings by Melanie Dew

sphere

SPHERE

First published in Great Britain in 2007 by Sphere

A CIP catalogue record for this book
is available from the British Library.

ISBN 978-1-84744-014-3

Typeset in Baskerville by M Rules
Printed and bound in Great Britain by
Clays Ltd, St Ives plc

Sphere
An imprint of
Little, Brown Book Group
Brettenham House
Lancaster Place
London WC2E 7EN

A Member of the Hachette Livre Group of Companies

www.littlebrown.co.uk
www.josiedew.co.uk

For Molly and Gary

Contents

Acknowledgements   ix
Maps   x

1   Auckland, 24 December 2003   1
2   Near Amodeo Bay, Coromandel Peninsula,
    31 December   11
3   Omokoroa, Bay of Plenty, 15 January   44
4   Te Kaha, Eastland, 25 January   63
5   Wairoa, Hawke's Bay, 4 February   81
6   Dannevirke, 12 February   94
7   Picton, Marlborough, South Island, 20 February   111
8   Kaikoura, Canterbury, 23 February   127
9   Moana, Lake Brunner, West Coast, 3 March   146
10 Lake Pearson, Selwyn, Canterbury, 6 March   156
11 Wanaka, Otago, 1 April   187
12 Timaru, South Canterbury, 20 April   200
13 Blenheim, Marlborough, 6 May   207
14 Wellington, North Island, 16 May   214
15 Parakai, Auckland North, 15 June   232
16 Rotorua, 7 August   281

Appendix: Equipment Department   333

Acknowledgements

Very special thanks to:

Mum and Dad, Gary Appleton, Melanie Dew, Beverley Bannister
Barbara Daniel, Simon Sheffield, Viv Redman and Sheena-Margot
    Lavelle at Little, Brown
Val Porter
Hilary Foakes
Mary and Barry Edwards
Stuart Webb
Jacquie Handley
Roberts Cycles: Chas, Andrew, Brian
The North Face: Éadaoin Hutchinson, Keith Byrne, Helen
    Samson, Tanya Bascombe
Lyon Equipment Ltd: Frank Bennett
Peglers: Dave Pegler
Owen Cycles: Owen, Jon, Phil
London Cycling Campaign: Rebecca Lack
Sam and Brian at Xynergy

1

Auckland, 24 December 2003

The minute I arrived it was time to leave – leave the ex-Russian ice-breaking cargo ship that over the past two months had transported me, not without incident, 15,000 miles across the boundless slosh of the Atlantic and Pacific to New Zealand, Land of the Long White Cloud. Only it didn't look so white at that moment. More a universal greyness of unpromisingly dank proportions. Well, I ask you! What a welcome to Christmas Eve and the height of midsummer (they're a bit mixed up with their festive dates and seasons, these Kiwis), with rain so heavy it would qualify for biblical matter. In fact, in light of the inclement weather it seemed prudent to stay where I was upon my ark rather than run the risk of drowning on land. Too bad if I had spent the last 55 days concerning myself with the very real prospect of sinking into the slop of the sea only to capsize in my tent on terra firma.

Donning full wet-weather battledress I shouldered my bike to descend the slippery and unstable gangway that swayed at a jaunty angle down the monumental side of the ship's hull. Once feet and wheels had introduced themselves to the forgotten sensation of stability proffered by the dockside, I flipped my bike up on to its double-legged stand and scuttled up and down the gangway several times in the hammering rain to retrieve a multiple of stuffed panniers from the poop deck. With all possessions accounted for, I formed them into a heap to the lee of a well-dented HAMBURG SUD container and took stock. Here I was plonked in the middle of Auckland, a scarily large-looking city of sky-scraping monoliths butting up against Waitemata Harbour – rank upon rank standing to attention as they rose up before me into the ominous murk.

It was early morning rush-hour and somehow I had to find my way among the swirl of scurrying streets. Navigating an escape route out of an alien city on two heavily laden wheels is daunting at the best of times but felt doubly so now, having just spent such a raft of days incarcerated at sea away from the bustling hustle of normal life.

Before I could launch myself into the throes of the throng I would have to fight my way across the hazardous battleground of the port, its vast expanse a busy blurry mayhem of dock-cranes, thundering cargo-carrying trucks and dementedly bleeping and flashing forklifts and straddle-carriers darting all over the place while either clutching or seeking their prey of much voyaged shipping containers. As these containers looked certain to turn any ill-positioned cyclist into pulp at the slightest provocation, I felt no immediate urgency to make an agitated mercy dash for the exit gate. Not that I knew where the exit gate was, mind you.

'It's way over there, mate,' said a matey chap who happened upon me from behind a cliff face of containers. 'But don't think about getting there under your own steam – it's too easy to get crushed in a place like this! And port authority doesn't allow it. Wait here and you'll be right, mate. A van will turn up to take you and your gear to the gate.'

Kevin Cooper was a project manager for Titan Marine Engineering Ltd and a self-confessed outdoor nut. 'Like most of us Kiwis, I guess,' he said, wiping the dripping rain from his fit, suntanned face. He had admitted to this alfresco addiction when espying my bike and mound of panniers and learning that I was planning on spending several months cycling around his homeland. 'Awesome!' he said. 'You'll have a *fin-tis-tic* time!' And with that he handed me his card, telling me to ring if I needed any help.

*

Before long I was dumped at the port gate, where I set about hooking and strapping and bungeeing a bewildering heap of bags on to my bike. Although I was burdened with exactly the same amount of luggage as I'd had when cycling to my ship rendezvous point all those blue moons and numerous seas ago, it had somehow expanded tenfold. I believe this is a phenomenon known in physicist circles as The Sod's Law of Voluminous Mass of Weighty Density Gone Round the Bend Bonkers. Also known as BABE (Blinking Automated Bag Extension) for short. Either way, I found myself struggling to house my mountain of kit in anything resembling a conveyable fashion.

Half a day later I had my bursting charges under some sort of control and wheeled my steed out on to Quay Street, where I prepared my unseasoned legs to mount up. Quay Street sounds like it should be a small, dainty and narrow cobbled byway lined with topsy-turvy olde worlde houses on one side where smugglers had once secreted their illicit contraband in intricate underground passages, and quaint brightly coloured tubby-girthed fishing vessels tethered to an ancient stone-walled harbour front on the other. Instead it's a big fast thoroughfare officially termed Main Urban Route 6 which, if followed in either direction, will filter you on to the truck-stonking State Highway 1 – a low-numbered but high-ranking swathe of tarmac that stretches the length of North Island: 1,098 kilometres (682 miles) from Cape Reinga in the north to Wellington in the south.

Luckily, tackling this stately highway on my wheels could wait. And a good thing too: wobbling around on my feet fresh off a lurching boat meant that I was in no fine shape to do battle with 50-tonne logging trucks. The wobbliness didn't last for long though as I swiftly substituted my sea legs with my cycling legs, bypassing the more unstable land legs (cycling, it seems, is the perfect antidote for ocean-swaying unsteadiness). I then spun myself the short distance down Quay Street to the big ninety-one-year-old neoclassical Ferry Building that, among all the foresting tower blocks of silvery glass and steel, sat solidly squat on the city's waterfront like a friendly fat red toad.

*

As I was in search of an address in a district called Bayswater I took off across the harbour (lovely view!) on board a passenger ferry to Devonport. Devonport is one of Auckland's oldest suburbs, a good 160 years old, which for a relatively new land like New Zealand is saying something.

It was still raining cats and kiwis as I wheeled my bike down the pier and along the waterfront. Everything was looking very Christmassy (glittery decorations wrapped around street lamps; piped carols emanating from shop doorways across the road, including an overload of *Jingle Bells*, or *Jungle Bills* as it seemed to mutate into in the Kiwi accent) though I couldn't for the life of me think why. Oh, yes. It was Christmas tomorrow. How could I possibly forget? Quite easily actually. Spending weeks crossing the Pacific encompassed by a blinding blue in sweltering temperatures on board a Russian tub does not a festive gander make.

Devonport looked decidedly affluent, beset with art galleries and craft shops and stylish cafes and costly looking boutiques all humming with the business of what I guessed to be a panicky last-minute Christmas shopping variety. I took off in a northerly direction up a main street lined on either side with quite fetching Victorian-type buildings. Quite colourful too. At the top of this road I was greeted by a rude shock in the form of a short sharp hill. Normally, my calf and thigh muscles rallying together in unison would not bat an eyelid at the prospect of carting me up and over such an insignificant blip of an incline. But present conditions were far from normal. My legs, used to a daily 50-mile pounding on my trusty-wheeled steed, had barely lifted a finger over the past two months at sea. Thus, a meal I made of a molehill. And quite aquiver I was too by the time I had summitted.

Before long I was bowling along down a road past a fire station that warned of its presence with a triangular hazard sign containing a picture of a Trumpton-style toy town fire engine complete with roof-strapped ladder. Nearby, on the same side of the road, I spotted a Methodist church. Outside the front door reared a plastic sliding-letter notice board declaring: 'ALL FRESH

SERMONS – NO SUMMER RE-RUNS!' So that was good to know. We don't want any of those stale repeats, thanks.

The road became festooned with weird-shaped trees with tortuous trunks ablaze with spiky red flowers. These flowers emitted the most heady scent of loveliness that I had smelt for a very long time. In fact, the trees' richly fragrant bouquet lay in such stark contrast to the acrid diesel fumes I had become accustomed to on board my Russian tub that I yanked on my brakes so that I might linger a moment to take a deep breath or two about their boughs. And as I did so I heard birdsong. But this was no normal run-of-the-mill song from your normal run-of-the-mill bird. Saying that, it did look a bit like a blackbird. Only it had what appeared to be a distinctive white ruffled pompom attached to its throat, giving it the look of a prize poodle primped for a show. Its song was a liquid call, impossibly pure and fluting, interspersed with an unusual repertoire of clicks, grunts and chuckles.

Following a few wrong turns down a maze of residential streets as wide as a ship and lined with fat concrete telegraph poles, I found the address I was looking for, minus the addressee. Jacquie, a friend of my dad's (they had worked together back in the mid-eighties when I was a fledgling cyclist getting lost in far-off lands) was currently seeing to a spot of emergency car repair. 'I won't be long,' she said when I rang her on her mobile. 'Maybe half an hour at the most.'

As a sudden full-blooded rain came on to join forces with the torrential wetness that was already falling from the leaden sky, I dived for shelter into the mouth of an open garage, part of a row of identical garages, and stood with bike, dripping and steaming, watching the raindrops bounce like mini bombs off the tarmac outside. The garage looked out over a driveway and into the kitchen of the one-storey wooden house opposite. In the kitchen I saw an elderly couple looking out of their window looking at me. They both bore an expression of perplexity as to just what the devil I was doing – a stranger on the block, standing astride a mount loaded to the gunwales in a garage that had nothing to do with me.

For all I knew it could have been their garage. Though I rather hoped it wasn't. I didn't really fancy rubbing any Kiwis up the wrong way on my first day. There would be plenty of time yet for that. So to put their minds at rest that I wasn't a terrorist disguised in Gore-tex, I pointed to the sky (indicating rain) and gave them a sort of 'bloody weather!' shrug-of-shoulder smile and a cheery wave – a gesture of comradeship that only succeeded in making them appear even more worried. Oh well, I thought, there's no pleasing some people. So I decided to read the paper instead.

On the way over here I had picked up a copy of the *New Zealand Herald* (Auckland edition). Casting an eye across the headlines on the front page I was a little surprised to read: '22 HOURS UP A TREE WHILE KILLER CROCODILE LURKS BELOW'. Flipping heck! There I was, thinking I was coming to a nice safe land famed for its profusion of innocuous sheep and devoid of any form of poisoning or stinging or limb-gnawing Aussie-style nature that can kill you in seconds, when what should I discover but a possible posse of immigrant crocodiles on my doorstep. But it always pays to read beneath the surface of the headline and that was when I discovered that the killer croc's place of residence was Australia. Two teenagers and a twenty-two-year-old man had been washing mud off their quad bike in the swollen Finniss River 80 km south-west of Darwin when the man, Brett Mann, was swept away. His friends swam out to rescue him, but were beaten there by a four-metre salt-water crocodile. 'I went past the croc, I didn't see it, Ashley [did and] screamed out, "Croc, croc". We just swam to the nearest tree and straight up we went,' said one of the teenagers. A couple of minutes later the crocodile 'showed off' the dead body of Mr Mann in its jaws, before stalking the teenagers all Sunday night and Monday morning.

Fortunately New Zealand is a little tamer in this department. Another headline on the front page of the *Herald* concerned a sample of the 6,000 emails sent to the North Pole this year from what I presume, and hope, to be the younger residents of New Zealand. The paper said:

Here are extracts from Santa's favourites:

'We will leave you a glass of milk and cookies because we know you will be very busy on Christmas Eve night and most of the takeaway shops will be closed.'

'I wish for peace on Earth and goodwill to all men and to win the Powerball jackpot.'

'We have some wrapping paper over and we thought you could use it. Please can you send an elf to fetch it tonight.'

'My dad won't put a possum trap in the fire because last Christmas he did.'

When Jacquie turned up we climbed up the outside steps to her top-floor flat. Despite being only two storeys high this flat felt like being in an air traffic control tower. Because we were in the tallest building in the vicinity (most surrounding houses were squat one-storeys) we had a wide sweeping view encompassing a nip-and-tuck of Shoal Bay, a busy tract of State Highway 1 laden with traffic filtering on to and off the Harbour Bridge and the house-crammed suburbs of Northcote, Hillcrest, Birkenhead and beyond. The relatively high towers of Takapuna were also visible, as was the magnificently distinctive low conical shape of Rangitoto, the volcanic island that floated on the skyline at the upper end of Tamaki Strait. By now most of the rain had cleared, leaving a stretched sky of scrubbed pale blue across which scudded weird-shaped dollops of fast-moving clouds. The clarity of the light was astonishing. Vibrant and undiffused, it gave everything a sharp and emphatic hyper-realist presence. In the areas where it simultaneously rained and shone, the sky reflected prisms of dazzling rainbows.

Jacquie, who was plonk in the middle of her forties, lived with two cats. One was a grey fluffball called Jemma who didn't like the look of me and my clobber at all and had scarpered out of the back catflap and not been seen since. The other was a short-haired and playful tabby called Milly. Jacquie was a bit loopy when it came to cats. Along with sleeping with her real ones, there were various cat-like ornaments dotted about the flat. Framed pictures of stately felines lined the wall of her bathroom and attached to her fridge were two magnets. One was of a cat with the words: CATS LEAVE PAWPRINTS ON YOUR HEART. The other had a picture of a rotund cat sandwiched amidst the request: PLEASE GOD IF YOU CAN'T MAKE ME THIN, MAKE MY FRIENDS FAT!! I felt like taking Jacquie aside and having a quiet word with her about her feline fetish, but as I barely knew her and as she had kindly offered to put me and my mountain of bags up in her home, it was probably best to keep my mouth shut. At least for the first night.

During an exploratory cycle this afternoon, I came across a number of corner stores (run by Chinese families) known as dairies or superettes. Sounds more like the name of a sixties girl band to me. I also passed gardens that frothed with colour. Jacarandas, with their trumpet flowers, and the tall nodding heads of blue and white agapanthus sprouted from every corner. Each block was a complete mixture of houses. Some were of utilitarian ugliness, many with corrugated iron roofs, others quite attractive weatherboard constructions with verandas and trailing vines. It seemed the rich could live right next door to the not so rich. One minute, grand house, big car, neat garden. The next, a home (usually a Maori's) of peeling paint, battered car, weedy flowers waving along the edge of a yard containing a dented deflated football and a bashed-about child's bike dumped on its side.

And everywhere, birds. More of those honey-toned ruff-necked black ones that Jacquie told me were known as tuis – or, on account of their white collar, the not so mellifluous-sounding parson bird. Mynahs were forty to the dozen too. At one point I counted eight mynahs making a major racket with their range of gurgling, squawking, clicking and harsh bell-like calls. With their cunningly fearless antics and yellow eye-patch masks, they resembled cat burglars hopping furtively about the roof of a low-slung house.

Down at Bayswater marina a swag of pied shags, perching stock-still on top of a row of sea-lapping piles, resembled scarecrows as they held out their bedraggled wings to dry in the frisky wind. A pontoon, open to the public apart from in high winds when big slappy waves off Waitemata Harbour flopped across the top, curved its way around a tidy sum of boats with names like *South Pacific Sunrise, Dividend, Yehudi, Samurai, Tintagel, Dream Chaser, Random Access, Sea Runner, LadyBird, Iconoclast, Elbow Room* and *Twice As Much.* The only people on the pontoon were a huddle of well-hooded Vietnamese fishermen. We got as far as exchanging 'harrows!' but conversation went no further as none of them spoke English. There were lots of big toothy smiles, though, and holding up of landed fish. These fish were not your normal Joe Bloggs fish to those of us who dwell within the upper reaches of the globe. An information board at the entrance to the pontoon bore etched pictures of some of the various fish likely to be hauled from these waters. Fish like kingfish, butterfish, blue cod, moki and tarahiki.

*

Across the road from Jacquie's flat lay a cemetery. A path led down the hill through the cemetery and on to a boardwalk that crossed a marshy finger of Shoal Bay swamped with mangroves – the sort of place you might imagine finding killer crocs if you weren't in New Zealand. But fortunately, as I'd discovered earlier, New Zealand doesn't have any crocodiles. Just lots of possum traps. And Christmas wrapping paper surplus to requirements.

Although this pathway was popular with dog-walkers and joggers and children on bikes, the whole area was something of an ornithological madhouse busy with all sorts of birds, including herons and kingfishers fishing and flitting about their business. There were also parakeets, or *kararikis,* as the Maori call them – their word for bright green. I was more used to coming across these birds incarcerated in cages in people's front rooms mimicking the theme tune to *EastEnders.* Seeing these parrots flying free was like watching an electrical storm. The yellow, blue, green and red streaks seemed to scorch the evening sky.

On the path back to Jacquie's I was overtaken by two stick-thin lycra-encased women speedwalking, their elbows pumping like chicken wings. Shortly after this I noticed a pair of trainers, tied together by their laces, dangling from the telegraph wires on the road in front of the cemetery. I took a photograph of them for the sake of posterity. Peering through my telephoto lens, they looked very lovely silhouetted against a sky burning red from the sunset.

2

Near Amodeo Bay, Coromandel Peninsula, 31 December

Well, that's Christmas done and dusted. And a good thing too. Saying that, I had a fine feast at Jacquie's uncle's house. I didn't so much have seconds as fifths. But then I was feeling a bit half starved after two months bobbing about on the ocean wave. Not that the food on the freighter was anything to cause a rumpus about; it just wasn't up to my usual cyclist quantities. Here, though, there was a quantity of food and a profusion of tastes that were hard to say no to.

A large crowd of people in buoyant Christmas spirit gathered around the long table at Jacquie's uncle's. I tried my best to be full of festive jollity, but my heart and head felt on another planet. Have done ever since I received the news on the ship that my nephews' nineteen-year-old cousin Jonnie was killed in a car crash six days before Christmas. I can't quite take in that the happy strapping lad I hugged merely days before I left home in October is now lying in a coffin in a cold wintry graveyard. His funeral was yesterday. I spoke to Mel, my sister-in-law (though she's a lot more sister than law), who is Jonnie's aunt. She said the church was packed, mostly with Jonnie's school friends. Mum and dad and my brother Dave, Mel's husband, were there too. It was a freezing cold dark and drizzly December day. Which makes it seem even more unreal when I'm sitting in dazzling light bombarded by sweltering sunshine and busy summer birdsong.

Because of this terrible happening, I don't feel I've been

particularly good company for Jacquie. But we've still managed to have a laugh. Especially at the amount I eat. On my first day with Jacquie I was well behaved and politely ate my food off a plate with a knife and fork. By the second day I had taken over the cooking (Jacquie was more than happy about this) and was eating out of her largest pasta bowl with a spoon. Over the next few days I rapidly progressed from pasta bowl to small mixing bowl to medium mixing bowl to deep bread-making bowl. Jacquie likes to tuck into her food while watching telly (usually Corrie, as *Coronation Street* is known over here) on the sofa. As I'm more of an eating-while-reading-person I sit at the table directly behind the sofa. The moment I plonk myself down at the table with my giant mixing bowl of food, Jacquie swivels round and looks at me in a state of shock. It's always most amusing.

Last night as I was packing my panniers ready for an early getaway this morning, Jacquie, who was watching the 6 o'clock news, called me in to come quickly and watch: one of the main news items was about how touring cyclists were being targeted by motorists throwing bottles at them from passing vehicles. The latest to fall victim to this missile-hurling pastime were two Swiss cyclists. The boyfriend had a bottle thrown at him from a car travelling at speed, and fell off. Apart from being a bit shook up he was uninjured. But his girlfriend, who was also the recipient of an airborne bottle, suffered a slashed ankle and a badly broken leg. They said how they had just spent the past few months cycling 5,000 km across Europe and the USA, but by far the worst drivers in their experience were Kiwis.

Jacquie was a bit concerned for my welfare. She thought maybe I should delay my departure until well after the New Year, as drink-driving is a huge problem in New Zealand and it would only exacerbate this sport. 'There're enough maniacs on the road as it is,' she said. But I was ready and rearing to go, and when I've got my sight set on things I don't tend to like to back down. Dogged stubbornness, my mother calls it.

So at dawn this morning I rolled up my sleeping mat and compressed my sleeping bag into its stuff-sack (Jacquie had offered me a sofa bed, but I prefer sleeping on the floor). After polishing off a substantial breakfast I loaded up my steed, gave Jacquie a big hug and was off, rolling into a dazzling early morning sun.

My original plan for leaving Auckland was to cycle south out of the city through the sprawl of traffic-laden suburbs. But the more I looked at my map of mile upon mile of mangled roads, and the more I heard about the undesirable driving antics of New Zealand's motorists, the faster I went off this idea. One of the surprising things about Auckland is that, though the population stands at around the one million mark (precious few people by world city standards), in terms of area it ranks as one of the largest cities on earth – a low-rise urban sprawl, straddled by the harbours of Waitemata to the east and Manukau to the west.

With a city surrounded by so much water I decided there must be a boat that could cart me out to greener lands. So one morning last week I cycled up the short but steep twisting road to the top of North Head, one of Devonport's two volcanic cones. From here I had a view of the whole harbour with its constant flurry of boats. Across the way lay the docks and downtown Auckland, dominated by the giant hypodermic-syringe shape of the Sky Tower piercing the sky. Over in the Hauraki Gulf floated a wide assortment of green-carpeted islands. Beyond them, sketchily purple in the east, rose a range of mountains. Peering at my map, I worked out without too much trouble that these were the backbone of the Coromandel Peninsula, a fattish thumb of land that extends northwards from the Hauraki Plain. Although the mountains looked a bit worrying for the likes of my legs (two cycle-free months on board a ship was not the recommended training for tackling the undulating topography of New Zealand – a country that is 70 per cent mountain), the Coromandel looked like a perfect spot to reach by boat.

Back at Jacquie's, I asked her if she knew of a ferry service from Auckland over to the Coromandel. She didn't, but said that it would be worth asking down at the wharf. So I did. After several enquiries among the flotilla of ferry booths on the waterfront I came across Glenys, who was manning one of these booths. She told me of a passenger ferry service that operated only over Christmas and the New Year and Easter and only on sporadic days and at sporadic times. As it was New Year there was a boat running, so I handed over $40 for me, and $10 for my bike, and booked myself on the 9 a.m. Fullers *Kawau Kat* ferry on New Year's Eve.

On board the *Kawau Kat* I strapped my bike on to the back railings outside the toilets. As I did so a man in a baseball cap, aviator sunglasses, shorts and flip-flops (or 'jandals' as I overheard someone refer to them), leaning against a railing while nonchalantly dangling a bottle of beer between his fingers, looked at me and said, 'That's some shit load of gear you've got on there, mate. I'm guessing you're either going to end up fit or fucked. There're some bastard big hills over there.'

With these encouraging words ringing in my ears, I climbed up the steps to plant myself on the open top deck in the wind and the sun. The ferry's engines grumbled into action and we took off out of the harbour past islands bushed in green and a yacht called *Stamp Machine* heeling over in the wind. An American man called Hank sat down next to me. He told me he was from Jackson, Mississippi, and asked if I had ever been to America. I told him I had cycled down the west coast a couple of times and across the country. 'But I never got as far south as Mississippi.'

'Whoa!' he said. 'That's some ride. Have any problems?'

'Not really. The worst thing was riding across the Prairies in tornado season.'

'I can believe it,' he said. 'You know what we say in Mississippi? That divorces and tornadoes have one thing in common – somebody's gonna lose a trailer!'

We landed on the Coromandel at a place called Te Kouma. Te Kouma consisted of a wooden jetty. That was it. One or two of the passengers were met by friends or family and driven away in four-wheel drives. The majority were scooped up in a waiting air-conditioned bus for a day tour of the local delights. Before long I was the only one left, standing with my bike beside a couple of battered pick-ups parked up on the side. I presumed they belonged to fishermen. One had a tailgate sticker stating: FISH-ING IS FOR LIFE – THE REST IS JUST DETAIL. The other one's sticker suggested that:

IF YOU WANT TO BE HAPPY FOR:
A DAY – GET DRUNK
A WEEK – GET MARRIED
LIFE – GO FISHING

I set off bumping along a track that soon gave way to a sealed road not two cars wide. A cliff face of jungle full of exotically whooping birds reared up on one side. On the other a languorous sea flopped on to the rocks. Soon I passed a sign that said: SUGAR LOAF LANDING. But despite having a good look around, I couldn't see any sugar loaves landing. All a bit disappointing.

I had managed a good five minutes' cycle (exhausting it was too) when I came across a beach. At the near end, beneath a shady tree, sat a simple plank for a bench. A perfect spot for a picnic. I leant my bike against the plank before noticing a fat knotted rope hanging from a wide bough off a big old tree nearby. On the spur of the moment I took a running leap at the rope, swung out widely into an admirable arc before narrowly missing being knocked out cold when I was flung back at speed towards the trunk. What fun that would have been: five minutes into my tour of the Antipodes, only to kill myself by an ill-timed Tarzan-style lunge on a rope. I don't think mum would have been too impressed.

After this rush of blood to the head I decided to take things a little more calmly and sat down on the bench to eat a bag of food. Moments later a big Toyota Land Cruiser pulled up with a bumper sticker that said:

EAT RIGHT
EXERCISE
DIE ANYWAY

Two men with two small boys clambered out of the vehicle. One boy chased after a football that his dad had kicked along the beach. The other boy made straight for the swinging rope. Both men made straight for me. One said, with a rising intonation that turned his declarative sentence into a question, 'Apologies for shattering your peace, mate! Looks like you were having a cruisy time before us buggers arrived!'

The other said, 'If you don't mind me saying, that's one fuck of a load you've got on that bike.'

They asked where I was going, so I told them I was heading around the peninsula.

'You be careful,' said the bloke who had a splotched face like a burger in a bucket of beer. 'The roads are a bloody madhouse this time of year. Not that I want to worry you, but you know this country's got the worst record for driving in the world. And being alone and all that too . . .'

His mate, who liked to start his sentences with 'If you don't mind me saying/asking', said, 'If you don't mind me asking, doesn't a girl like you have no boyfriend?'

'Yes.'

'So why's he not out here with you?'

'He might be by May.'

'May? Jesus! You'll have another one by then!'

'Or had another few!' laughed the burger-face bloke.

Soon after this promising encounter I hit State Highway 25, also marked on my map as a 'Heritage Trail'. Heritage of what? I wondered. Road-kill victims?

Rolling into the 'township' (as it seems quaintly to be called) of Coromandel, I read a roadside sign informing me that: CORO-MANDEL LION CLUB WELCOMES CAREFUL DRIVERS. WE HAVE TWO CEMETERIES, NO HOSPITAL.

Coromandel looks a bit like something out of the Wild West. The sort of place where you could imagine a gun-slinging cowboy suddenly flying through the swinging doors of a bar to land in the gutter. This probably has something to do with it being an old gold-mining town. There was a lot of kauri milling round here too. The township took its name from the storeship HMS *Coromandel*, which sailed from the Bay of Islands into this harbour in 1820 to take on kauri spars for the Royal Navy. The tall, straight kauri pine trees were greatly valued by mariners and the densely forested hills around Coromandel made ripe pickings for the timber mills to plunder. Despite the kauri, the town really only became famous in the 1880s when gold was discovered and people flocked to the area, pushing a virtually non-existent population up to a soaring 10,000. Some of the old Victorian and colonial buildings still line the short and slightly ramshackle main street.

These days Coromandel doesn't so much attract people to gold as to an alternative lifestyle. The place was full of conservationists, galleries and craft stores, pottery shops, woodcarvers' studios, furniture workshops and bumper stickers proclaiming NUCLEAR-FREE NEW ZEALAND – MAKING A DIFFERENCE. There were a lot of crystals and spiritual healing and vegetarian cafes too. I took a short spin around the town, riding past places like Fowl and Fancy Art and Craft, Kowhai Watercolour Studio, Kapanga Krafts, Gold Diggers Liquor Store and Furey's Creek Motors. As I leant my bike against the wall of the small Four Square grocery, with its green and yellow fascia and fifties-style logo, an anxious-looking man came up to me to warn that it wasn't a good time of year to be on the roads because of the amount of drunk drivers, who apparently like to get 'as pissed as a Sheila on a glass of wine'.

'We've usually got about a thousand, say, two thousand people at most, living up around this way,' he said. 'But come Christmas and New Year that number swells to around forty thousand. It's the kids and the hoons you got to really watch out for.'

'Hoons?' I said, thinking it was the way he pronounced hounds. 'You mean dogs?'

The man laughed. 'No, I mean the hoons. The yobs, the louts, the delinquent boy-racers. They're the hoons. No respect for anyone.'

After buying a bagful of food at the Four Square I pushed my bike around the corner to a park and sat at a shady picnic table.

Someone had left a local paper on the table so I flapped it open and read the headline:

RECORD NUMBERS OF POLICE ON PENINSULA

More police than ever before are patrolling the peninsula this summer and new legislation will allow them to better manage the crowds. Operation CoroMass kicked off this week and Acting Eastern Area Commander John Kelly says the new laws should make their job easier. New 'boy racer' legislation and the inaugural 24-hour liquor ban mean more police will be out during the day. 'What we're saying is, come and have a good time, drink your alcohol but don't be out on the streets with it.'

The new 'boy racer' law allows police to impound cars for 28 days if drivers are charged with sustained loss of traction, more commonly known as doing 'burnouts' or 'donuts'.

Mr Kelly says many of the police have been through refresher courses including practising with riot equipment. 'Touch wood we don't have to use it.'

Operation CoroMass and riot equipment were not quite what I was expecting of New Zealand. I was banking more on a surplus of sheep (a reputed 48 million of them in all, compared with 4 million people) than something akin to an inner city battleground.

While I was contemplating this thought a man in his fifties and a sunhat came up to my table and said, 'Glad to see you've got the right idea by sitting in the shade. You can't be too careful of our sun. Most dangerous in the world. See this . . .' and he rolled up his sleeve to point at a darkened speckled splotch mark on his forearm. 'The makings of melonoma. No doubt about it.'

A woman called across to him from beside the toilet block.

'That'll be my wife,' he said. 'She's always after me to rattle my dags!'

'Rattle your what?' I said.

'Dags. Means get a bloody move on! At least it does when you rattle them!'

Jandals, hoons and rattling dags. Not to mention another word

I seem to have learnt: grundies – not a family in *The Archers*, but a pair of underpants. Men's, I believe.

I was pushing my bike across the grass and back on to Kapanga Road when a man stopped me in my tracks and said, 'Don't tell me you're going to ride that thing across the mountains?'

From where we stood in the street, you could see a huge mound of Coromandel's great catapulting hills rising up behind the town. A road was just visible snaking its tortured way up the side of one of the inclines. Occasionally a toy-sized vehicle could be seen crawling upwards, advancing in slow motion. This was the continuation of State Highway 25 and led across the hills to the east coast. On my map the road was marked as 'minor road unsealed'. After telling the man that yes, I was, but not quite yet, as I was heading north first, I asked him if he knew what the condition of the road was like.

'Good as gold,' he said. 'It was metalled only six to nine months ago. My son worked as a foreman on it. Doesn't mean to say the gradient has got any easier, though. Just the thought of driving up there exhausts me!'

The road north out of Coromandel Town towards Colville was busy with hoons in noisy cars with exhaust pipes the size of the Mersey Tunnel. There was also a whole procession of big four-wheel drives, most of them pulling a boat behind them containing fishing-rod holders in the cockpit. None of the drivers appeared to have any idea how to pass a cyclist, or else they just didn't care, overtaking me on blind corners of narrow uphill winding roads. This inevitably led to me having overly close encounters with the sides of their trailers as the owners erratically slewed their tail-ends in towards me when they met another vehicle travelling in the opposite direction, trapping me up tight against the steep and unforgiving hillsides.

Every campsite I passed was packed with tents and boats and 4WDs and motorhomes and rowdy clumps of guffawing lads. I didn't fancy spending New Year's Eve among such a hullabaloo so after riding through Papaaroha and Amodeo Bay I dived into the roadside jungle (or 'bush' as they call it in local tongue).

Here I put up my tent among a forest of enormous tree ferns with feathery umbrellas at least two storeys high with fat trunks that looked as if they were made of giant pineapple skins. It was a top spot for slumber, surrounded by extravagant foliage and tropical-looking birds and jungle noises. And at the bottom of the cliff came the swash and slap of the sea as it collided with the shore.

Coromandel, 3 January 2004

The last few days have sent my legs into wobbly shock syndrome. Instead of reacquainting my muscles gently back into the cycling swing of things, I stormed north up the winding and hilly and corrugated gravel dirt road to Fletcher Bay. Fletcher Bay is within catapulting distance of Cape Colville, the Land's End of the Coromandel Peninsula. Studying my map back in Amodeo Bay, I had pondered on my two options: cycle the fifty-odd kilometres to Fletcher Bay fully loaded with kit, or leave everything except survival rations of food and water and tools and clothes in my tent and do a commando-style raid on the area – in and out in a day.

I opted for the commando raid. But not before I had moved from my secluded camp spot and cycled down the hill to the Anglers Lodge Motel and Holiday Park. Here I found a little space for my tent up the tiered hillside overlooking the sea. I decided if I was going to ride a hundred unconditioned kilometres through the heat of the day along what was certain to be a hard and dusty track, then I could at least treat myself to a shower when I got back.

The ride from Amodeo to Colville was all tarmac but not without its severe ups and downs. One hill fell away so steep and straight that by tucking in my elbows and hunching down on my drops I notched up an eye-streaming 46 mph. On the approach to Colville everything looked lush and vibrant with fields an Irish green. Road kill seemed to comprise mostly splattered possums and some comical-looking birds that my pocket bird book told me were pukeko, or purple swamp hens. These were goose-sized birds with large clownish scarlet bills. They were not really purple at all but mostly a deep iridescent indigo blue with a coating of greenish gloss on the back and the wings and undertail coverts of pure white. Their downfall was that they looked like they went in the wrong queue for the legs, standing as they did on fragile orange-red twigs of stilts that were out of all proportional length and strength to the rest of their body. Their feet resembled huge clawed starfish. The alive pukeko I'd seen walked very awkwardly, as if they were drunk or suffering from a severe bout of haemor-rhoids. I think they were perhaps suicidal. They certainly didn't appear overly gifted when it came to road sense. I'd watch them on the side of the road, dithering, then darting uncertainly backwards and forwards as if summoning up courage for an opportunity to cross. After a long gap in the traffic, they would see a vehicle coming and decide to play chicken with it before embarking on an untimely skaddling across to the other side. Most of course never made it.

I wasn't quite sure what to expect of Colville, but I was expecting to find more than I found: a boxy-roofed general store. Apart from the odd house dotted here and there, plus a Buddhist retreat complete with stupa, that was it – the sole sum of bustling Colville.

Colville used to be known as Cabbage Bay. Some say this was because Captain Cook came this way and insisted his crew eat the young leaves of the cabbage tree as protection against scurvy. Others say that it wasn't the cabbage tree (*ti kouka* in Maori) that the crew ate, but the nikau palm, parts of which can also be eaten. Whatever the truth or half-truth of the matter, the cabbage name stuck (to the tree, not the bay) even though the cabbage tree looks nothing like a cabbage but more a spiky palm tree clump.

Sitting in a time warp on a shaded bench outside the store perched two old men, one in worn denim dungarees, the other in overalls, having a smoke and a chat in between chewing the cud. They looked like part of the furniture, though more like the sort of sight you'd expect to find at an isolated roadhouse out of 1930s dustbowl America.

Meanwhile, all around continued the thrust of modern life. Fat, aggressive 4WDs, some spanking new, pulled up in the dust outside the store. Colville store may be small, but its status lies in being the Last Store before Cape Colville and the northernmost tip of the peninsula, and the tills within were humming. Apart from an ageing hippie bloke in sandals with a long silvery ponytail and wearing something jangly and loose-fitting, most of the male customers were shirtless and shoeless. Though the women tended to keep what little tops they had on (it was hot outside, topping 35°C) they too didn't seem to favour shoes. But then, even back in the township of Coromandel, shod feet were thin on the ground. Maybe it's a back-to-nature peninsula thing. There again, I did notice a number of shoeless people wandering the upmarket streets of downtown Devonport. At this barefoot rate, I felt New Zealand was going to give birth to a whole generation of horny pads.

The store wasn't big, but was one of those places that manage to sell everything from fencing wire to bulk-bin health foods and fish bait to homeopathic remedies, plus all the everyday essential groceries in between. A sign on the wall informed the customers that: EVERYTHING IN THIS SHOP IS FOR SALE – EXCEPT THE STAFF (ALTHOUGH EVEN THAT'S NEGOTIABLE).

On the wall outside the store was a much-used noticeboard. Here's a selection of the local happenings of note or services on offer. One was a request to keep your eyes open for the rare Coromandel striped gecko. 'You can help solve the mystery of one of our least known lizards,' said the DoC (Department of Conservation) leaflet. 'Only three have ever been found.' Next to this was pinned a business card from someone called Catherine Hill, 'Marriage Celebrant'. I can't say I'm too sure what a marriage celebrant is. Could it be someone who chivvies up a celebratory mood for a newly wedded couple when one or both of them realise they should have acted on impulse and done a runner rather than walk down the aisle? Or could a celebrant simply be some sort of advocate for celibacy, and what Catherine Hill was really championing was a connubial shag-free fest? All this was probably what came as part of the package anyway when you booked in for a stay at the Mahamudra Buddhist Retreat Centre, which its advert recommended as a boon 'For Universal Unity'.

If arboreal matters were more your cup of tea and you were after a little tree-lopping, planting or surgery, then look no further than The Green Commandos for 'All Tree Services'. Made the task of branch-trimming or tree-felling sound positively exciting. I wondered if the Commandos arrived on the scene by parachute or approached your premises by taking you by surprise after running zigzag fashion close to the ground through thick undergrowth while dressed in Desert Storm army fatigues. And what about when they commenced their limb-slaughtering mission – was there much maiming and collateral damage to neighbouring foliage?

On an entirely different tack was the card appealing to (presumably) women to reduce consumption and waste by using 'Washable Menstrual Cloths'. Apparently these menstrual cloths were all about 'Positive Menstrual Education'. The advert invited you to acknowledge that it was 'Your Blood Your Planet Your Choice'. To which some might say, 'Right on, sisters!'

Attached to the end of Colville store I found a little open-sided porch containing a small bank of red mailboxes numbered with the locals' PO Box numbers. Stencilled on the wall of this porch, and to let you know in no uncertain terms what the country stood for, was the word: ECONATION.

The dirt road began shortly after leaving Colville. A woman in her twenties and a sundress was walking along the road and stopped me to ask how far away the store was. She looked very hot. Her deeply suntanned skin glistened with sweat. She kept making little plucking motions at the front of her dress where the material was stuck to her chest. I told her the store was about a kilometre up the road and asked where she'd walked from. 'Oh, not far,' she said. 'I'm staying at a friend's batch. I need some smokes so thought I'd walk.'

'A batch?' I said. 'What's a batch?'

'Oh, you know. A holiday home. A place to chill.'

Since this little encounter I have investigated the word 'bach', pronounced 'batch'. A man in the campsite in Amodeo Bay told me that a bach was sometimes no more than a wooden shack that had been in the family for a good generation or two. On the other hand you could get a bach that resembled more a palatial water-side residence – big buck-costing second homes that city dwellers tended to snap up. Apparently a bach was originally a bachelor's pad at a work camp but had since become something of a Kiwi institution. Just to complicate matters further, in the South Island a bach was known as a 'crib'.

All this explained a slightly mystifying programme that I'd heard on National Radio called *Rainy Day at the Batch*. It was a sort of *Desert Island Discs* with a famous person (at least in New Zealand) being interviewed. But instead of the interviewee's ten top tunes being played, there were only two on *Rainy Day at the Batch*. Which I now know was really *Rainy Day at the Bach*.

The narrow dirt road was hard work for cycling, being an almost continuous rumble-strip of skull-rattling corrugations. On the bursts of steep hills the gravel and stones were so loose and deep that it was impossible to turn the front wheel. If you didn't hit these patches at the right angle or in the right gear you would simply slide off the edge. Sometimes the drops were not the sort of drops you would want to drop off.

The sun beat down. Bike and body became caked in dust. It stuck thick to my skin. It stuck thick to my chain. The day became so hot that the heat flowed through my helmet like melted butter. The coast soon became rocky and rugged and fringed with ancient pohutukawa trees clinging to the inhospitable rocky coastline by way of gnarly long twisted roots and a tangle of fibrous aerial roots. These trees, their leafy canopies ablaze with magnificent crimson flowers, had turned the sea blood red by sending garlands of the windblown flowers swashing upon the eastern tides. Jacquie had told me that because pohutukawa trees burst into their fiery red blooms around December, they were known as Christmas trees. Even though they looked nothing like Christmas trees. More like a contortion of multi-limbed old men with a thick coiffured barnet of red. Cycling up this coast might have been perfect timing to catch these trees at their flamboyant best, but it wasn't so good for the holidaying traffic. Wave upon wave of 4WDs charged past my elbow – Isuzu Bighorns, Mitsubishi Pajeros , Nissan Safaris, Nissan Patrols, Nissan Pathfinders, Toyota RAV4s, Toyota Highlanders, Toyota Land Cruisers and Lexus V8s. Most of them sported private licence plates: IN D MUD; OH 4 MUD; I HOOK (below which was printed in small capital letters: ONLY THE BIG ONES). Some towed fishing boats, or 'tinnies' as I overheard someone calling them, with names like *Bandit* and *Hookie 1*. Each vehicle kicked up a storm of dust and a fusillade of stones and gravel. Not one driver slowed their pace to pass me. Whenever a vehicle bore down on me in its cloud of dust I had to dismount and heave my bike over to the edge of the road, turn my head away and screw up my eyes to prevent them getting filled with grit. Each driver peppered my body with a painful shrapnel of sharp stones zinging off my skin. Oh the joys of doing battle with people's domestic air-conditioned tanks!

Apart from this, the rest of the ride passed fairly uneventfully.

The scenery remained spectacular, becoming even more dramatic the closer I got to the top with Mount Moehau, Coromandel's highest mountain, soaring towards the sun at the peninsula's narrowest point. According to Maori legend, this nigh-on 3,000-foot peak is home of Turehu, a short, fair-skinned being, though they say that not so much as Turehu's footprint has ever been found. But I've spotted something akin to this description, albeit sealed in surfing gear while climbing out of a Bighorn with a glazed expression.

At one point I passed an old wharf and old quarry and an old building. Actually, this building wasn't so much old as 'olde' as it was called Ye Olde Stone Jug. That means that both ye wharf and ye quarry were olde too as they were obviously all part of ye olde same era. (I have since learnt that this area was famous – in New Zealand – for its quarrying of granite at the turn of the twentieth century. This granite, which faces a fair few prominent buildings around the country, is considered to be as good as Aberdeen stone, though I think many an Aberdonian may beg to differ.)

I continued onwards and upwards over Fantail Creek with its shingly beach, before the road clutched at straws as well as the steep coastline past Goat Bay. Another big climb was the order of the day as I veered inland until I popped out at Port Jackson where the ragged hills rose straight from the shore. Much as there was nothing goat-like about Goat Bay, there was nothing port-like about Jackson. No ships, no docks, no cranes, no containers, no straddle-carriers. Just an open crescent of sandy beach and, at most, two houses. I heaved myself over the hills for about another five kilometres to Fletcher Bay, where the road dribbled itself to near extinction. The only way to continue round the eastern flank of the peninsula was to join the Coromandel Walkway, a track that would take me through to Poley Bay and Stony Bay. For this I would need either a pair of sturdy hiking legs or a lightweight mountaineering steed. As I was in possession of neither I did an about-turn to head back the way I'd come. But not before eating the contents of my front left pannier and having a quick rest in the shade.

Before leaving I went on a wander and came across a hand-written sign that someone had propped against a rock. In big colourful capitals and alongside an arrow that pointed in a sky-wards direction, it said: CAPE COLVILLE. STOP: WE'VE RUN OUT OF LAND AND SUPERLATIVES!! Another sign alongside warned: WATCH OUT FOR THE HAIRY MAN! And there I was thinking I was supposed to be looking out for short fair-skinned legends and rare lesser-striped geckos. It was all getting a bit confusing.

By the time I arrived back at my tent I was in need of not much more than a shower and sleep. As it turned out, the shower was a lot easier to come by than the sleep. This is because when I flopped on to my sleeping bag it was still light and the camp-ground still noisy. Things clattered and clunked. People barbecued and banged car doors. Dogs yapped, barked and growled. Children played and laughed, shouted and cried. Others screamed. Especially the babies. Because it was so hot, I had left the outer flap of my tent open with just the mosquito door between me and the night. Propping myself up on my elbows I watched a little girl lugging a squalling baby about by the armpits. Close by another baby with a screwed-up face was having some-thing of a fit. The young mother jiggled the baby boy sharply against her shoulder. The baby's face was puce red. Spikes of damp hair lay plastered to his forehead. The baby's crying had reached the stage where he had to fight to breathe, pausing frequently for deep, hiccupping breaths.

The woman walked off with the baby and her space was filled by a man on a mobile. Or cell phone, as they call them in these parts. The man positioned himself about ten feet from my door. On his head he had a thatch of hair that stood up in thick tufts, like wind-tossed grass.

'Hiya bud,' he said in a shout, verging on a yell, 'I got yer mis-sage. I giss you were pissed when you sint it! Yeeah, bist I done is a five pounder. Bit Conner caught a tin pounder. Yeeah, that's good for round here, mate!'

The one-sided conversation of various sizeable landed fish continued in a strong Kiwi accent for several more minutes. At last the man rounded off the phone call by saying, 'Yeeah, bist I git bick to the tint. Just thought I'd touch base. Talk agin soon. Yeeah. Good on yer, bud. Be seeing yer.'

When he came off the phone, he turned to his mates sitting around the barbie and multiple chilly bins throwing back the piss (local parlance for beer) outside their 'tint', and shouted, 'Hey guys! Rob sizz he caught a twinty-five-ind-a-half pound snipper in Doubtless Bay. Jeez, that's some big fish!'

Finally I fell in to a dreamless sleep punctuated with the noisy goings-on of campground life. Later in the night I found the crescent of a tangerine moon suspended in a clear sky upside down. It's hanging upside down again tonight. Either I'm just very tired and am seeing things not as they really are, or else something strange happens to the moon by the time it reaches New Zealand.

Something else that's strange about the night is a haunted call that emanates from the surrounding forest of bush. At first I wondered if it was the Hairy Man of the woods, or possibly even my mother out on the search for me, but then I discovered it was nothing more sinister than an owl. Though a bit of an odd-sounding owl both in name and in call. The Maori term for this owl is the *ruru*, whereas the Pakeha (non-Maori) know it as the morepork. 'More-pork, more-pork' is the repeated and sometimes prolonged call of the morepork (with a little serving of crackling on the side), though in truth it actually sounds less like 'morepork' and more like a curdled 'quark-quark'. It's a lovely sound to hear, though not a patch on our horror-film whoop-de-whoo tawnies.

On my way back through Coromandel township, I stopped up the road from the Four Square to eat some food in the same park that I had stopped in on my way north. This time the person to come and sit down at my picnic table was a German student from Münster studying business studies for a year in Auckland. He wore a silver polished bicycle chain as a bracelet and a skull and crossbones T-shirt. He pulled the T-shirt on in my presence, covering up the body of a light-starved tulip. He told me he thought New Zealand was not a good country for cycling. 'I ride my bike a lot in Germany,' he said, 'but I would never ride here. The country has too many hills and mountains. But even worse than the mountains are the drivers. They are very terrible and dangerous and there are no cycle paths. I have travelled around New Zealand by car but I think by bicycle would be too frightening.'

This evening I am camping just outside the township in an orchard of oranges and lemons and plums belonging to the Tui Lodge backpacker hostel. Earlier on I was leafing through a copy of the *New Zealand Herald* when I spotted an advert warning readers that:

THERE'S ANOTHER OFFENDER YOU SHOULD BE AFRAID OF. You're more likely to be killed by a speeding driver than any criminal. Last year they took the lives of more women than rapists, more of the elderly than home invaders and more children than paedophiles. Yet we seem to largely accept the speeding driver's behaviour – some of us even oppose measures proven to curb it. And although the driver does not have the intent of the other offenders, the end result is just the same.

Kuaotunu, Coromandel Peninsula, 4 January

New Zealand appears to be doing quite a good job at killing its citizens (and visitors) in two ways. One, as I'm discovering, is by vehicle. The other is in the water. New Zealand, being a country of islands (about 700 in all), has a lot of water. This means it also has a lot of coastline (15,811 km). As no part of the country is more than 130 km from the sea and as it is also crammed full of lakes and rivers and fjords and waterfalls, the water plays a huge part in most people's lives. Sailing, boating, fishing, swimming, surfing, diving, canoeing, kayaking, water-skiing and jet-skiing, plus a whole host of other aqua-filled occupations, are all watery activities that come as second nature to most New Zealanders. Whereas the

British may spend an inordinate amount of time standing in a queue or caught up in a motorway snarl-up (both pursuits having become something of a national pastime), New Zealanders prefer to pass most of their time if not on the water, then beside it or in it. The only drawback to this is that every year sees a disproportionate number of people being unintentionally drowned (on average 130) in comparison with the size of the population (4 million). This death rate is about double the rates for Australia and the United States. In New Zealand, the leading circumstances of drowning are swimming, followed by fishing and boating. I've only been in New Zealand ten days, but already I've noticed that the media here cover boating accidents and beach mishaps the way British newspapers cover floods and hosepipe bans and leaves on the line – as a seasonal event involving lots of comparative statistics. In the news today, I heard on my radio how twenty-four people have already drowned this summer.

Talking of summer, the last few days have been sunny and hot with temperatures stuck in the mid-thirties. But that's just here on the North Island. The South Island, which logically should be colder seeing as it's further from the equator and closer to the South Pole (it's only a mere 2,000 or so miles away), has been sweltering at a record 40°C. Christchurch has just had its driest December since records began in 1864. This drought might be all very well for the pursuit of water sports but isn't such good news for the country's hills, where wildfires have been burning out of control. So the papers are not only full of the latest drowning, but also pictures of leaping flames, scorched land and blackened hills.

From the Tui Lodge I cycled out on to State Highway 25, also known as the tourist-themed Pacific Coast Highway. Even though I was nowhere near the Pacific Coast. Actually I was; it's just that it felt like a very long way away due to a large hurdle lying in my path before I reached it: 370-metre Whangapoua Hill. As I cycled towards the foot of this sizeable mound on legs not yet feeling completely at home with life a-wheel, Whangapoua Hill looked a lot more mountain than hill – a fact not helped by my coming away from my tent spot with several kilos of windfallen plums and oranges crammed into my already weighty panniers.

But as mountainous curvy-bended hills go, it was a fun one for cycling. It might have been only about a thousand feet up in the air but the temperature had plummeted by the time I arrived at the top, though after my perspiring efforts I was far from cold in T-shirt and shorts. Motorists, on the other hand, who were climbing out of their vehicles at the scenic outlook to take some scenic snaps, looked decidedly chilly.

'You look hot!' said a multi-clothed couple as they wandered past. Turned out they were from Reading (Berks).

'Ah, Gateway to Basingstoke!' I said. They asked if I knew Reading.

'I've cycled in and out of it a few times,' I said. 'But it's not a very nice place on a bike as it seems to be constructed entirely of roundabouts.'

The man laughed. 'Yes,' he said. 'Reading can be a very confusing place. Even now when I drive somewhere I have to stop and think and work out which way to go!'

The Reading couple wandered off to take some pictures, leaving me to ponder how you can travel 15,000 miles across the world to a wild hilltop in New Zealand only to find yourself talking about the roundabout blight of Reading.

The downhill swoop was tremendous – despite the fact that it suddenly decided to start raining – and I skimmed past blurred hillsides of pink-ochre earth.

The rain had stopped by the time I arrived in Matarangi so I went for a swim in the Pacific. Matarangi was a good example of a fine stretch of beach ruined by a dull complex of expensive holiday homes. A number of suntanned blokes in shades were driving their big city surfboard-topped 4WDs across the sand. Some just sat in them going nowhere, engine burning, staring moodily out to sea.

It's funny to think how development changes things. Quite a few hundred years ago, the first wave of Polynesians (ancestors of the Maori) arrived by outrigger canoes on the Coromandel and eventually lived peacefully in coastal encampments, fishing and hunting moa. These big wingless birds became a major food source for those early settlers, who used their skin and feathers in clothing, the leg bones for making fish hooks and harpoon heads and the eggshells as water containers, until they finally hunted them to extinction. By the time the Yorkshire-born navigator Captain James Cook appeared on the scene in the *Endeavour* on his grand voyage of exploration in 1769, there were no more moas and the Maori tribes were well established all over. Cook sailed right around the peninsula and wrote that the land on the west coast, close to the area that he called 'the River Thames', was the best he had seen for colonisation. Soon after Cook came the loggers with their two-man cross-cut saws to fell the colossal forests of kauri. Hot on the loggers' heels were the kauri gum-diggers and the gold-seeking miners. By the end of the nineteenth century, nearly all of the area's natural resources had been plundered. Today you get the hordes of holidaymakers following the NZTB (New Zealand Tourist Board) themed coastlines and heritage trails. And you get the surfers parading their bodies of sheet muscle or showing off their wheels on the sand.

Tonight I'm camping beside a sluggish river at Black Jack backpackers in Kuaotunu. Kuaotunu is a big improvement on Matarangi. It's got cliffs, hills, bush, beach and hardly any people. There's just a small store across the bridge called Kuaotunu Store and Liquor and a ramshackle garage that runs guided quad-bike safaris for those who like that sort of thing.

Up near the river I came across an information history board. Until this point I had been vaguely wondering the meaning of the name of this place – Kuaotunu – and now I discovered it actually had several meanings, though this particular information board, being a bit guarded with its information, was only giving one of them away: the one that translated as 'roasted young eel'. But the board did reveal that in pre-European times the Ngati Karaua people cultivated the land and fished the surrounding waters and that in 1889 gold was discovered in the area of the roasted young eel. As a consequence, the *tangata whenua* ('people of the land') departed from their ancient *kainga* ('the places my feet have trod') and left the area.

One of the reasons I decided to camp here at Black Jack was that there were free kayaks for use by Black Jack residents. I've only kayaked once in my life (cycling around Hawaii I met a man who put me to sea in his kayak, resulting in my nearly being knocked for six by a breaching whale) so I thought it was about time I gave it another go. Black Jack's owner, a friendly man called Carl, handed me a life jacket and a paddle and then left me to my own devices. He said I couldn't go too far wrong. Oh no?

Before tackling the surf crashing on to the beach (certain capsizing monsters of waves if ever I saw any) I thought I'd first test the paddling waters by heading up river. All went well for the first fifteen minutes. Lots of shade-dappled water. Lots of busy birdsong. All very peaceful. All very lovely.

Then I went aground. Just like that. A large shingle bank had reared up suddenly beneath my hull. No warning, no nothing. Not even a lighthouse. I tried shoving myself off with the end of my paddle. I moved, but not enough to get underway again. I tried wobbling from side to side. This caused a mini flurry of wavelets but not enough to free me. So I half stood up, lifted a leg over the side, stepped on something sharp and fell in. All this was watched by a handful of cows who had stuck their heads through a hole in the hedge. They didn't look overly impressed. But then cows never do.

Soon after this a dog got wind of me and charged along the riverbank barking and yowling. Then it turned into an aqua-dog and swam with menacing intent towards me. I paddled furiously away, but the dog kept coming for me, swimming as fast as if it were attached to its own inbuilt outboard motor. In the commotion I became ensnared in the branches of a fallen tree, resulting in a momentary power struggle between the tree, my paddle and the webbing of my lifejacket. The snarling hound lunged towards my arm with bared teeth but I managed to ward it off with the paddle. This was more excitement than I needed so I took myself off to sea instead. Apart from being swamped by a wave all went well and I spent many hours happily paddling up and down the coast.

Hahei, Coromandel Peninsula, 7 January

Today I heard on the news that the Met Service had registered a record-blistering high of 41°C in the South Island town of Darfield. Things weren't looking quite as hot up here this morning. When I stuck my head out of the tent I found that a dark, slaty grey day had descended and a light drizzle was falling. Carl told me they don't call drizzle drizzle, but pizzle. 'We don't usually get this sort of rain,' he said, looking disgruntled at the sky in his shorts and wellies. 'When it rains it usually hammers down!'

The road from Kuaotunu climbed up a winding and heavily bushed hillside for several twisting and turning kilometres. Despite the gloom, I would have thoroughly enjoyed the ride had I not had 50-tonne logging trucks thundering around the tight corners on top of me. These huge trucks are scary brutes to hear careening around a bend from the rear. The drivers don't take kindly to cyclists. You don't want to be in their way, which I usually am as the Coromandel roads are mountainous and narrow with nowhere to pull over to let the trucks pass; you have either a sheer drop on one side of the road or a steep wall of cliff on the other. Blind corners or not, logging trucks won't drop down a gear or two to wait behind, no matter what might be coming the other way. Their method of tackling a mountain with so much weighty wood on board is to take a running leap, hitting the lower slopes at full whack in the hope that the log-swaying momentum will take them up and over. Cyclists are treated like possums: it's up to you to get out of the way or else you're pummelled into the tarmac.

Descending the mist-shrouded mountains, the pizzle turned into a fine rain that felt like pins sticking in my eyeballs as I squinted ahead into the rushing headwind. But by the time I was rolling alongside Buffalo beach and into Whitianga township the sun was beating down again. Whitianga looked like a very busy palm-tree-lined resort. Like the township of Coromandel, its normally small population had swelled to mammoth proportions, popping the 40,000 mark. Because Whitianga sits bang on the shores of Mercury Bay, the town is a big game-fishing base for tuna, marlin, mako (blue pointer shark), thresher shark and kingfish. I've no idea what a thresher or a blue pointer shark looks like (apart from maybe blue and pointy), but the thought of this area being a magnet for sharks was good enough reason to steer clear of the water.

I cycled around the town for a while, passing watery and fishy-themed eateries with names like On the Rocks, Reel 'Em Inn and Snapper Jack's. After topping up food supplies at New World supermarket, I rode down to the Narrows to join a queue of tourists waiting to board the passenger ferry (a small launch) for the five-minute crossing over to Ferry Landing. As this ferry would shave off 30 km of logging truck road, I hoped there would be room for my bike among the crowds cramming on to the boat. There wasn't, but the boatman and the packed passengers took it upon themselves to treat it as a challenge to haul me on board anyway. During this tightly squeezed encounter I learnt a new word to add to my Kiwi vocabulary. A shirtless male passenger, rammed up against the bulbous aft end of my bike said, 'What a lot of stri-iitcheees you've got!'

'What a lot of what?' I said.

'Striiitcheees.'

None the wiser, I tried to think what he meant by 'striiitcheees'. Strict teas. Stripped knees. Striped cheese. Striptease. Ah, that must be it. He obviously thought I had the potential to perform a handful of stripteases for dramatic effect. What, here? Now? In front of all these compressed boating folk? Oh, all right. If you insist.

I was about to start seductively removing my bike helmet with a kinky little twist of my head when I thought I'd best check one more time on my striptease striiitcheees. 'What is a striiitcheee?' I asked.

'These things,' he said, twanging one of the many bungee cords tethering a mountain of kit to my rear rack.

I have now added striiitcheee, or stretchy, to my Antipodean list of confusing words.

In the car park on the Ferry Landing side, a number of coaches pulled to a pneumatic halt. Ferry tourists climbed on board to be carted off to wherever tourists go. Talking of tourists, the first and the most famous tourists to visit Mercury Bay were the Polynesian explorer Kupe and Britain's Captain Cook – both fine navigators. Kupe got here first by some 900 years, all the way in his canoe from an island near Tahiti just to take a look (the exploratory skills mastered by these early voyaging Polynesians were so fine that they have been described as the Vikings of the Sunrise). When Cook reached these parts he anchored in Mercury Bay (which takes its name from the planet whose transit Captain Cook and his party of scientists observed during their anchorage here on board the *Endeavour*) and was so taken with the place that, in the name of King George III, he declared New Zealand a British Colony. What days those must have been when you could turn up in a new land and think: Nice here, isn't it? Let's be having it then.

Hahei, 8 January

Tonight I'm camping at Hahei ('outward curve of Hei's nose' – another ancient explorer man, I'm told), said to have the best beach on the Coromandel. It certainly looks very lovely: a long expanse of white sand tinged pink by shells, shaded by sloping pohutakawa trees in blazing red bloom and protected by a higgled bastion of offshore islands. I've found a nook for my tent among a bit of bush on a hill overlooking this beach and as I lie here now there is no sound but the wind and trees and the omnipresent sea.

On the talkback radio station Newstalk ZB (not to be recommended) there has been nothing but talk of Steve Irwin, an Aussie with his own television show and zoo in Australia. It seems that overnight his fame has turned to international notoriety, having sparked controversy after he used his month-old son Bob in a crocodile-feeding show at his zoo. From what I gather, he didn't actually feed his son to the crocodile. Though apparently it was a close thing. Steve entered the 'croc pen' with Bob in one arm and a chicken in the other. Steve then dropped the chicken into the jaws of a four-metre crocodile. Everyone's now talking about this act as an 'open-and-shut case of negligence'. Child welfare groups and members of the public are up in arms and have criticised Steve for recklessly endangering his son. Some callers on Talk Radio are likening him to Michael Jackson, who held his baby over the edge of a balcony. the *New Zealand Herald* quoted an editorial from *The Australian* evidently none too impressed with Steve's behaviour. 'The croc tamer's bravado at his Queensland zoo last week for the entertainment of visitors is looking all the more pathetic after his lame defence of his one-month-old son's partic-ipation in the act. Talking of animals that can lunge in a split second and that have reportedly chased people up trees, Irwin said he had "a safe working distance with that crocodile" and "it's all about perceived danger". He also left himself open to a charge of over-confidence by declaring it would have taken a meteorite to upset his balance. Then, referring to the baby, he said he wanted his children to be "croc savvy".'

On another talkback station, Radio Pacific (also awful), there's more talk of Steve and his actions. They are also debating some-thing else: immigration. Every caller launches into a diatribe of racist rants. One man finished off his call by saying, 'If we've been good enough to let these ragheads into our country and they don't want to become Kiwis, then they should do the proverbial and bugger off!'

Opoutere, Coromandel Peninsula, 9 January

Sailors Grave Road came and went. As did Pumpkin Hill Road, Mount Paku (an ancient *pa* site, or fortified Maori village – this one complete with the legend that you won't return from the top for seven years, though it took me about fifteen minutes) and the Twin Kauris. In the overdeveloped beachside town of Tairua, I stopped at the quiet tourist office. Two women behind the desk asked where I was from and what did I think of New Zealand. I said hilly and full of bad drivers (I'd just had several near misses). 'Unfortunately we have a reputation for being bad drivers,' said one of the women apologetically. Her friend told me about an advert that was on TV a few years back showing a family man, all loving sweetness, kissing his family goodbye as he set out for work. Once behind the wheel though, his whole persona changed. He sprouted horns and became a snarling monster, speeding, bad overtaking, shouting and swearing, shaking his fist. When he arrived at the office he returned to being a good-mannered and considerate man. But on the drive home the devil was reincarnated, cutting people up, steam pouring out of his ears. The minute he stepped back through his front door, angelic child in his arms, he was all sweetness again.

Tairua is a twin-town with Pauanui, Tairua Harbour separating the two. Pauanui is even more of a luxury retirement and holiday resort than Tairua, where only the rich reside. I read in the local paper that at this time of year the population of Pauanui went from around 750 to 18,000 people, which only translated into a lot more angry drivers on the road with horns. I took off over Opoutere Saddle (New Zealand tends to call its hills saddles) and then, not long after I passed 'K9 'N' Katz – Homestay for Pets', I turned off to secluded Opoutere, riding down a road that hugged the shoreline of Wharekawa Harbour – flowering pohutukawa trees on one side, towering pine-covered hills on the other.

There was not a lot to Opoutere – no shops, no petrol stations, no upmarket suburban monstrosities. Just a pine-shaded campground, a hostel, a handful of houses clinging to the hillside and a five-kilometre expanse of wild white beach. I was aiming to camp somewhere down on this beach, known as Ocean Beach, but just past a driveway with a sign pointing upwards into the sky with the words STUDIO AT TOPADAHILL, I spotted a garden that looked like a perfect place for a tent. A sun-faded blue picnic table sat at the bottom of the garden shaded by an orchard of apple and orange trees. A few feet away across the quiet road lapped the gentle slap of waves of the bird-crowded harbour. An indiscreet sign advertised that the house at the top of this garden (a garden decorated with interesting lumps of metal sculptures) offered 'Backpacker Accommodation'. A long-haired man in a cowboy hat answered the door. This was Rusty, ex-motorcyclist ('I used to ride a Triumph, but sold it in a fit of madness'), carpenter, sculptor and blues-band fan. He told me no one had ever asked to camp in his garden before, but he didn't see why I shouldn't now that I had. I've just had a shower up in Rusty's bathroom and am now lying flat out in the orchard listening to the swash of water as it hits the shore.

Opoutere, Coromandel Peninsula, 10 January

Among the many places that Rusty had travelled he said this was the best place he'd ever found to live. He'd been there twenty years now. Bought this place for next to nothing. 'It was a wreck of a hovel but I built it up over the years. It's now worth quarter of a million bucks. That's because it's all the rage to live in Opoutere these days. Property prices have gone through the roof. It's bloody ridiculous. But I can't say I'm complaining!'

Before I left, Rusty handed me a postcard with a picture of a butterfly sunbathing on a sunflower. The printed words on the back said:

As we seek the pathway of sunflowers in our life,
The seeds of happiness and contentment grow stronger.

All a bit deep for me. Easier to grasp were the address and phone number Rusty had written on the back. He told me to contact him if I ever needed any help.

My plan was to get a good few miles under my belt today. Good intentions are one thing, but actions are quite another. My actions this morning took me in quite the opposite direction from the one I intended. This was because I fancied an early morning saunter alongside the roaring surf and seething wash of Ocean Beach. But before I made it to the beach I passed a track leading up to the hostel – a big white building overlooking the harbour and virtually surrounded by encroaching bush. Ten minutes after packing up my tent at Rusty's, I was putting it back up – this time beneath a peach tree in the orchard behind the house.

The hostel was run by an amicable couple, German-born Rosemary (an ex-teacher) and John, an Englishman and ex-engineer from Stroud, Gloucestershire. When they first got married they lived in London and then Canada. New Zealand has now been home for forty years. 'When we moved here,' Rosemary said, 'our standard of living went up by three-fold.'

I liked Rosemary. She had quite a silly sense of humour. When I was checking in and having a chat with her, a man (a bit of an oddball who had obviously rubbed Rosemary up the wrong way) came in to check out. When he'd left, Rosemary turned and said to me, 'We're always happy to see people. Some when they arrive. Some when they leave!'

The hostel offered free use of kayaks so I spent half the day paddling among the black swans and multiple bird life of Wharekawa Harbour. The water was clear and sparkling and shallow in places. At one point as I was bobbing about in the water peering over the side, I saw the flattened diamond-shaped body of a stingray sweeping itself off the sandy bottom with a few swishes of its whiplash tail. At low tide a wide patch of the harbour turned to mudflats, drawing a smattering of locals and tourists into its glutinous midst with buckets and spades to dig for the harbour's supplies of plentiful shellfish, including something called *pipi*.

At the harbour entrance end of Ocean Beach and tucked among the dunes was a bird sanctuary and breeding ground for the shore plover, pied stilt, bar-tailed godwit, variable oystercatcher and endangered New Zealand dotterel. There was a roped off area with a handwritten sign saying: 'NESTING DOTTERELS – please respect the fence and give the little dudes a chance!'

Birds as dudes. That's not a name you would get the National Trust calling them. Walking the length of sparsely populated Ocean Beach, I spotted more rare species – this time not so much dudes as nudes. Seemed the top end of the beach was an unofficial naturalist area. Mostly of men. I tried to avert my gaze as one man strode brazenly along the shore towards me, coconuts swinging gently in the wind. Further along I saw a man with nothing on lolling beneath a sun umbrella he had stabbed into the sand. The wind was no match for this umbrella and one gust later the umbrella had taken off, somersaulting along the beach. The man took off after it, the more dangling part of his anatomy slapping in a pulverising fashion from side to side. He then tripped up on a small piece of driftwood and, legs splayed, went crashing to the sand, whereupon I had the misfortune to observe an area of his body where the sun don't shine.

Back at the hostel I met a Japanese man (thankfully clothed) preparing a bowl of noodles in the kitchen. He told me he was from Osaka ('*Ah so, desu-ka?*') and worked as a fitter on the Toyota car plant production line. At least he did until he gave up his job to travel around New Zealand for a few months by bus, though he told me he could get a job back at the plant anytime. When he asked if I had ever been to Japan and I replied that I had spent eight months cycling around the country by *jitensha*, he became very animated and wouldn't leave me alone. He even tried to crawl into my tent, which I thought was a bit forward for a Japanese man.

The only other tent at the hostel belonged to a middle-aged German man called Klaus. He was on a bike kitted out with front and rear Ortlieb panniers. 'I carry precisely zee twenty-five kilo of gear,' he told me proudly. Klaus said he had flown to New Zealand from Berlin, arriving in Auckland on the 23rd of November. He was due to fly home next Thursday. Like my Toyota car plant man, Klaus became quite excitable at the prospect of me travelling alone by bike. So we did a bit of comparing of notes. Like me, he was not too impressed with the drivers down here. 'I have found zee traffic makes for very stressful cycling indeed.'

We both agreed that uphill left-hand bends were not good news in New Zealand. Most drivers raced up the hills with no thought that there could be something up ahead hidden around the corner travelling much slower. 'Usually I like to lose myself in zinking when I cycle,' said Klaus, 'but when I hear zee big truck coming from behind I have to hold zee handlebar tight like ziss,' (quick demonstration) 'and also I am taking my feet out of zee clip pedals. Ziss does not make for a relaxing cycle.'

Klaus was a software man. He told me I needed to do away with my diary notebook and to get a mini computer like his (another demonstration) into which he'd logged his whole itinerary before he left for New Zealand. And he'd kept to it rigidly – day by day, kilometre by kilometre. He left nothing to chance, computing in the nearest tourist offices, accommodation info, even bus time-tables which he'd downloaded from some site while sitting at home in Berlin.

'What happens if you like the look of another road rather than the one you are on?' I asked. 'Are you allowed to divert course?'

'Ziss is impossible,' said Klaus, looking at me as if I must be mad. 'I have no need to do so.'

During the night two hissing possums fought over peaches in the tree above my head. One fell out of the tree and landed on my tent. Gave me quite a shock it did. I thought it might be Klaus trying to get into my haus.

Waihi Beach, The Coromandel, 14 January

Opoutere was one of those places in which you thought you were only going to stay a night and ended up spending the better chunk of a week. At least it was if you were not attached to a Klaus-style schedule-strict computer that dictated your every move.

Next stop was Whangamata, though I didn't stop long. It was another one of those holidaying places whose population exploded at this time of year. Rusty said that unless I enjoyed being submerged by crowds of surfers and boogie boarders and holiday homeowners and boy-racing hoons, then don't linger there as the population of 4,000 shoots up as much as tenfold in January. It also seemed to be full of rented campervans (Maui and Britz and Kea Campers and Breakaway Libertys). There were lots of private licence plates doing the rounds too: LIVIN IT; MAJIC 1; BOLLIK; B NICE – this last one on a battered old hippy bus.

I bought a paper and read how four women had suffered severe burns after using a public toilet in Christchurch. An acid-like substance had been put on the seats of the toilets. Police were now appealing for help from anyone who might have seen anything suspicious. In the *New Zealand Herald*, Sergeant Lewis Corbett said, 'This is a very serious incident. These young women may need plastic surgery.'

Think I'll stick to the fine art of darting behind a bush.

The weather has been all at sixes and sevens with itself today – clammy and humid with the sky a drag of dirty grey rag. Every so often, and when I least expected it, I got pelted by a torrential downpour. Then, just outside the old gold-mining town of Waihi, I was overtaken by four hoons in a Subaru Legacy with a noisy exhaust. As they roared past in a burst of erratic acceleration, one boy, with a face like a broken crag, spat at me and another threw a beer bottle. Both missed. The spit flew over my head while the bottle smashed against a roadside rock like shrapnel.

3

Omokoroa, Bay of Plenty, 15 January

Today I passed through the open-air art gallery town of Katikati (Maori for 'nibbling'). In 1991 Katikati had something of an inferiority complex moment. It fretted over its small size and non-descript status. It thought that, because it was boring, it was being overlooked by tourists. So in order to become a little more eye-catching, it decided to rebrand itself as a mural town. Katikati is a typical New Zealand town, architecturally uninspiring, the buildings not built out of the land as in Europe or India or Africa, but imposed upon it. The favoured building materials seem to be laminates, concrete, fibre cement, steel frame roofs and plastic-coated tin shaped to look like timber. Now in Katikati every wall of every uninspiring building has been smothered in a mural, and the town is also promoting itself as The Gateway to the Bay of Plenty.

Despite having left the Coromandel Peninsula behind, I didn't get very far today. After packing up my tent on Waihi Beach I joined State Highway 2, the only road down the coast. This road was the stuff of horrors, heaving with heavy traffic. It carved its obnoxious path through acres of orchards – lemons, oranges, kiwis, nashi pears, avocados. When I stopped at a roadside stall to buy five avocados for $2 the stallholder told me that this stretch of road between Waihi and Tauranga was one of the worst in the country for car crashes and deaths. I wasn't surprised. Dotted at regular intervals along the roadside were small forests of white wooden crosses – memorials to all those car-crash victims. One corner had five crosses planted on it. All the victims were teenagers. And all of them male.

Billboards were strung out along the road warning drivers of the hazards of speeding and drink driving. One said succinctly, 'DRINK DrIvE', while one from the emergency services pleaded: 'GIVE US A BREAK!' Another was a cartoon of a bird saying: 'PSSSSSSST – HAVE YOU HEARD? – DON'T DRINK AND DRIVE!' Then there was the one that asked, 'YOU'RE A LONG TIME DEAD SO WHAT'S THE HURRY?'

I read in today's paper about the latest Land Transport Safety Authority (LTSA) figures, showing that most fatal or serious injury alcohol-related crashes in New Zealand happened in rural areas – 270 per year compared with 170 per year in the cities – despite the fact that less than a third of the population lives in the country. Most of those killed in country areas were locals, and 82 per cent of rural drunk drivers who crashed were male.

After being passed too close by one driver too many today, I gave up on cycling much earlier than normal and veered off Death Highway 2 down a dead-end road. I'm now camping in a field lined with big blue balls of hydrangea bushes bordering an orange orchard. A hippy bus is parked at one end. It belongs to Sally Hutchings, a woman in her late sixties or early seventies. And slippers. Sally's bus was once a school bus in Auckland. But that was about forty years ago. When the school bus was replaced with a more modern version, Sally and her husband Steve bought the old bus and gave it a complete overhaul and refitting. They put in beds, bookshelves, tables, couches, gas cooker, fridge and a pot-belly stove. Then they spent years travelling around the country. As well as being keen bussers they were also keen bikers. As were their two sons. All went well until two years ago when within the space of a few months Sally lost her cat, husband and son. John, her son, was killed on his motorbike. 'He was a speed merchant,' said Sally. 'He just loved the feel of going fast.' Sally was working on a strawberry farm at the time. 'I was in the nursery when I saw John fly by on his bike. He gave me a huge wave like he always did. That was the last I ever saw of him. He just lost control. The odd thing was that he didn't have a cut on him. And his helmet was untouched. They think he simply died of massive shock. His pillion rider walked away fine. The pain of that year though was unbearable. Still is.'

Paengaroa, Bay of Plenty, 18 January

New Zealand seems to be doing strange things to me. I drop by a place to have a quick look around and the next thing I know several days have passed. Sally's field was like that. I used it as a base to go on exploratory missions. One of these was to the long thin island of Matakana – an elongated strip of mostly Maori land of dusty tracks, dense forests of radiata pine, plantations of kiwis, avocados and corn, battered cars with no licence plates, a 24-kilometre stretch of pristine beach overlooking, at the time, a froth of clouds on the horizon, and a small store called Tubby's. The wharf on the ferry side was also busy with young Maori boys, as supple as whips, leaping off the piles into the water.

To reach the island I cycled down to the end of the road from Sally's where a sign said, 'Welcome to Omokoroa – A Lifestyle Village for the Over 55s'. But the small store down by the jetty in Omokoroa wasn't so much filled with over 55s as with suntanned boys in baggy swimming shorts. Outside the store an estate agent board belonging to Rex Harrigan Real Estate had an unusual approach for trying to win interest in its properties. For a west-facing house the details were headed: 'LOOK AT THAT SUNSET!' Then there was 'PEACE AND PROSPERITY' for a house situated in the back of beyond; 'TIMBERRRRR!!!!' for a house made of logs; 'LET'S GET PHYSICAL!' for a gym for sale and 'GO NUTTY!' for a house set among an acre of pecan trees. Enough to put anyone off, I'd have thought.

Today has been another hot clammy day in the thirties but compared with what's going on in Australia it's positively cold.

Queensland is currently trapped in such a heatwave (yesterday the mercury rose to 49°C) that goldfish are apparently exploding by sizzling to death in their tanks. I read in the paper about a man who worked at the Birdsville Hotel in the state's southwest, commenting how the goldfish died when air-conditioning at the home of a local resident broke down. 'The house got so hot,' he said, 'that the water heated up and the two fish in there just blew right up.'

I've been back on Death Highway 2 today. I've also been to Bethlehem. No stars or wise men in this one, just a non-descript huddle of homes with a dangerous junction and a convenience store inconveniently situated on the opposite side of a road busy with mean-looking logging trucks that would stop for nothing.

Further along I stopped at a country market to buy a kilo of bananas for a dollar. Opposite the store three white crosses sprouted from the verge. Each was a miniature shrine shrouded with plastic windmills of flowers and toys. All the names on the crosses were girls. The woman in the market told me the girls had stopped here to buy some fruit and ice cream. They had just set off again when their car suddenly veered into the path of a logging truck. 'The log truck steamrolled the car,' said the woman. 'It was a terrible mess.'

Next came the sign: WELCOME TO TAURANGA 'SIMPLY SUPERB'. Simply superb for what? Bottlenecks? Traffic jams? Dangerous junctions? Superbly unattractive buildings? All of these, from my observations, would qualify nicely for the city's motto. Tauranga District is the second-fastest-growing local authority area (after Queenstown) in New Zealand. It was busy with traffic and busy with building. Nothing about the place made me want to stay so I beat a hasty exit down a long American-style strip of commercial buildings – garages, auto shops and car showrooms. Hundreds of acres of fields at the Papamoa Beach end of Tauranga were marked out with pegs and strings into 'exclusive sections'. Close by, large 'exclusive' homes and vast gated communities were mushrooming out of the land. The road slicing through this building frenzy acted as a racetrack for hoons. They accelerated past in their souped-up cars adorned with spoilers, aerofoils, fat wide wheels, expensive paint jobs and private plates written with things like: O HONEY; 2 B SURE; LESURE; GAYE; SKI TOY; LUVV IT.

After filling up on food supplies in Bayfair's Countdown super-market, I burst back out on to Death Highway (to heaven) 2. If I'd thought there were a lot of logging trucks north of Tauranga, there were even more now. For the second time in two days a truck ran me clean off the road, an experience that made my heart feel as if it was marching in jackboots. Today's *Herald* had a letter in it written by Derek Rudge of that mural-overload town Katikati. He wrote:

> We are an English couple spending a few months of each year in your beautiful country. We love nearly everything about New Zealand, except for the appalling driving standards, particularly by some truckers. It is no wonder so many people are killed on your roads when drivers insist on 'tailgating' – hovering a few metres from your rear bumper, looking as if they are going to overtake but rarely doing so. As a professional truck-driver for some twenty years, I am particularly ashamed by the dangerous and intimidating tactics employed by some of your truckers. As an example, on Wednesday at about 10 a.m., on State Highway 2 driving from Katikati to Tauranga, my wife and I were nearly forced off the road by one such menace, who evidently didn't think 100 km/h was fast enough so sat about 2 m away from our rear bumper. One day he's going to kill somebody and, unfortunately, it probably won't be himself.

Trying to look as big and visible as possible, I passed through the slightly stomach-unsettlingly named town of Te Puke, which actually means nothing more harmful than 'the hill'. I can't say I saw much of a hill at Te Puke, but what was impossible to miss was the shockingly large cross-section model of a sliced kiwi. It was at least two storeys high and looked like an enlarged version of a cat's bottom. Apart from the fact that it was green. Te Puke is home to this giant kiwi, officially known as the Kiwifruit Slice Viewing Tower (for those who feel so inclined, it's possible to stick your head out of the top), because Te Puke is 'Kiwi Capital of the World'. This title seemed to have been nicked from China, because the furry kiwi used to reign solely in China. In 1906 Chinese gooseberries, as they were then known, were introduced to New Zealand. It wasn't until the 1960s that a handful of New Zealand's horticulturalists experimented with the Chinese gooseberry and developed an international market for it under a new name – kiwifruit. This area of the Bay of Plenty provides the perfect growing conditions for kiwis and in the 1970s and early 1980s, boosted by strong demand and high prices, many of Te Puke's farmers became millionaires from a harvest of only a few hectares.

The giant Kiwifruit Slice Viewing Tower dominated Te Puke as well as Kiwifruit Country, an information centre-cum-theme park where you could pay good money to go on a guided tour of the extensive kiwi orchards (both gold and green varieties!) and game park by riding in a 'kiwikart' – a sort of golf cart pulling a train of kiwi-shaped carts. Further punishment was on offer in the shop and restaurant where you could sample kiwi wine and kiwi chocolate.

I was more anxious to rattle me dags and battled onwards into the knifing wind. Perhaps this was the wind euphemistically known as the Kamai Breeze. This understatement refers to the strong winds that blow over the Kamai Ranges (a large ridge of inland mountains seen from Te Puke) and was blamed for bringing down an airliner in 1963, killing twenty-three passengers and crew.

The shores of the Bay of Plenty were one of the first landing sites of the long-ago Polynesians, but the place was given its present name by Captain Cook. His description proved prophetic because, apart from all the acres of kiwi, the sunny climate is just the ticket for growing avocados, passionfruit, tamarillos, citrus and other subtropical fruit. Pumpkins also seem to flourish in the area and as I cycled southwards I passed a line of pick-ups parked along the hard shoulder, their rears overflowing with pumpkins. The sellers didn't appear too concerned with making money from their rotund produce. One sign propped up against a rear wheel arch said: 'PUMPKINS – ALL YOU CAN CARRY'.

Being such a prolific fruit-growing area means that there are vast quantities of fruit to pick. This means that armies of fruit-pickers are needed. The majority of these fruit-pickers are from the Philippines, China, Thailand, Vietnam, Cambodia, Malaysia. The campground on the outskirts of Te Puke was like a refugee camp – squalid and dirty and crammed with decrepit moss-stained caravans housing a scrum of exhausted bodies. A wild medley of washing lay draped across every surface: chain-link fences, caravan doors, car doors, roofs and windscreens. Much of it had been blown off its original perch and was flapping about on the ground among the litter.

Ten kilometres south down Death Highway 2, the campground (with motel attached) at Paengaroa junction where I had found a little space to put my tent was similarly full of fruit-pickers but marginally cleaner. This was because Robert, the owner of the site, spent half the day cleaning up after them. 'They're a filthy lot these Asians,' he said. 'I advise you to get in the shower and the kitchen before they all come back from work. They don't seem to realise that you put toilet paper in the toilet, not throw it all over the floor. And I'm not quite sure what they get up to in the shower but it's definitely not just showering! As for the kitchen – strewth! The whole place looks like a bombsite after they've finished cooking their dinner!'

The pickers may not have been the tidiest lot on the planet, but that didn't mean to say they weren't kind. One woman retrieved a pair of my cycling shorts for me, blown for six off my makeshift bike-brake-cable washing-line, while a man gave me half a pot-load of cooked rice.

Over the last few years there'd been an influx of immigrants from Asia. Walk down Queen Street in central Auckland: English language schools springing up all over the shop and Pakeha faces well in the minority. I found all this mixture of people very interesting, but many New Zealanders were not happy about it. Every night talkback radio was full of die-hard Kiwis ranting about the 'invasion of Asians'. On Christmas Eve, the day I arrived, the *New Zealand Herald* had devoted half a page to 'AUCKLAND'S CHANGING FACE'. 'God save our filthy Queen St' read the headline. A photograph at the top of the article, showing a basement area in Queen Street with a bright neon sign lit up with the words 'EAT ASIAN – 9 SPECIALIST FOOD SHOPS', was captioned: 'ALIEN-ATED: Readers feel intimidated by the Asian presence downtown and decry the lack of parking.'

The previous day the paper had invited readers to write in with their thoughts of Queen Street. Here's a small selection of their responding letters:

My thoughts on Queen St today? After being born and bred in Auckland, I, like many hundreds of thousands of New Zealanders, decided that the changing face of the country, and more so Auckland, was an insult on the Government's behalf and decided to move to Perth.

I once thought my hometown Auckland was the best spot on Earth, and used to love heading into Queen St, but over the last five to ten years, I couldn't think of anything worse.

If I wanted to live in China, I would emigrate there. I am not alone in my thinking – although there are a lot of gutless people out there who say the reason they leave New Zealand is to pursue further opportunities abroad. Yeah, right.

So, due to the Government's open-door immigration policy, expect to see a tide of 'True Blue' Kiwis leave our shores as they search for a place where they can live and raise their kids without being beaten up by Islanders or being caught in gunfire from Asian triad gangs.

Brent Becroft

Queen St is appalling. Instead of creating an international-destination city, our idle local body planning and Government policy have left Queen St a destitute hub of cheap and tacky Asian crap.

What do we want in Queen St? Some decisions, mainly. A policy to limit the number of kitsch Asian stores selling junk would be a good start.

Phil Coop

In a word – crap. It is turning into a mini-Asia with crap clothing and gadget shops everywhere purely catering to the students . . . What about the rest of Auckland? No wonder everyone heads to the suburbs.

Lyndal Kelly

I agree about the Asians. I don't want to appear racist, but I have become increasingly reluctant to venture out at lunchtime because of them. They hog the footpaths, congregating in large groups outside doorways and entrances of the countless English language schools, and do not seem to have the courtesy to move aside and let people past.

Some of these groups can be quite intimidating, and I'm no chicken. I have travelled in densely populated countries such as India.

Margaret Howe

That phrase 'I don't want to be racist, but . . .' is the beginning of a sentence I've already heard a lot in New Zealand. But like any-where, these 'racist, but . . .' people tend only to surface in newspapers and on the radio. I think people who don't rant on about their 'racist, but . . .' views tend not to be too bothered by the changes.

Whakatane, Bay of Plenty, 19 January

This morning as I was packing up my tent, Robert asked which direction I was heading. I said East Cape.

'East Cape?' he said. 'I'd give the place a miss if I were you. Especially on a bike. You need a four-wheel-drive for the place. I drove around it in my SUV. The place is awful. There's nothing there. No stores. Nothing. The roads are bloody terrible too!'

East Cape is the North Island's easternmost extremity, an out-on-a-limb lump of land that protrudes into the Pacific. On my map this protuberance looks lovely for cycling. It's full of coves and steep coastal winding roads and mountains. There are no cities, not even any major towns. Just small communities. I think I'll ignore Robert's advice.

More roadside crosses and shrines decorated the verge. More dead teenagers. In New Zealand you can legally start driving at fifteen. Schoolchildren behind the wheel. It's not a reassuring sight when you're cycling along with no other protection around you but air to be overtaken by a driver who looks like they should be in double maths. Although 15–24-year-olds make up only 16 per cent of the driving population, they account for around 30 per cent of crashes.

Unusually for New Zealand, the ride from Paengaroa to Whakatane was hill-free. Most of the way it was as good as flat. A few kilometres past Pukehina ('unwell hyena'?), Death Highway 2 slapped itself against the coast. For some reason the traffic levels petered off even though this was still the main drag down the coast. What's more, I had a tailwind. First wind yet to strike me from the rear. What joy a tailwind can bring! It gladdens the heart and lightens the head and powers the load. I powered along past clumps of flowering fennel six feet high as the waves crashed on to Kohioawa Beach. Overlooking the road on the other side stood craggy sand-hardened cliffs topped with ancient pohutukawa trees clinging on with a knotty entanglement of tortuous roots.

Further along, Death Highway 2 suddenly veered inland at Matata ('motherly potato') leaving me to continue whipping along the coast on Route 30. Just because it was no longer State Highway 2 didn't mean that all dangerous driving came to an end. Roadside billboards warned passers-by of the hazards of drinking and driving. 'STAY ALIVE, SOBER DRIVE,' said one. Another had a photograph of a smashed car complete with dead body. Only the car and body were made up of broken bottles. The caption read:

'DON'T GET SMASHED THIS SUMMER'.

Near the Rangitaiki River, I stopped at another roadside stall situated outside a house. I bought four stubby cucumbers that were
more the shape of conch shells. I was standing beside the stall,
simultaneously admiring the view of the distinctive volcanic cone
of Mount Edgecumbe as well as the truncated shape of my cucumbers, when the cucumber-producing woman spotted me from her
house and invited me in for a cup of tea that came in a mug on
which was written: 'DANGEROUS WORK CAN BE SAFE IF RISK-
MANAGED'. Best not to, if you ask me, otherwise you'd do
nothing and go nowhere. Anyway, the woman wanted to know all
about me and where I was going. So I told her. To everything I said
she replied with the expression, 'That's for real!'

Further on up the road (but not a lot further, mind) I stopped
again, this time at R&B Berry Fruit Farm. As its name suggested,
R&B Berry Fruit Farm grew berries. Strawberries, raspberries, bil-
berries, blueberries. I bought a fruit smoothie and a one-kilo
mixed punnet of berries for $5 and ate the lot sitting at a picnic
table outside their shop. As I ate, a disgruntled man pulled up in
a Toyota Starlet Glanza and got out to buy one of R&B's fruit
smoothies. Then he got back into his car to eat it, staring straight
ahead. He wore a baseball cap that told me to BE WARE.

R&B Berry Fruit Farm was run by Richard Manktelow and his
wife Barb. Unlike the Be Ware man, they were both very friendly.
I said I had never heard the name Manktelow before.

'It's an East European name,' said Richard, 'though Barb and I
are actually from Kent. The Gillingham and Gravesend area. But
we've been here forty years.'

It seemed their berry farm was very successful. Most of the fruit
was exported to America. There was another cheerful woman who
worked in the packing shop. She had purple hands. 'This is my
summer job,' she said. 'In winter I decorate cakes. I like to have a
finger in every pie.'

Using the toilet in the warehouse I found a sign on the back of the door that said in both English and Maori: 'PLEASE WASH YOUR HANDS. HOROI O RINGA RINGA'. Amazing how the Maoris could make a mundane pastime sound so enjoyably musical, like a campanologist's bonanza.

I'm now in Whakatane. I've noticed in New Zealand that something strange happens to places whose names start with a 'Wh' as they come out as a 'Fff'. On the Coromandel when I told people I was heading for Whangamata they looked at me a bit oddly before saying, 'Oh, you mean Fahng-a-ma-*ta?*' I wasn't so sure that I did, but sometimes it's best to agree that yes, you think you were meaning something that they thought you meant, even when you didn't mean anything of the sort.

To my unconditioned mind Whakatane comes out either as Whack-a-tane or Whack-a-tar-knee. Judging from the local way with words, this is completely wrong. Pronounced correctly Whakatane comes out as Fuk-a-ta-*ne*. In similar vein this means that all the other places that begin with a 'Whak' (Whakarongo, Whakamara, Whakapourangi, Whakapapa and so on) come out as Fuk-a-something. How the early missionaries ever coped with such shocking pronunciation I can't imagine.

'I shall act like a man' – that's what Whakatane means. These words came about back in the fourteenth century on the arrival of the *Mataatua*, a lead canoe from Hawaiki (the Polynesian homeland whence what became the Maori tribes are said to have migrated at various times over the centuries by double-hulled canoe and thought most likely to be Ra'iatea in the Society Islands), at the local river mouth. Legend has it, in the legendary way that legends have things, that the men went ashore, leaving the women on board the canoe, which began to drift back out to sea. Touching the paddles was *tapu* (sacredly forbidden in a taboo sort of way – *tapu* is where the word taboo comes from) but Wairaka, the high-spirited daughter of the Chief Toroa, took the matter into her own hands by grabbing a paddle and shouting, '*Kia whakatane au I ah au!*' ('I will act as a man!'). A bit of ferocious paddling ensued as others followed her lead and the canoe was saved. What a relief.

Whakatane, Bay of Plenty, 22 January

There, it's happened again. I turn up in a place to spend half an hour and next thing I know a few more days have been brushed under the carpet.

Whakatane is where I've been and where I still am. Maybe because Whakatane is a base for big-game fishing, most of the private licence plates round here exhibit a piscine theme: FISHEZ; A FISHA; GO2 SEA. There's no shortage of boy racers either with their wide exhausts and thick heads accelerating with a squeal of wrenched rubber between one set of traffic lights and another. One racing boy, whose licence plate read 2 FAST 4 U, turned out to be not too fast for me. I caught him up on my bike when he became marooned between two trucks at the lights, pointlessly revving.

I'm spending every night camping beside the river at Whakatane Motor Camp and Caravan Park. The camp is half full of resident caravans that are home to a busy assortment of Maori, the other half given over to campers and motorhomes. On one side of me I have a game-fisherman in a 4WD stuck with a bumper sticker that declares: 'Work is for those who can't fish'. On the other side I have a Maori family in a big Wendy house-style tent. There are three gorgeous dark-haired children with big brown eyes: ten-year-old Elijah, eight-year-old Jesse and five-year-old Lily. They all seem intrigued with my compact tent and spend half their time clambering in and out. Lily keeps hugging my leg while the boys fire me with technical questions. Why do I have so many water bottles? What do I put in them? How many gears do I have? How do I know where to put everything? How many countries have I cycled in? What do I do when it rains?

Their dad is a thickset Maori, a working bloke with a big smile, who told me, 'I might get me a haircut, eh?' and who likes to say 'gidday' and 'bro' (a Maori term of endearment) to me a lot. He's a logger and goes off every morning at dawn to log in the forests. The family are from Rotorua though they want to move down here to Whakatane if they can find anywhere they can afford, as they say it is much nicer than Rotorua. I said it probably smelt better too. They agreed. Rotorua, sitting on a sulphurous pile of bubbling volcanoes, is famous for smelling of hard-boiled eggs. Talking of Rotorua, there was a bit in the *New Zealand Herald* about how the Grumpy Mole Saloon, a bar in Rotorua, was under scrutiny by its national franchise owner after complaints about jelly-wrestling. It seems a group of patrons walked out 'horrified' after a member of the audience was offered a $130 pair of sunglasses to strip off and join two women dressed only in bras and G-strings wrestling in a pool of jelly.

The other day a Belgian man on a Canondale bike and carrying only fourteen kilos of kit turned up at the campground. He was cycling around parts of New Zealand for three months but was very disappointed with the country. He thought the drivers were terrible and he also found New Zealand to be a very boring place. He felt once you had seen one town you had seen them all. 'After 6 p.m. they turn into ghost towns,' he said. 'Everyone is indoors watching TV. I have travelled in Cuba and Thailand and Spain where everything is alive for twenty-four hours a day. Also for scenery, you cannot beat Europe. For trees you have the Black Forest, for mountains the Jura, Carpathians or Alps. And everywhere has the ancient history.'

Canondale Man was also disappointed because he had just arrived back from a boat trip out to White Island but had been unable to land for a guided tour as the seas were too rough to dock, though he said the boat ride was fun. White Island, which I could see when I stood on the bank behind the toilet block, is New Zealand's most active (and only marine) volcano, smouldering 50 km off the coast. Around the beginning of last century, the volcano had a sulphur mine within its crater. At least it did until 1914, when an eruption killed all the miners on the island. Nowadays Whakatane is a busy hub for tour operators offering guided tours to, and on, the island by boat, plane or helicopter. Canondale Man was surprised I wasn't willing to fork out between $100 and $400 to have an up-close encounter with this island, but I just couldn't get excited about paying a lot of money to sit with a lot of excitable people while listening to the guide's inevitable repertoire of stock jokes. Anyway, the postcards this side of the water gave me a good feel for the place, which saves having to fall into a fumarole.

Sitting in the coastal heart of the eastern Bay of Plenty, Whakatane is supposed to be one of New Zealand's sunniest locations, averaging 2,500 hours of sunshine a year. Can't say I've seen much of this well-advertised sun – more like wind and rain. But then maybe this is an unusual glitch as a lot of the middle to lower North Island is currently having a burst of unseasonably bad weather, especially Napier and Wellington, with floods, tornados, uprooted trees and no sailings across the Cook Strait. Luckily I've put my tent on a slightly tussocky hummock, but my Maori neighbour's tent has turned into a muddy quagmire. I saw a Maori man from the residential end of the caravan site, which is even more waterlogged than this end, walking about in canoes for shoes. They looked like extra large Moroccan slippers, curled up like sledge runners at the toes.

   The blowy weather doesn't seem to be deterring the fishing folk. They're all out in force. But then Whakatane is currently holding the Holden 2004 Open Tuna Tournament. The town's streets are clogged with recreational fishing boats, some huge and squatting precariously on seemingly insubstantial trailers. The local papers are full of fishing talk. I'm not quite sure what it is about the people who fish around here, but most of them seem to have a fish theme in their names. I've been reading about Goose Haddock, president of the Whakatane Sportfishing Club, who talked about the first of the game fish caught by one of the club's junior members – seventeen-year-old Cody Herdman. By all accounts, last year's tournament was a poor affair as the tuna stayed away in their droves. But this year, day one alone has put paid to any worries about a repeat performance as twenty-two yellow-fin were weighed, with Ash Gordon's huge 112.6 kg big-eye tuna (the record for Whakatane Sportfishing Club was a 133 kg tuna caught back in 1988, so this one is the second biggest) said to be 'raising eyebrows' around the country.

This evening I walked along the riverfront to the weigh station on the wharf. Throngs of spectators crowded around the excitable weigh master (as he's called) and the huge hook scales. This weigh-in event, where the fishing boats pull up at the wharf to unload their day's catch, was an unbelievably popular affair. The event drew such a crowd of people that special tiered stands of seats had been erected to house them all. Children were as enthralled as the adults. One little girl with a small heart-shaped face, riding on her father's shoulders, looked completely spellbound by the whole procedure. Being small I managed to wiggle my way forwards in the crowd to stand behind the row of children at the front. The fishermen all seemed to be in shorts and sunglasses and bare feet, walking about in all the scaly fishy gunk on the wharf. Each boat's prize catch was hooked by the mouth and with much fanfare the weight was shouted out, to cheers from the crowd. The fisherman then stood beside his suspended catch to have his picture taken by the official photographer. It seemed smiling was not the thing to do. They just stood there in their shades besides their unbelievably huge fish (some were four foot long by two foot wide) looking mean and tough like a prize-fighter before he goes into the ring. It was all most amusing.

While I was down at the weigh station Ash Gordon pulled up with his 112.6 kg big-eye tuna. It was the size of a shark. Talking of sharks, it wasn't just tuna that were turning up on the scales; there were also marlin, yellowtail kingfish, albacore and mako sharks.

All week the local radio station has been talking about nothing but fishing. One morning I was in my tent having breakfast and listening to the radio when I learnt how you can tell the difference between a big-eye and a yellow-fin tuna, something that up until now I have been able to get through life very nicely without knowing. From the outside a big-eye and a yellow-fin look much the same. So if you really want to know what you've got you need to dissect the fish, for it's within the liver where the difference lies. One of the tuna has a smooth liver while the other tuna has a liver that comes with striations. But I can't remember which type of liver belongs to which tuna. Sorry about that.

Opotiki, Bay of Plenty, 24 January

One morning in Whakatane I went for a walk up the bush-clad hillside to Kohi Point accompanied by the hovering flit of fantails performing their feats of flight in pursuit of insects and the clicks and croaks and grunts and rattles and wheezes and chuckles and honeyed tones of the tuis and bellbirds. Then the skies broke and a torrential rain fell so I ran back down the hill to town, where I went to have a look around the local District Museum and Gallery on Boon Street. As the rain drummed on the roof I peered at lots of Maori language prayer books, war belts and hatchets, loggers' axes and saws. There were also lots of old typewriters, the type of things you find at car boot sales back home. More interesting were the 'Woman GAY carefree home perm' and the 'HIP & SITZ bath' and 'The Veedee Vibratory Massage Device'. This latter exhibit came with a note typed by the museum: 'The Veedee Vibratory Massage Device was unfortunately incomplete so the museum staff were unable to try it out'.

Saucy devils. But then it's probably a good thing that it was incomplete because, judging from the picture on the box, the vibratory device looked like a hand-operated eggbeater. There was another picture showing a woman egg-beating a man's back as he held on tightly to the back of a chair, though I'm sure men's backs were not the only part of the human anatomy that got whisked with vibrations.

From Whakatane I hauled myself up and over the hill to Ohope (Maori for 'place of main body of army') and on to Ohiwa (apparently 'place of watchfulness' though it sounds more like greeting of surprise) Harbour, with a magnificent backdrop of native black beech trees and mangroves. On I went through Cheddar Valley (where on one fast descent an angry wasp became lodged in my helmet before reappearing on the inside of my sunglasses, resulting in the execution of an impressive emergency stop) and past the junction of Toone ('Geordie for town') Road. I'm now in Opotiki, easternmost town of the Bay of Plenty and 'Gateway to the East Cape'. The town itself is full of the usual uninspiring boxy building architecture, the usual New World and Four Square stores, the usual Caltrex service stations and Star Mart convenience stores. I believe the most exciting thing to have happened in Opotiki was about 140 years ago when the Reverend Carl Sylvius Völkner was hanged and then decapitated by Maoris convinced he had passed information about their movements and fortifications to Governor George Grey. And that's about the sum of the place.

Yesterday and all of today I propelled my way by kayak up and down the Otara and Waioeka Rivers and out to sea. I've been camping at Opotiki Holiday Park where there are two motorhomes belonging to two retired couples, both of whom are spending several months driving around the country. I've noticed that many motorhome owners seem to have a custom whereby they paint their generally corny and ill-spelt travelling motto on to their vehicle's bodywork just above the windscreen. The mottos of the motorhomes here say *Good e-nuff!* and *Whatta Life!*

Until this evening, I was the only tent here, camped on a grassy patch beside a bank of trees that were blowing merry hell in the frisky wind. There are now another three tents, all belonging to cyclists. One of these is a lone American man who looks very vexed about something and spends all his time in the TV room. Another belongs to a middle-aged couple on Bike Fridays. They too are American and don't seem to be very content with New Zealand. The woman keeps moaning to me about the wind. On a brighter note are John and Alison Rankin, the couple in the next-door tent. They are both Kiwis, in their mid-to-late forties, and feel wholly positive about all that lies before them. This is because they are just about to spend a few days cycling around East Cape ('a test run', they call it) before going home to Hamilton where within the next two months they will pack up their belongings, rent out their house and give up their jobs before heading to Nepal for a spot of trekking and then to London, where they plan to get jobs and save up some money to buy some good bikes before setting off on a long cycling expedition.

Tonight I was lying in my tent tuning through the various radio stations when I came to rest for a moment or two on Radio Pacific (one of the talkback stations). I heard the woman presenter talking about having seen a trailer to a film, but instead of the word 'trailer' she used the word 'shorts'. 'I saw the shorts to that movie,' she said. It took me a moment to work out what she was talking about. Then, to everyone who rang in she said, 'Good on yer,' followed by 'Awesome!' Even if what the callers were doing or saying wasn't awesome at all. As she was signing off for the evening she said to her listeners, 'You have a neat night now!' A *neat* night! Well actually, I'm going to have a very untidy one, thank you. I've got my sheet sleeping bag in a right old twist and I've got food and panniers all over the tent. You should get over here – it's an awesome sight.

4

Te Kaha, Eastland, 25 January

On my way to Tirohanga ('Lane Gyratory System') I passed a sign that said 'LITTER IS unlAWFUL' and then another sign (handwritten this one) pointing down a track that said:

PIG DOG
TRAINING SCHOOL
BOOKBINDER

Could this mean that down the track there lay a pig-style dog, a training school and a bookbinder? Or did it mean that there was a training school for pig-dogs, or even dog-like pigs that were capable of a little bookbinding on the side? It was a job to know.

I was now on the part of the Pacific Coast Highway that is State Highway 35. This meant that for the time being I had left Death Highway 2 to veer inland through Waioeka Gorge over the mountains to Gisborne while I followed the relatively quiet coast road around East Cape.

I'm camping in the old whaling settlement of Te Kaha ('to car hire' – verb). These days the place is more a draw for fishermen. The campground is awash with rods and boats and fishing nuts with their tinnies called things like *Aqua Holic* and *Y Knott*? The licence plates of my two neighbours spell LAND EM and SQUIDZ.

Tonight I was invited to eat some of the barbecued catch of the day by some people nearby who had a big tent and an even bigger 4WD (with a sun-visor motif on the cab roof saying: BORN LUCKY). A woman and three blokes. All loud and raucous and drunk on what looked like a mixture of whisky, vodka and beer. One of the blokes was called Jeff, pronounced Jiff. To his lift, I mean left, slouched a man with a buzz cut and a knocked-about face. He was liberally embellished with tattoos and was called something like Hunt or Hurt or Hiirt. He told me I was 'fucking crazy, man' to travel alone around New Zealand without a knife on me. By knife, he meant a *big* knife. I think we were almost talking machete. Then there was Monty, hunched over in his seat, noisily crunching on crayfish bones and hungrily sucking out their flesh and juices like Neanderthal man, his face covered with the remnants. He looked like he had used his face as a weapon while doing battle with a giant live pincer crayfish. But no, the blood was merely put down to a bad shave earlier in the evening.

Monty told me that all Kiwis hate cyclists. 'That's because we're always in a hurry to get places and cyclists slow us down. There're a lot of crazy people out there who wouldn't think twice about hitting a cyclist. If I was you, I'd keep right over to the lift, man.'

Jiff told me that he had some friends who had always fancied cycling around New Zealand. 'But after the second day they gave up and rented a car. They said cycling was too much hard work and the roads were too bloody dangerous.'

Oruaiti Beach, Eastland, 26 January

The past two days' riding were a scenic delight. The weather behaved a treat and the sea sparkled as dazzling as crinkled foil. The road clinging to the rocky coastline was rugged and lined with flowering fennel and cloaked crimson with pohutukawa trees. Birds cackled and whooped from the bush-thick hillsides. It was an up-and-down ride full of narrow one-lane bridges painted green and white. At one point I passed the 110-year-old Raukokore Anglican Church jutting out from the road almost into the sea.

With its distinctive small white-clapboard frame and stubby little steeple like a witch's hat, it stood a lonely sentinel between the tarmac and the waves.

Apart from the odd fisherman or farm or splash of Maori children leaping into a river, the area was empty of people. In fact, this East Cape region is one of the most sparsely populated areas in New Zealand, rarely visited and considered to be something of a backwater. SH35, which took decades to build, was a continuous sinuous mix of steep and twisting climbs up to headlands, dropping down across rivers to inlets and coves or beaches strewn with enormous chunks and trunks of driftwood bleached white from the sun. From a distance so much stricken wood, splayed limbs angled in tortuous positions of torment, looked like a fallen army, as though some terrible battle had taken place here on the sand. Most of the timber had come from the towering hills of the heavily forested hinterland and been washed down the many rivers along the coast.

Traffic was either 4WDs pulling boats or battered pick-ups and cars belonging to locals. Nearly every home I passed had an old sofa on the front porch and a pile of car corpses stacked in the backyard. Every now and then there was the skeleton of a vehicle, its bodywork an epidemic rash of rust and extensive blisters of coppery corrosion, left to rot on a plot of land or a riverbank. The few and far between communities were mostly tiny settlements, some with pubs advertising 'LION RED – The Measure of a Man's Thirst'. Others had an impressive carved *marae* (meeting house). The land is predominantly Maori and signs warned that if trespassers were found on this land without permission they would be shot.

For a road that had virtually no traffic on it there seemed to be a disproportionate amount of tyre-squashed possums. Maybe, like those pukeko swamp hens, possums are suicidal and throw themselves in front of vehicles. After seeing an advert in the window of one of only two small stores I'd passed since leaving Opotiki, I thought maybe I should scrape the possums off the road to earn some money. The advert said:

POSSUM FUR & GREEN SKINS
(For Sliping)
We are buying hand plucked and machine plucked
possum fur.
For $60/kg
Let us help you make extra money from your trapping/poison-
ing programmes.
Fur must be:

- An average length of 25cm
- Clean with no contamination (eg bullets, staples)
- Dry to the touch (we do not buy water)
- Keep H/P and M/P separate

Skins must be open skinned and rolled into balls before freezing.

Phone Sue and Steve on—

Brush-tailed possums were introduced into New Zealand from Australia in 1837 to establish a fur trade, but got rapidly out of hand. There are now more than 70 million possums (17.5 per person!) running havoc throughout the country, falling out of fruit trees on to unsuspecting cyclists' tents, slaughtering ground-dwelling kiwis and chomping through more than 20,000 tons of native vegetation a night with blithe indifference to the principles of conservation. People are out there in their gardens and the back blocks (remote areas) shooting and poisoning and trapping them whenever they can. As a result you can now wear possums in the form of jumpers, skirts, gloves, hats, scarves and socks.

A few years ago a retired North Island farmer came up with a new approach to New Zealand's least-wanted pest. His motto seemed to be: If you can't beat 'em, eat 'em, or at least persuade pets to. The result was Possyum, a gourmet casserole of possum meat, vegetables and jelly that is packed with high levels of heart-friendly polyunsaturated fats. The farmer, Bryan Bassett-Smith, says dogs love it. He also doesn't mind the taste himself. 'It's good on crackers – just needs a bit of salt.'

*

Here at Oruaiti ('yes, I'm fine thanks') Beach campground I met a mouthful in the form of two Belgians on bikes. They were Diane and Günter Vercammen-Brems from Oostmallebaan and their laden bikes were even heavier than mine, which is always reassuring. They were even using large Ortlieb rear panniers on the front for more capacity. Günter blamed me for getting him in this cycling mess after reading one of my books. Neither him nor Diane much liked the North Island. The South Island, they said, was a vast improvement. 'But still we are very disappointed with the amount of traffic and standard of driving,' said Günter. They were hurrying now for Auckland to catch a plane to Alaska. 'Alaska?' I said, 'In January? Isn't that going to be a bit cold?'

'Yes,' they said. 'Very cold.'

And then we went to bed.

Te Araroa, Eastland, 27 January

There was an article in today's *Herald* headlined: 'CYCLIST LOSES FIGHT FOR HELMET EXEMPTION'. Wearing a helmet when cycling is law in New Zealand. I wasn't very happy about this when I first got here because I don't like being forced to do things. I think something like wearing a helmet should be a matter of personal choice. Although I've had various helmets for seventeen years, I've probably worn one for about 10 per cent of that time – always at night, always in bad weather, always on roads so full of traffic that I think I might die if I don't put one on. None of which, I admit, are very good reasons, but then that's up to me and not some man in a suit who sits in an office and drives a car. But since I've been in New Zealand, land of bad drivers, I've been wearing my helmet – only occasionally taking it off when inching my way up a mountain in direct sunshine with sweat streaming down my face. I don't mind my helmet any more. In fact, most of the time I hardly even notice it.

But Patrick Morgan was obviously not a happy helmet wearer. Last year he had applied to Wellington District Court to overturn a decision by the director of the LTSA declining an application for exemption. It seems the director can grant an exemption on a case-by-case basis for religious, medical or other reasonable grounds. Patrick said that the helmet-wearing regulation was discriminatory. He also claimed that helmets lacked protection and they could lead to increased risk of spinal and brain injury. The director obviously thought he was talking rubbish. This resulted in his application being refused.

The traffic has tapered off even further. Just the odd Maori wagon and the occasional logging and stock truck. Adjacent to Cape Runaway at Whangaparaoa (cusp of the East Cape where, the story goes, the warriors in the *Tainui,* one of several ancestral canoes loaded with settlers from Hawaiki, first stepped ashore about 650 years ago on the land that they came to know as Aotearoa) the road finally turned inland and was a lovely lonely stretch of green hills and small mountains and farmland and forest interspersed with lots of cows, rivers, fennel and honeysuckle. The road plopped out at the sea again at Hick's Bay. Hick's Bay was originally named Te Wharekahika, but was renamed after one of the crew of Cook's *Endeavour.* Quite a lot seems to have gone on in Hick's Bay. It once had a port and freezing works (in Kiwi-speak, a slaughterhouse or abattoir) and was the home of Tuwhakairiora, the most famous of Ngati Porou fighting chiefs – though I think Tuwhakairiora came a little before the freezing works. Then, in 1830, the new European settlers were celebrating the marriage between a Pakeha and a Maori girl when an enemy tribe launched a surprise attack and ate the wedding guests.

Talking of Maori, I was just packing some freshly purchased produce away into my panniers outside the Hick's Bay store when at the sound of a gallop of hooves I turned my head to see two Maori men riding bareback, one with a small boy holding on tight, clattering up the dusty road. Just the local method of transport for coming to pick up their mail.

A short sharp shock came in the form of a steep headland I had to climb in a sun-induced sweat before hurtling at breakneck speed down the other side to Te Araroa ('boat ashore'). But before I embarked upon my swift descent I stopped at a scenic outlook at the top of the headland. The minute I arrived a Chinese student in a hire car turned up at the same spot. He couldn't speak a word of English but when he came grinning and proffering his camera and pointing at me I took it that he wanted me to take his picture accompanied by the attractive scenic backdrop. I was wrong. Instead he wanted to take a picture of me. 'What do you want to take a picture of me for?' I said. 'You don't know me from Adam!'

The boy just grinned some more and pointed to where he wanted me to stand – not with the scenic backdrop as I had imagined, but beside his Hertz hire car. There was not even a hint of the dramatic view before us, just me and a maroon blob of metal. I could have been standing on a patch of scrubland on the outskirts of Uttoxeter for all you knew. I dutifully took up position beside his car. 'I'm not feeling at my best!' I warned, aware of the oily chain marks tattooed across my shins and sweat-soaked hair stuck to my forehead. As I held my unflattering pose I tried to imagine the scene back at his home in Nanchang or Chengchow when showing his holiday snaps to his extended Chinese family. 'So, Wang Woo,' his uncle-once-removed-three-times would say in a teasing tone when they got to the picture of me, 'Who's this then? Some floozy you picked up on the road?'

And Wang Woo would say defensively, 'No, not at all. She said her name was Adam.' Which would result in everyone becoming very confused.

Tokomaru Bay, Eastland, 28 January

Today's been a bit of a busy day. I spent the night, or part of the night, camping in Te Araroa – site of the oldest (600 years) and one of the largest (with twenty-two trunks) pohutukawa trees in the country. At 3 a.m. I crawled out of my tent to cycle over 40 km on a bumpy dirt road to East Cape (the most easterly point in New Zealand) to see the sunrise. The sun rose, only I didn't see it.

Momentary cloud cover the minute the moment arrived. Nice lighthouse though.

Back in Te Araroa I packed up my tent. This was covered both inside and out with the cockroach-like carcasses of a nocturnal invasion of cicadas, two of which got stuck to my face. Then, as I was strapping on my bags, I met an Austrian man on a bike. He must have been in his fifties and looked like a mad professor with long white electrified hair flying in all directions. Speaking in slightly stunted English, he referred to the mountainous day we both had ahead of us not as a 'hard' day but a 'strong' day. When he looked about his tent and saw the amount of clobber he had yet to pack away into his panniers, he said, 'Every morning I see all this and have little bit panic!'

I've ridden 120 km today – most of which have felt uphill. Apart from hills, some of which have names like Gudgeons and Letterbox, here's what came my way: burning sun and melting heat, torrential rain, waves of truck-passing spray, waves in shoes, fennel, maize, cows, multicoloured beehives, logging trucks, forests alive with the deafening clatter of cicada chatter (this was before the rains came), spectacular ornate Maori church at Tikitiki which was near the burger-selling Kaui Kart which was near the Barry Avenue petrol station, horseback-riding Maori, Rastafarian Maori. The latter I came across in Ruatoria, centre of the Ngati Porou tribe, where many Maoris have taken on Rastafarian colours and beliefs. The Ngati Porou ancestors were renowned for striking fear into the hearts of their enemies. The tribe still has something of a rough-tough image and Ruatoria has a reputation in New Zealand as a belligerent cowboy town with spates of machete and arson attacks.

By the time I arrived in Ruatoria the rain was still waterfalling out of the sky and I was so wet that I went to warm up in the Blue Boar Tavern on the junction up from Piggery Road. The Tavern was owned by TeAo and Duke Henry and was full of Maoris. The men were all big blokes, many of them loggers having stopped early for the day because of the rain. One was a big bull of a man with a strong spade-shaped chin and face muscles that seemed to be made of knotted wood. Everyone was incredibly jovial and friendly and bidding me *kia ora* (hello, good health, good luck). I was given a big mug of steaming hot tea by one of the women, who wanted to warm me up. She was going to give me coffee but then she said, 'Yous Pommies like tea, eh?' Maori English is very enjoyable to listen to. It's not so much an accent as a speech pattern with a distinctive rising intonation of each sentence ending with 'eh'. It also seems to have the odd plural and surprise, like when Duke asked me, 'How's yous doin', bro?'

A man called Gary, a logger who had lived all his life on the East Cape and was married to chain-smoking Rita, wouldn't allow me to cycle down the road to the local Four Square store to stock up on supplies. 'Yous ain't goin' out in that rain, eh?' he said. This wasn't so much a question as a statement. And that was that. He drove me down in his wagon instead and sat in it while I went to do a shop. Then he drove me back to the tavern again. He and Rita wanted me to come and stay the night in their house up the way. But I was keen to get going even though the rain was still hammering down outside. As this point a man called Grant pulled up at the tavern in a Liquor King van. He was here to deliver a few crate-loads of drink before driving the 140-odd kilometres back to Gisborne, where he was manager of the Liquor King store. A number of Blue Boar regulars took Grant aside and before I knew it they had got him to pack my bike on board his van to give me a lift to Gisborne. Not what I wanted at all! But arguing with a tavern full of well-wishing Maori is not easy, so I climbed up into the Liquor King cab and squashed up alongside Leticia, Grant's girlfriend, on the bench-seat and off we went, sluicing through the floods of rain.

Before I asked Grant to stop out of sight of the Blue Boar Tavern to let me out, I learnt that Grant and Leticia had only moved down to Gisborne from Auckland six months ago and that Leticia had spent two years doing, as she put it, 'the OE thing'.

OE? I thought. What's that? Old English? Oxford English? Organised Evacuation? Overtly Exuberant? Ordained Evangelical? Overhead Eiderdown? Origami Egg? Osteopathic Elephant? It was a job to know. So I made some enquires.

'Overseas Experience,' said Leticia.

Although New Zealand is a very spacious country for the size of the population, the population is so small that most young people can't go anywhere without meeting someone who knows someone who knows them. This can seem a bit claustrophobic so they tend to head off around the world for about three years with a rucksack, most of them ending up in the UK. Leticia had done this and spent two years living in Portsmouth, where she worked on the cross-Channel ferries to Le Havre.

Grant begrudgingly agreed to dump me at the side of the road in the rain despite telling me, 'You're bloody nuts, mate!' He gave me his address and told me to come and stay when I made it to Gisborne. I cycled back in a Blue Boar direction to redo the bit that had passed me by in the Liquor King van.

Hills came, hills went, but the rain remained as I aquaplaned through Papawera ('he's over there'), Hiruharama ('Bananarama's brother'), Takapau ('I've taken one, thanks') and Te Puia ('or not Te Puia, that is the question'). And so to Tokomaru Bay, a shabby and crumbling seaside settlement cupped in a cliff-framed bay that had seen better days. It had seen a busy wharf and freezing works, now quiet and derelict. It had also seen a cyclone. This struck in 1988, destroying many of Tokomaru's old wooden buildings, including the Te Puka Hotel, now risen from the debris in the shape of the Te Puka Tavern.

I'm lying behind the petrol station in the Mayfair Camping Ground, which, despite its grandiose name, is a bit of a dismal-looking place (not helped by the oppressive rain) with dirty toilets and kitchen. The only other people staying are an elderly couple in a pop-up caravan who have come for the fishing, or 'fushing' as they call it. The wind is doing strange things tonight – one moment my tent is being buffeted senseless and a loose slab of corrugated iron on a nearby shed roof is singing like a banshee, and the next everything is quite still. Apart from the sea, that is, which sounds boomingly loud all the time.

Tolaga Bay, Eastland, 29 January

From Tokomaru Bay to Tolaga Bay – the grand distance of 40 km. Well, it was a bit hard to get going this morning. It rained most of yesterday, it rained all of last night and it was still raining when I woke up within my dripping cocoon. So I did the only thing I could do in the circumstances – I turned over and went back to sleep.

The morning then formed a pattern: wake, hear rain, eat, sleep, though at one point I performed a little variation on the theme and clipped my toenails. Finally the rain abated and the sun came out – tentatively at first, but then with sumptuous gusto. Then it was all hands on deck and a desperate drying of all possessions in the sun that had turned from watery to milky to skin-witheringly hot.

The escape from Tokomaru Bay involved a steep 3 km climb over Purau Saddle followed by a steep descent. It was on the steepest part of this descent that I came across a woman with a STOP/GO sign standing ahead of some roadworks that had closed the road down to a single lane. As I was plummeting at high speed towards the woman she stood with the GO towards me. Then, when I was only about fifty feet away, she flipped the sign around to STOP. When you're falling full pelt down a mountain with half a tonne of kit on board on a road that has suddenly turned to gravel, a sudden stop is not the easiest manoeuvre to pull off without much skidding and steaming of brake blocks. So instead I continued careering past the woman while calling out, 'SORRRYYY – CAAAN'T STOP!' All I hoped was that there wasn't a logging truck rumbling towards me round the bend. I tore round the bend and there it was – all fifty logging tonnes of it, growling up the hill towards me. The only way to get past it was to dodge through a slalom of cones dividing the one open lane from the roadworks lane, navigate through two heaped piles of grit, a JCB and a steam-roller and then bounce up back on to the road again into the black cloudy fuelled wake of the logging truck. Compared with my morning of eating and sleeping and nail-clipping, this manoeuvre felt the height of excitement.

The rest of the ride was comparatively uneventful as I glided down the valley of the Hikuwai ('questionable hiccup') River past fields of maize and courgettes interspersed with rotting car wrecks to Tolaga Bay. Tolaga Bay was a quiet town with a straggle of houses and stores straddling the road. All the streets were named after Captain Cook's crew, as Cook cast anchor here in 1769. When I pulled up outside George and Mildred's, a small grocery store situated a few stores along from The Snarler Parlour – Tolaga Meat Supply (now closed down), a large Maori woman was waddling in hot pursuit of a bevy of chickens making a break for freedom down the main street. As soon as a logging truck came rumbling through they scarpered off in all directions.

I'm now camping down at the beach alongside the wharf that marches 660 metres out to sea on an army of stilted legs. When Tolaga Bay was a thriving port, this wharf (much-heralded as the longest wharf in the southern hemisphere) hummed with coastal shipping activity. I was about to go for a swim when I noticed a headline in the local paper warning that a 4½ metre great white shark had been spotted off Gisborne. As Gisborne is only about an hour's swim away for a shark I decided to concentrate on washing my socks instead.

Tolaga Bay, Eastland, 1 February

I arrived here last month and I'm still here, even if it was only three days ago. In between several lengthy bursts of washing and walking, some more cyclists turned up. They were John and Alison Rankin, the couple I'd met back in Opotiki who were about to head over-seas on their extended OE. They told me that about ten years ago they had travelled around Europe in a camper van and then when they were living in Taupo (in South Island) they met some keen cyclists who became their friends. As a result the friends got them into cycling and so they went touring around southeast Asia by bike. They had read one of my books, which didn't appear to have put them off cycling, so that's good. John said he was in the process of writing his own book, currently titled, *Work Sucks – Let's Go Cycle-touring* and that he had an uncle in England who worked in publishing, so John was relying on him for a helping hand.

This morning in the campground kitchen I came across a pile of the past week's papers stacked in the corner. As I ate my porridge I leafed through the various copies of *New Zealand Herald*. There was a lot about the 'foreshore and seabed issue' (Maori are laying claim to rightful ownership when for all New Zealanders it has been a generally accepted truth that the sea and its contents belong equally to all) as well as the views of John Tamihere, the Land Information and Associate Maori Affairs Minister, on the 'Maori right to choose place names'. Because of their *whakapapa* (a Maori's oral family history), John Tamihere said Maori had rights to name places and landmarks and he was keen to see Auckland's name changed to Tamaki Makaurau, the Maori name for the area, though he said he would not 'die in a ditch' for it and agreed it would change only when the country was more mature. There was also a lot about the 'controversial race relations speech' made this week by the National Party leader Don Brash.

More eye-catching than all of this were the words I spotted in the advertisement section of the Bay of Plenty's *Bay Trader*: 'Barbed wire, 2 rolls, swap for Mongolian nose flute'.

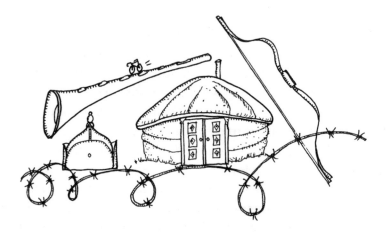

It's still the 1st of February but after a few hours of cycling I'm now in Gisborne. Arriving here was a bit of a shock to the system – like being hurled back into the chaos of civilisation. Although Gisborne is more large town than city, it feels like a metropolis after riding through the wopwops (remote area) over the last few days. In Maori the area around Gisborne is known as Te Tairawhiti – 'the coast where the sun shines across the waters'. Because of its proximity to the International Date Line, Gisborne is the most easterly city in the world (*whiti* means east) and it makes the most of being the first city on which the sun rises.

In similar fashion, Gisborne blows its trumpet as being the place where Captain Cook first set foot in New Zealand – at nearby Kaiti Beach in Poverty Bay. Poverty Bay acquired its distinctly misleading name from Captain Cook when he found little to feed his crew on here and discovered that the area 'did not afford a single article we wanted, except a little firewood'. Poverty Bay is now far from poor, known for its warm summers and fertile alluvial plains, and is a farming, viticultural and horticultural hub.

I was going to drop by on Mr Liquor King when I spotted John and Alison wandering along Gladstone Road just up from the Pak 'n' Save supermarket. They told me they were camping down near the docks. After cycling along to Liquor King and finding Grant not in, I went down to camp at the dock site too. Alison and John were sitting at their tent-side picnic table and drinking wine out of their unbreakable and collapsible travelling wine glasses and invited me to join them. By the end of this little session I had discovered quite a lot more about them – especially John who, along with being a food buyer for supermarkets, had also had a stint at being a wine shop owner and a forester. For most of the 1980s John had been a policeman. That's how he met Alison. She was working as an accountant in an office opposite John's. Both offices had glass walls so they could easily see each other. Three policemen worked in John's office. They all knew Alison was single so when the police office party was coming up John held up a big handwritten sign against the window that Alison could read. Together with their office extension number it said: 'WHICH

ONE OF US DO YOU WANT TO GO WITH TO THE POLICE PARTY?' And all three policemen stood against the window trying to look alluring. Alison pointed at John's mate Paul. 'Because he was the only good-looking one,' said Alison. But for some reason, when the party came, John went instead of Paul. 'That was twenty years ago!' said John.

John had spent some time in the CIB (the New Zealand version of the CID), mostly based in Rotorua. There was always a lot of trouble going on – mainly between rival tribes and gangs of Maori. He told me about one particular Maori man, a Rastafarian nick-named Diesel Dick who used to soak rags in diesel and then set fire to buildings – often public buildings like supermarkets. Once he even burnt down a fire station. John's CIB mates were sick of Diesel Dick and wanted to teach him a lesson so they kidnapped him and beat him up. Which doesn't sound like the brightest move for a CIB man to make. Perhaps they weren't overly blessed. Anyway, not surprisingly, Diesel Dick made an official complaint and the CIB men were all arrested. I'm not quite sure what happened after that except that John left the police because he found it too stressful. But his policing definitely put him in good stead to be an attentive citizen of the community. Several years ago, when he had a stint at living in London, he was working in his wine shop in Wandsworth when a man came in and put a £300 giant bottle of Moët & Chandon under his jacket. A giant bottle of champagne is not the wisest thing to try to conceal beneath a jacket and the man attempted to walk out of the shop with the bottle sticking out of both the bottom and top of the jacket. John saw the whole amateurish smuggling operation take place and found it quite amusing how anyone could be so blatantly stupid. He chased the man down the street. The man turned round and tried to bash John with the giant bottle but nearly fell over with the weight of the thing and just ended up feebly throwing it at him instead. The bottle landed on the ground but didn't break. 'Champagne bottles are made of strong glass to withstand pressure,' said John by way of explanation. The man then ran off down the street. John took off after him and performed a spectacular rugby tackle on his assailant of which he was sure the All Blacks would be proud. He held the man to the ground until the police arrived.

Another time in Wandsworth, he and Alison had just been for a long run and were still in their running gear when they saw a man running down the street with a handbag tucked under his arm. Just up the road stood an old woman angrily shouting and shaking her stick in the direction of the fleeing man. John gave chase to the handbag man – a pursuit that involved vaulting over walls, running down alleys, leaping steps and careering across people's back gardens. It sounded just like something out of Starsky and Hutch. I was waiting for him to say how he cornered the man by jumping off the roof of a two-storey building to land, unscathed, on the bonnet of a car, preferably a Dodge Charger with 01 on the side. But the fire brigade came to the rescue. An attentive crew on board a fire engine noticed the chase and saw the handbag man run into a cul-de-sac. So the firemen blocked off the entrance of the cul-de-sac with their engine. The handbag man saw the fire engine and turned to run into the dead-end street only to find John standing there looking mean. Handbag Man, who John said was a huge bloke built like a rugby prop forward, decided he stood a better chance of escape the John end of the street and charged at him like a frenzied bull in a china shop. John fended the man off before tackling him to the ground in similar vein to Champagne Man and then bashed his head against the pavement to 'quieten him down', as John put it. John had a lot of loose change in his pocket which in the ensuing struggle rolled all over the ground. When the police arrived they thought the coins were part of the money the thief had nicked so put it all back in the retrieved handbag. 'So in the end,' said John, 'the old woman made a profit!'

Unless I end up cycling in completely the opposite direction from the one I'm intending, I don't think I'll be bumping into John and Alison much after Gisborne; they are returning home to Hamilton before heading to Nepal and London, while I'm riding south to Wairoa and beyond. As with most things, John had a few stories to tell about Wairoa, one of which involved rival Maori gang 'warfare'. Apparently not that long ago a gang member was beheaded and his head speared on a pole and left on the edge of town for all to see. 'Be careful when you're down there,' said John. 'It's a rough area.'

Morere, edge of Wharerata Forest, 3 February

Gisborne was hit by a mini monsoon yesterday. All day water poured from the sky as if from a bottomless bucket. As merely sprinting to the campground toilet block involved a severe soaking, I decided to leave tent disassembly to a drier day. As did Alison and John. Instead I wandered around a few museums, stocked up on food and sat in the camp kitchen chatting to Alison and John.

On the radio last night there was news of a man somewhere down south stabbing his two children to death before killing himself. This morning the paper headline was: 'KIDS DEAD IN BEACH STABBINGS'. What's happened to the supposed fluffiness of this land?

To head south I had to ride out of Gisborne in a northerly direction (to skirt Poverty Bay) past HAIR WE ARE hairdressers and Granny Tarr Street before hitting the dreaded Death Highway 2. No sooner had I rejoined this road than a carload of boy-racing hoons squirted past me with a contemptuous throaty roar. Further up the road they performed a tyre-squealing donut before racing back down the middle of the road. As they burnt past, one of the boys spat at me from a backseat window.

On top of this there were stock and logging trucks a plenty. The landscape since leaving Gisborne had gone from vineyards and orchards to farmland with sheep-stations to forest. Or put another way, it had gone from flat to flipping hilly. The highest of these was the Wharerata ('I'm up here!') Saddle. With saddling great hills there are down points in so far as you have to go up them, but then come the highs when you have to go down. The high of the Wharerata Saddle came in a stepped descent. On one of these steps the road fell straight downwards, carving a swathe through a forest of radiata pines – pines that were being enthusiastically logged. I was plunging down this saddled step, catching glances of my handlebar-mounted computer (38 mph, 39 mph, 40 mph, 41 mph, 42 mph . . .) when, despite having one-and-a-half lanes of empty tarmac on which to pass me, a logging truck, approaching from the rear, ran me clean off the road. It all happened very fast. When the truck thundered alongside I had two choices: either be sucked under the rear wheels or be pushed off over the side and down a deep and steeply sloped embankment. I thought I stood a better chance of survival there, so went bouncing off at an angle into its rocky grounded midst, expecting to end up arse over axle. Happily I hit the bottom while still saddled upright. I checked my heart for signs of life, counted my limbs and, finding all intact, made my way out – a procedure that involved unhitching all my panniers and clambering back up to the road with them one by one, followed by a laboured dragging of muddy rock-bashed bike.

Tonight I'm camping in a tangly thicket of native coastal forest across the way from Morere hot springs. I've just been wallowing in the rain in a hottish pool of the mountain stream that is rushing down through some rocks below my tent. Surrounding the area is a whole host of nikau palms which, despite the rain, make the whole place appear decidedly tropical. Nikau palms don't look like your normal run-of-the-mill palm tree at all – more like an elongated feather duster. The name 'nikau' might be derived from the disappointment the Polynesians felt when they first settled in New Zealand and found the country lacking in their main foodstuff, *ni kau* being Polynesian for 'no coconuts'.

5

This morning in Morere I met a man wearing a T-shirt emblazoned with the words: 'TRUST ME – I KNOW WHAT I'M DOING'. Well, I'm not so sure myself. He was manoeuvring his motorhome in a lay-by and reversed into a picnic table. Sustaining a dent in his rear-end didn't seem to overly concern him though. In fact he was more disturbed by the news that I was heading for Napier. 'Jesus, mate,' he said. 'You don't want to go down there on a bike. I've just driven up the coast that way and there're some bastard big hills!'

Hills were the last thing on my mind today as I've had enough rain on my plate to fill a lake. It started out as sudden full-blooded rain and seems to have stayed that way. Apart from waterlogged, the road from Morere to Wairoa was mostly down with a few ups and then a rolling flat with another up and down at the end. I'd gone from mountain forest to valley to coastal farmland and lagoons loaded with black swans to town.

Wairoa ('because I've lost my sail') sits either side of the broad Wairoa River. If you come to New Zealand and fancy looking for the Wairoa River then it is quite understandable that you could become very disoriented and confused as there is a Wairoa River up near Auckland at Clevedon, a Wairoa River at Dargarville and a Wairoa River and Pa (not 'father' but fortified Maori village) at Tauranga. To add to the chaos, there's a Wairau River, Wairau Valley, Wairau Bar and Wairau Pa at Blenheim, a Wairua River near Whangarei and a Waitoa River near Hungahunga.

There's a lighthouse sitting in the middle of the main street in Wairoa. Obviously the town must suffer from so much rain and floods that it's something of a navigational hazard for cars as well as washed-up shipping. Ah, I've just discovered from the campsite owner (whose catch phrases are 'good as gold' and 'way to go!' – example: *Me*: 'Here's $10 for my tent spot.' *Her*: 'Good as gold!' *Me*: 'I'm planning on cycling to Napier.' *Her*: 'Way to go!') that the town lighthouse, built in 1877 of solid kauri, is not there as a warning light for aquaplaning pedestrians, cyclists and drivers, but was relocated from nearby Portland Island at the tip of Mahia Peninsula purely for historical value. What a disappointment. I rather like the idea of traffic navigating their way through the flooded streets past the likes of the Write Price supermarket and Oslers Bakery with the aid of flashing beacons, water-wings and depth sounders.

Wairoa, 5 February

I'm still here because it's still raining. Hard. I told the woman at the campground desk that I was going to stay another night and she said, 'Good as gold!' Then when she asked me what I was going to do today and I said I was going to the sports centre for a swim, she said, 'Way to go!' The sports centre swimming pool, by the way, was Olympic size and, apart from a very large Maori woman wallowing about like a giant seal in a swimming cap that looked like a herbaceous border, completely empty. Maybe the residents of Wairoa (which is actually Maori for 'long water') prefer to swim in the streets instead. They are certainly wet enough.

Talking of residents, apart from a sumo-sized man with a full-face tattoo dressed heavily in a black denim shirt and black jeans and crumpled leather motorcycle boots, I haven't seen any signs of Maori territorial tribeland warfare material. Nor have I seen any severed heads speared on sticks. I'm feeling quite let down.

This evening in the campsite kitchen I met a sixty-two-year-old Irish woman from Dublin called Iris. Irish Iris was garrulous and jocular but never opened her eyes wider than a slither – letting in no more light than a slanting chink in a Venetian blind. She's a retired schoolteacher and she told me that she had always said that when she was sixty she was going to go travelling. Then when she hit sixty she got some sort of serious illness and had to put her plans on hold. But as soon as she was better she sold her house, her possessions, her everything, including her car. 'It's the first time I haven't had a car since I was seventeen,' she said. 'And it's wonderful. Very liberating!' She was now travelling everywhere while she got a house built in Melbourne. 'I chose the house from a catalogue. I wanted to buy a house in an area that I had never seen so that I wouldn't have any preconceptions about the place.'

Kotemaori, Hawke's Bay, 6 February

Here's the headline news back home: nineteen Chinese immigrants
were drowned while picking cockles in Morecambe Bay,
Lancashire. Though they thought it could have been as many as
twenty-three. And here's the headline news here: Helen Clark (the
manly prime minister of New Zealand) was attacked on a Maori
marae (tribal meeting place) while Don Brash, the National party
leader, had mud hurled at him.

And here's the headline news in *Hawke's Bay Today*: 'POKIES
TAKE $2.3 MILLION FROM WAIROA'. When I first got to New
Zealand I thought maybe pokies were the equivalent of our pikeys –
otherwise known as tramps, travellers, gypsies or mischievous ne'er-
do-wells, depending on whom you talk to. So I thought maybe the
pikey-like pokies of Wairoa had been hoodwinking the locals out of
pocket. By a few million. But then I discovered a poky is not so
much a person as a fruit machine. Big money-grabbing ones at that.

Another up-and-down day full of gorges and steep saddles –
some of which offered fine sea views. The day was windy and the
land was wild and rugged and green and every now and then I rode
through heady wafts of wild fennel and honeysuckle and flowering
gorse growing alongside the road. All day there had been no towns,
not even solitary stores. Apart from logging trucks, and
motorhomes nicknamed things like 'J & RUBY', 'STRESSLESS'
and 'FOOTLOOSE', the only sign of modest modernity was a railway that followed me all the way, occasionally ducking and diving
out of sight through a number of hefty hills. Yet I didn't once see a
train on this track. This seemed a terrible waste as it would have
been a fantastically dramatic train ride, especially when the track
crossed the spectacular viaduct at Mohaka.

I was planning on riding the 120 km from Wairoa to Napier
today but then I got distracted. I had just cycled past Kakariki Pit
Road when I noticed a hand-written sign mentioning something
about a cyclist's hostel called The Bothy. Turning off the road down
a long dirt road I found The Bothy looking very bothy-like – small,
simple, stone and remote. It belonged to moustachioed Hamish

and Elsa MacLean and sat squat and sturdy in the middle of a vast sheep farm in the hills.

Hamish told me that doing up the bothy as a place to stay had only been a recent idea. 'I've hardly advertised as I want it to be a mostly word-of-mouth place,' he said. 'Which probably explains why I've only had about ten people to stay since I opened up last October! My plan is to target real travellers – mostly cyclists. I don't want any noisy parties of people and I'm not interested in back-packers. They've all turned a bit soft, if you ask me. In my day backpackers hitch-hiked everywhere. Now all they seem to do is drive around the country in hired cars or cars they've bought. And they call themselves backpackers!'

Judging from the visitors' book I was the third cyclist to stay this year after German Felix Ebner and Scotsman Gary Mochrie from Glasgow, who wrote, 'Follow your nose in this country and you'll stumble on something special and unique ... a fantastic memory – CHEERS!'

The bothy was painted blue and cream on the inside and green and primrose yellow on the outside. It had a handful of bunks, a small kitchen with an old Airco pull-handle fridge (the sort of thing that would fetch a small fortune on the streets of Notting Hill), a shower with shiny corrugated iron for walls and a floor of hand-picked stones from the nearby Mohaka River. There was even a selection of cassettes: Midnight Oil, Phil Collins (no thanks), Talking Heads, Split Enz and The Bucks 'Dancing to the Ceili Band'. Although I made the most of the toilet, shower and kitchen, I slept in my tent behind the bothy – not because I didn't fancy the bunks, I just preferred sleeping outside with the wind-rustling palm fronds and the mournful call of the morepork.

Hamish was originally from Scottish stock though he'd been in New Zealand most of his life. 'I've had the farm for forty years,' he told me as we sat in the courtyard outside his kitchen drinking tea as various biting insects landed on me for their blood-sucking feast, 'though in between I've buggered off here and there. I lived on the South Island for a while building what we called 'mud' houses – earth houses. I've also spent a couple of years travelling overseas. I went to see what Scotland is like as my family come from the Highlands. But I didn't find the people very friendly. They were fine to have a drink with in the pub, but apart from that they didn't want to know. Edinburgh was better because of all the students. As for the English, I found them very standoffish – friendly enough when in the pub or out in the open but they don't invite you to their homes. It's not like here in New Zealand. I suppose because there are so few people out here in the country in so much space that when someone appears you welcome the company with open arms. My nearest neighbour lives just across the river as the crows flies, but he's ten miles away by road.'

Hamish had a whole heap of farm dogs, one of which was called Rain. I spotted two cats. When the fluff-ball called Wookie tried to sneak into the house, Hamish shouted, 'Get outta there you little bugger!'

I mentioned to Hamish the railway I'd been cycling beside all day, and all the trouble men had gone to in order to build bridges and viaducts and slice through mountains, yet I hadn't seen one train on the tracks. Hamish told me that when the railways were nationalised there were about four trains a day on this line. 'Though you did wonder if you were ever going to make your destination,' he said. 'Sometimes it could take all day just to travel fifty miles. Then it was privatised and the network was bought by an American outfit who wasted no time in closing any sidelines and stripping the passenger rail services back to nothing. Now I think the Americans have sold it to an Aussie who's not interested in it at all. Not so long ago all the logs used to be carried out of the forests by rail. Now, as you've probably noticed, it all goes by road. It's stupid really as we've got all the infrastructure there and yet it's all going to waste.'

Lake Tutira, Hawke's Bay, 7 February

I noticed a lot of free-ranging goats in the hills around the bothy. Hamish said they would have their use if they ate all the gorse. 'I've got a big gorse problem on this farm,' he said. 'It's a pain in the arse. I'm going to get a helicopter in to spray it all. My green friends say, "You can't do that!" but I say, "You try and stop me!"'

There I was this morning thinking how I would easily cycle the 70 km to Napier today, if not quite a bit further. And yet I'm still not there. More distractions I'm afraid.

The ride was spectacularly hilly, plunging in and out of gorges and canyons. In some places the road was so narrow and rocky and winding that when a logging truck squeezed by, in order to prevent being swept under the multiple of wheels or pushed over the edge into the gorge, I just took a deep breath and hoped for the best. So far I've survived, but it's a close shave.

Somewhere near Putorino ('put a rhino where?') – a veritable metropolis with a population of 300, a pub and a dairy – I found myself bowling along through the heady wafts of a eucalyptus grove, its trees standing to attention in their Gulf War camouflage. Like gum and eucalyptus groves everywhere the trees had left their shed bark, shed twigs and shed branches untidily over the ground. When I cycled over this heap of debris it made a lovely crackling noise and smelt like a nasal decongestant.

It was still early by the time I arrived at Tutira, but the lake here looked so appealing that I thought Napier could wait, so I put my tent up on a hill overlooking the water in the DoC site (water tap and long-drop toilets). I spent the rest of the day walking in the high hills around the lake. Lake Tutira is a wildlife reserve and ornithological hotspot for spotting black shags, welcome swallows, harrier hawks, black swans, whitefaced herons, New Zealand king-fishers, New Zealand scaups, New Zealand shoveler ducks and New Zealand dabchicks. Never mind dabchicks, you've got to be a dab hand to identify that lot, like Peter. Peter was camping in a nearby tent with his twelve-year-old son, Zac. 'We're having a "boy" week-end,' said Peter. 'Fishing and camping and kayaking while my wife and daughter are elsewhere.'

Peter, who had some sort of banking business, was originally from Boston. For a while he lived in London in Notting Hill Gate and loved every minute, but his wife (who I think was now his ex-wife) hated it. Peter now lived in Napier, as did his wife, who lived elsewhere in the city. I'm not quite sure who his children lived with. All he'd said about his daughter was that she was seven going on fifteen. I sat beside the lake with Peter and Zac for quite a long time this evening. Zac was busy catching cockabullies (tiddly fish) in a plastic bread bag that he waded into the weedy edge of the lake with to scoop through the murky water. Every so often he scurried back to us to hold up his bag (which was fast springing leaks) to show me his latest cockabully catch. Then he'd upturn the bag into the water and start again to catch some more.

Napier, Hawke's Bay, 8 February

This morning I awoke to heavy rain clattering on my tent. A man sleeping with his daughter in a camper van on the other side of the trees told me that he moved to Hawke's Bay from High Wycombe (where he was doing something with wood glue) fourteen years ago and that this is the wettest January/February he'd ever known. 'I've never seen the hills looking so green,' he said. 'At this time of year they are usually a parched yellow.'

Peter and Zac gave up on the day early. After piling the kayaks on to the roof of their car they were ready to head back to Napier. Peter offered me a lift. 'You don't want to be out in weather like this,' he said.

'And there're some stink horrible hills – like mountains – to get over before Napier,' said Zac. 'One of them's called the Devil's Elbow.'

Despite the rain bouncing off the road in front of my wheel and water cascading down my neck, the Devil's Elbow turned out to be a fun hairpin ride of relatively high altitude. My only complaint was the amount of stock trucks and trailers. They came swishing by in thick spray leaving me even wetter and dirtier, with the stench of animal fear on the wind.

Places came and went – Kawaka ('forceful hitting of automobile'), Waipatiki ('Well, why not pat her?') and Onehunga ('solitary starving'). The last twenty-odd kilometres to Napier involved labouring into a socking headwind, but at least it was as flat as a tray.

Just over seventy years ago I would have been cycling through water along this stretch; it was known back then as the Ahuriri Lagoon. But then at 11.50 a.m. on 3 February came the earthquake of 1931, measuring 7.9 on the Richter scale – the biggest ever in New Zealand's recorded history – which over the space of two-and-a-half minutes twisted and buckled the land with dramatic effect. The two major shocks (there were 525 aftershocks over the following two weeks) were so violent that they were felt throughout the country. Unfortunately for Napier it sat virtually at the epicentre. As a result the city lost 258 people to the eruptions of the earth but gained 5,000 acres of new land when the quake threw the seabed above sea level – uplifting the land level in some areas by over two metres. Trawlers were left high and dry in the lagoon and fish floundered on the mudflats. In some ways Napier did quite well out of this new shift of uplifted seabed as the airport now stands on part of this swathe of naturally reclaimed land.

Near the airport, on the opposite side of the road, I rode by what looked like a hugely industrial paper mill with high-pressure wisps of steam emanating from various pipes and funnels – a steel Krakatoa threatening to blow. Traffic came thick and fast as I approached the city, drenching me in oily road-soaked spray. Practically every other car was an upmarket SUV with kayaks on the roof and bikes on the rear. It was Sunday and people had obviously given up on the weather and their planned day of play and were heading back to the city to take cover. Some of these vehicles, especially the Toyota RAV 4s, had customised covers on their rear-door spare wheels. One was a cartoon of a cowboy wielding two pistols in hand, pointing the barrels of the guns into the face of the driver behind. The words on the cover said: 'BACK OFF!' Another wheel cover was a picture of a cartoon duckling and simply said: 'BUGGER!' One SUV had a bumper sticker that warned: 'IF YOU GET ANY CLOSER I'LL FART'.

In urgent need of stocking up on food supplies, I stopped at the big Woolworths supermarket in the middle of town. Most supermarkets in New Zealand have rows of bulk bins – big dustbin-like tubs of cheaper-priced food complete with scoops so you can shovel how ever much you fancy of a substance such as cereal or dried fruit, nuts and oats, sweets and biscuits into a plastic bag. I was in the middle of busily excavating the contents of the porridge oat bulk bin when I was simultaneously spotted by Peter (minus Zac) and Brian and Karen, a couple I didn't know but who apparently knew me after reading my books. It all suddenly got very complicated because Peter wanted me to come and stay with him, but then so did Brian and Karen, who upped the offer by saying they would like to take me out to lunch. After cycling over various elbows of devils in torrential rain and fighting into an exhausting headwind, it all seemed a bit unreal to be half-submerged in a bulk bin while being fired with kindly offers. In the end I turned everyone down and went to find somewhere to camp. Then, once the site had been located and tent assembled I rode off on some visiting rounds.

First stop was Peter, who lived in a huge house on the hill overlooking the sea and a jumble of rooftops. Zac was there and we all had tea and chatted a while before Peter had to take Zac off to chapel. Then I cycled off towards the airport, where I found Brian and Karen in a rented house that they called 'the shed'. They both hailed from northern England. Brian liked bikes (he had about five of them, including a red Moulton) and music – he used to have an instrument shop on Merseyside for many years but never made any money. 'Bike shops and music shops are much the same,' said Brian. 'They both attract good and interesting people, but as far as I can tell, there's no money in either of them.'

Napier, Hawke's Bay, 10 February

After the earthquake had shaken Napier to the ground, the city had to be rebuilt almost entirely. It was the 1930s when art deco was at its height of popularity and this is the style in which the architects chose to go a bit overboard in raising Napier from the ashes. As a result the city now possesses one of the most significant collections of these buildings in the world, making the town look sunny and bright – even in the rain. It was a pleasant surprise to find a New

Zealand town so architecturally distinctive from all the other samey places I'd seen so far.

Just past the Grumpy Mole Saloon on Tennyson Street I came across a museum. Inside I wandered among the exhibitions and artefacts on Maori art and culture, colonial history and dinosaurs. I also came across a nineteenth-century shark-tooth sword that had come from the Kiribati Islands (those tiny atolls just below the Marshall Islands). The sword was made of coconut wood, fibre and hair and lined with sharks' teeth, making the weapon razor sharp. These swords weren't so much designed for killing as for shredding skin and weakening the enemy. I found this an unusual approach of warfare and imagined a Kiribati warrior running up to his enemy and saying, 'Don't worry, mate, I'm not here to kill you. I just want to have a go at shredding your skin.'

Not surprisingly the museum had quite a big section on the earthquake. I read a cutting from the *Auckland Weekly News* headlined:

FEARFUL DEATH – WOMAN IN CHURCH PINNED UNDER GIRDER.
One of the most tragic incidents at Napier occurred at St John's Anglican Cathedral. When the first shock occurred, communion was being conducted. Almost without warning the walls caved in and although most of the congregation were able to escape, several were trapped. An elderly lady, Mrs T. Barry, was pinned beneath a fallen girder, but was not killed. Rescuers immediately noticed her plight but all efforts to lift the huge girder were unavailing. Then the flames broke out and gradually drew nearer and nearer to the stricken woman. Hoses were used but in a few minutes the water supply failed. Finally it was realised that she had no hope of escape and in order to save her from a frightful death by burning a doctor administered a large dose of morphine. Death was inevitable, but at least it was without pain.

Waipukurau, Hawke's Bay, 11 February

Those in officialdom don't talk about Napier just as Napier, but as 'the twin cities of Napier and Hastings'. Hastings lies a short way down the road from Napier and suffered as equally flattening devastation in the earthquake as Napier. From here I was planning to cycle to Cape Kidnappers, said to be the world's only mainland gannet colony – up to 15,000 of these torpedo-diving birds occupy the sheer cliffs of this eroded promontory at this time of year.

All started off well enough. I rode as far as Clifton, where the road ran out and then, as it was low tide as planned, started out walking the ten kilometres along the beach. But then the rain came (the weather forecast for today had been bright and sunny but I've discovered New Zealand forecasts tend to be like British ones – the weather people tend to get the weather right, it's just that they tend to put it on the wrong day; tomorrow will be glorious, I'm sure, as heavy rain is forecast). The further I plodded, the heavier the rain fell and the more the cliffs became obscure. So I turned round and traipsed back to my bike.

Death Highway 2 was horrible today – trucks, trucks and more trucking trucks. None of which was helped by the rain. There were lots of very stupid drivers, too, doing lots of very stupid things. And I had another carload of boy-racers spit at me. When I stopped to use some public conveniences in Waipawa ('questionable cat's feet') I met a man cleaning out the toilets and he said, 'There're a lot of SOBs on the road.' When I finally worked out that he meant sons of bitches, I said, 'I quite agree!' It's always nice to have an agreeable moment in a toilet.

So what else has happened today? Well, not a lot really. I stopped at a very friendly bike shop in Havelock North where I bought an extremely stretchy striiitcheee. And I found some sturdy mole-grips lying in the road. They weighed about twice as much as my tent but I put them on board anyway because, you never know, they might be useful.

The sun came out for a very brief excursion when I was cycling through an expanse of orchards. If Napier was known for its vineyards, then Hastings was known for its fruit trees – much of the fruit appeared to be sold at fantastically low prices at the side of the road. One roadside stall I passed was selling 10 kg of peaches for $10. In other words about 35p a kilo, or about 17p a pound. This was so cheap how could I say no? I couldn't, so I bought 10 kg, which amounted to about five times the weight of my tent. But unlike my tent, they were edible.

Somewhere near Pukehou ('unwell half-built house') I cycled through a white cloud of butterflies, many of whose flight paths had been sent into disarray by the speed of rushing traffic so that they ended up littering the road like confetti. The two fields bordering the road were full of cabbages and I think it's fair to surmise these butterflies were cabbage whites.

Since I've been in New Zealand I seem to have passed a lot of fields or patches of wasteland piled high with those windowed boxy plastic lids that fit over the beds of pick-up trucks and turn them into campers. And judging from today's observance of traffic, they seem to have all been on the road. Maybe there's a pick-up camper-mobile convention taking place somewhere.

But far more exciting than a posse of pick-ups was seeing two freight trains on the track today. In fact, this sight was such a pleasant surprise that I had to stop to take in the scene for full appreciation value.

Tonight I'm camping between a railway and a main road. There's also a dirt road running alongside and it's on this road that the town hoons are racing and spinning their cars. I've erected my flimsy abode among a stack of permanent residents in beaten-up caravans. This site is situated just down from a farming supply store with its fetching display of reapers, threshers, cultivators and harrows. The town's called Waipukurau. In Maori the ubiquitous *wai* means water or stream, whereas *pukurau* means a fungus soaked in water before eating. So Waipukurau means something like 'river of edible fungus'. All this gets a bit complicated so the locals simply shorten Waipukurau to Waipuk, which in a way only complicates itself even further because there is a Waipuku up near Mount Taranaki as well as a Waipu just north of Mangawhai Heads. Both Waipuk, which was formerly a Maori *pa* site, and its near neighbour Waipawa were founded as farming settlements and the two have been rivals ever since.

6

Dannevirke, 12 February

Just in case you're wondering where I am now, I'm in the region of the lower North Island known collectively as Rangitikei–Manawatu–Horowhenua–Tararua. Otherwise called a mouthful. But this mouthful pales into insignificance compared with the name of a nearby small hill known as Taumatawhaka-tangihangakoauauotamateaturipukakapikmaungahoronukupokai-whenuakitanatahu. This hill, which is just down the road from Porangahau, rates as the world's longest place name and apparently translates as 'the brow of the hill where Tamatea of the big knees, who slid, climbed and swallowed mountains, known as "Landeater" and who travelled over the land, played his flute to his loved one'.

And so from a Maori-themed land to a Nordic one. In the early nineteenth century the plains and hill country east of the Ruahine and Tararua Ranges (the big long line of lumpy mountains off to my right as I cycle south) were covered with forest and thick primeval bush so dense that the back-breaking work of clearing the land with axes and fire and the consequent struggle to farm the area discouraged all of the settlers who arrived in the 1870s, apart from the hardy Norwegians, Danes and Swedes. They established such towns as Norsewood, which is just up the road from where I am now in Dannevirke ('Dane's Work'). I thought Dannevirke might look like a smorgasbord of Scandinavia, the local people wandering the streets with platinum hair and Viking cheekbones.

Instead the town looks just like any other rural New Zealand town and the locals, rather than looking like Sven or Aha, are indistinguishable from any other Kiwis.

Last night it rained so hard with the wind blowing such a flapping gale that I had to get up and get soaked to find a rock to whack my tent pegs in as far as they would go. This morning, on the radio's 'local news brought to you by Credit Union Bay Wide', I heard reports of severe flooding around Masterton and Wellington causing extensive road closures. Oh dear, because that's just where I'm going.

Today I had one of those rare opportunities when I could divert off course from Death Highway 2. That's because round here there's a choice of roads to take between Waipukurau and Dannevirke. I was going to go the long way round via that very lengthy-named place of large slippery knees, but when a local sheep farmer told me that the dirt road down that way was completely flooded, I took a shorter alternative. And very unexpectedly lovely it was too. Soon out of Waipukurau I turned off to Hatuma ('that you, mum?') and wove my way among a medley of lanes empty of traffic apart from the odd farmer's pick-up and steel Fonterra milk tanker with their 'I TURN OFTEN!' warning signs across their tailgate. This is sheep and cattle country. The rumpled blanket of green pastures and hills are full of sheep stations. Not just a fluffy handful of sheep like back home, but vast cascades of undulating wool. The sheep pens apparently have a capacity of 50,000.

Some of the roads around Hatuma were very English-like, lined with tunnels of oaks and grand old houses in big grounds set back from the road with names like Holyrood and Arundel. Then it all got a bit wilder, with the road plummeting down into mini chasms carved through with a river followed by a slow clamber back out of the valley. A rarely sighted freight train passed me today, chugging along in slow motion with over thirty wagons attached. The only fast-moving thing around here was the red New Zealand post car (private plate: YA MAIL) charging around from pillar to post, pausing only for an arm to pass out of the car window and shove a handful of mail into American-style mailboxes of tubular metal, some customised into shapes of sheep. A small armed flagpole (occasionally made into a sheep's tail) indicated to the farmhouse situated up the track and well out of sight that the mail had arrived.

Something else moving fast in this wind was the ubiquitous clumps of pampas-like toetoe grass, their feathery fronds waving about in the maniacal breeze like a frenzy of raised arms at a rock concert.

Eketahuna, Taraua, 13 February

Shivering in my tent last night (it was uncannily cold) waiting for the weather forecast to predict a day of sunshine (rain), Radio Pacific kept getting interrupted for the live racing report so all I learnt was how She's a Trouble Maker was on the brink of over-taking Pam's Passion on the finishing strip. Quite riveting, I can tell you. That's why I fell asleep never learning what the elements were going to throw at me today.

More white crosses of car crash victims continued to line spo-radic bursts of Death Highway 2 like wild flowers did on other sections. Thankfully I only had a short truck-sucking canter along this traffic-hammering strip today before I veered off on to a con-fusion of quiet country roads through virtually non-existent settlements before being jettisoned back into a scene of busyness at Pahiatua, whose main street is like some towns in America – about a mile wide. If you want to cross over it's a good idea to allow your-self a good twenty minutes to reach the other side. But unlike America, which just likes to build things big for the sake of it, the size of this street has a reason for its being. When Pahiatua was founded in 1881 in the heart of Seventy Mile Bush, the extensive centre strip of this street (now made into gardens and rest areas) was originally planned to carry the railway line that eventually took the route on the outskirts of town.

*

Outside New World supermarket a man came up to me and said, 'You German?' When I put him straight he said, 'It's just that practically everyone you see touring on a bike around here is German!'

Studying my bike in detail he then said, 'That's a good sit-up you've got.'

For a moment I thought he thought I was riding a sit-up-and-beg when really I had a touring steed complete with drop handlebars. And then I realised my stumbling block. He had pronounced a very Kiwi sit-up for set-up.

'In 1999 I cycled for sex months around Europe,' he told me. 'Didn't go to the UK, mate. Too bloody igg-spin-sieve!' The man no longer cycled because of a dicky hip. Before I disappeared into New World he said, 'Mind how you go. Motorists hate cyclists here!'

Half an hour later I was perusing the leaflets in the tourist office when a woman came in wielding a $10 note in her hand. She looked at me and said, 'Is this yours?'

I said, 'No.'

She said, 'Is that your bike outside?'

I said, 'Yes.'

She said, 'Well, I found it by your bike so you might as well have it. You look like you need it more than me!' And with that she thrust it into my hand with a smile.

From Pahaitua I was planning on diverting course across the mountains to visit the mother of a friend of my sister-in-law in Palmerston North. But due to all the rain and floods the road through the Manawatu Gorge had been closed and the locals informed me there had been equally severe landslides on the quieter route to Aokautere. Instead I continued south and so here I am now in the heady delights of Eketahuna ('elephant crossed with a hyena in possession of an estimated time of arrival'), camping in the poky municipal campground. It's dark and dingy and deserted. One of the reasons for this is that no one wants to come here. Most people see Eketahuna (pop. 579) as being a place on the way to somewhere else. In fact, in New Zealand Eketahuna is used as an aphorism for a boring nothing-ever-happens back-of-beyond. The campsite here in Eketahuna (which I've just discovered means appropriately 'to run aground on a sandbank') isn't improved by being in this dark and gaunt tree-shrouded dip. It's all a bit depressing. There's a comment in the damp visitor's book in the shabby kitchen that says that this site would be a 'good place for a revolution'. I'm not quite sure about that – the surrounding land is mostly mud and swamp, because last night the nearby river burst its banks and flooded most of the site. You can see how high the water rose by the tide level on the trees and where the water stirred itself into the soil and formed dark oozing mud. There's also a detritus of flattened rushes and driftwood and debris.

After a prolonged search, I finally managed to find the owner, a bit of an odd man, who lives in a house some distance away. He doesn't seem to take any pride in the place but he has let me sleep in one of the small cabins situated just slightly up from the flood mark. The cabin is the size of a small shed with two bunks and a table and chair. But it is cold and dank so I'm sleeping in my tent in the cabin instead. More cosy that way.

I haven't got a good feeling in this place. There's a track running right through the site which is open to the public for access to the river. It's just the sort of place in which you can imagine something horrible happening at night. If I had the energy I would move on. Instead I'm battening down the hatches and keeping an ear out for any rain and sounds of rising water. The owner says there's no rain forecast for tonight, but I'm not sure I believe him.

Masterton, Wairarapa, 14 February

What a night! All went fairly well, albeit sleeplessly, until 12.45 a.m. when a carload of hoons arrived on the scene. They disappeared down the track for a while before returning to do donuts in the mud, revving their engine and blasting the horn with their lights on full beam. They finally got bored of this and took off at speed up the hill.

Then the rain started.

It hammered on the roof as fast and resonating as an army of Sado drummers. As it was completely pitch black outside I had to keep monitoring water levels with my head torch. When dawn finally arrived I ran down the mud track in the thundering rain to find the brown river looking as if it was about to burst its banks any moment. It was high and wide and moving heavily towards the sea. It was not the sort of river into which you would wish to fall. It would pull you under in seconds.

It was a huge relief to be up and away from Eketahuna this morning, even if the weather was being more than a touch assertive. Tattered clouds scudded across the sky as if in a speeded up film. The wind screamed up the street. Once out in the open all hope of cycling was out of the question. It was wind you could lean on. The rain fell so heavy it was like cycling through a carwash. The swash and suck of the big trucks on Death Highway 2 only added to the hazardous conditions. So I pushed my bike, though even then I was blown clean off my feet. At the earliest opportunity I turned off on to a quiet side road that twisted and ducked its way alongside swollen rivers and flooded farmland. Huge herds of cattle and sheep had clambered up the hillsides to keep clear of the river's menacing water, frothing and foaming below.

Entering Mauriceville I noticed a sign that said: 'Historical Site 400 m'. When I arrived at the site wondering whether perhaps the Vikings had strayed this far or whether Hannibal had marched his army of men and elephants over a Southern Alp as well as a northern one, all I found was a run-of-the-mill locked-up village hall with a faceplate indicating it had been built in 1897. This sort of thing happens quite a lot in New Zealand. Another time I'd passed a similar 'historical site' sign only to discover it was indicating a nondescript blip in a lay-by marked by a boulder with a plaque to commemorate a man who had planted a handful of trees near the lay-by at the end of the nineteenth century. Then there's the plaque I noticed in Devonport. It said: 'ON THIS SITE IN 1897 NOTHING HAPPENED'. At least Kiwis have a hearty sense of humour about their fledgling land – the last country in the world to be settled.

By the time I arrived in Masterton I was completely soaked. These last few weeks I seem to be continually trying to dry out, if I'm not being busy getting wet. I'm now camping in the rain at the motorcamp down by the river. Despite being the 'height of summer', there's only one other tent here, a tiny-toy blue wedge of triangle that is dwarfed by the size of the tent's owner's 4WD parked alongside. I don't know why they simply don't sleep in the vehicle – it looks like they would have a lot more room to manoeuvre. And be drier to boot. The 4WD couple are looking miserable with all this rain. They are so averse to getting wet that even though it would be far quicker to run, they clamber into their Landcruiser to drive all of twenty yards to the toilet block. And when they're in the toilet block they leave the engine running. I ask you! Some people, eh?

Since I wrote the above I have had to bail out and move tent and belongings to another patch of ground that is marginally less sodden. Despite this sludge of grass being the highest point of the campsite, I'm not sure how long I will last here. The ground all around is beginning to drown. Over the last few hours the rain has been coming down perpendicularly, with a sort of measured intensity as if it were driving nails into a coffin lid.

Masterton, Wairarapa, 17 February

Masterton may be the chief town of the Wairarapa but it's not really the sort of place you would make a special effort to visit – not, that is, unless you have a particular interest in sheep. It is said of Masterton that the town lies dormant for eleven months of the year, only waking up in March for the international Golden Shears sheep-shearing competition. Apparently this is *the* sheep-shearing competition of all sheep-shearers, attracting hundreds of competitors from around the world and thousands of observers. Since the inaugural competition in 1961, the Golden Shears has become a national institution: at the competition's peak during the 1960s and 1970s, seats to the event were sold out twelve months in advance. I never knew watching a sheep being shorn could be such a draw. But it seems much appreciation can be had observing the skills and physical strength of the 'gun shearers' who are able to strip a sheep of its fleece in under a minute, without a cut or a ridge. What's more, sheep shearing has entered the world of professionalism with big prize money, corporate sponsorship and shearers adopting fitness and training programmes as gruelling as those for any top athlete.

I was still a few weeks too early to catch this grand ovine spectacle, but not to worry – there were other arresting sights to catch in Masterton. In a swampy park across from the motorcamp, a half-hearted rock concert tried to take place for a while, involving a handful of scroungy, beatnik-looking groups dressed in rags and tags jumping around in the mud making a lot of noise. The patchy audience comprised mostly boy-racing hoons who, if they weren't getting completely off-their-heads drunk in the park, were noisily tearing up and down the town's main streets in their fat-exhaust cars with licence plates shouting unnecessary things at you like: DEAFENZ; ONE OFF; BLITZM.

Another interesting pastime to be had in Masterton was to wander around the town observing how many of the shop names like to substitute an 'S' for a 'Z' in their spelling. Notable examples included the video shop 'VIDEO EZY' (motto: 'The choice is Ezy'). Hairdressers appeared particularly partial to this pursuit, as observed in the salons named 'MENZ' and 'HOWZ YA HAIR'. Well, as you've asked, not too good thanks. But then having a cycling helmet strapped on top of your barnet through thick and thin does not make what was bad before any better.

You might ask why I'm spending so many days in the heady delights of Masterton (this is my fourth day). Let me assure you that it is not a matter of choice that I am here, but a matter of necessity. That's because Masterton has been effectively cut off from the rest of civilisation owing to the biggest floods in history to hit the region. Along with the rain, which has been falling constantly for the past few days, there have been gales and hurricane winds gusting up to 120 km/h. The campsite has turned into a lake so Mike, the owner, told me to sleep in the TV room. As my tent is freestanding, I've erected it in the corner of the room. Means I can still sleep in it while drying it out, which is most satisfying. Also means I can lie in my sleeping bag in my tent watching telly. This is the life, I tell you, though the only television I'm interested in is the news – saturated by the floods – and the weather forecasts. Front after front seems to be hitting the lower North Island. More gales are expected to lash the region with strong, cold southerlies forecast (it's odd to think of southerlies as being cold, but then, being upside down, they are blowing off Antarctica) along with more heavy rain, plummeting temperatures, thunderstorms and hail. Oh joy!

The weatherman Bob McDavitt (who for some reason is called the Met Service ambassador – I can't imagine Michael Fish or John Kettley earning such a title) said, 'We are having June weather in February.' I'm not quite sure how I manage this. For years people have told me that if I ever cycle around New Zealand, I should make sure I'm there during February as it is the perfect summer month with glorious settled weather. Instead I have managed once again to end up in a country on my bike and attract the floodiest, stormiest, windiest, wettest, most horrible weather on record. The locals are saying to me that February is not usually like this, that it is usually hot and wonderful. And then they apologise for it being as it is – as if it's *their* fault, when really I'm the one to blame. I bet if I hadn't come to New Zealand, this summer would be just perfect. Sorry about that everyone.

Just outside the TV room is a large man-made turf bank (though it's currently looking not nearly large enough) and on the other side of this bank flows the Waipoua River. The bank is called a stopbank and Mike told me that the council spent a small fortune building it after the Waipoua burst its banks a few years ago following days of heavy rain, when it completely flooded the motorcamp, including all the buildings and cabins. Mike told me that this stopbank is far higher and wider than the previous stopbank. 'We won't get any water coming over the height of this bank,' he said. I hope he's right.

The first day I arrived here the Waipoua River was looking boisterous, brown and fast. And full. In the early hours of this morning I was lying in the dark in my tent in the TV room listening to the rain on the roof and the bedlam of howling wind knifing around the corners of the building, when I became aware of another noise slowly overriding all of this. It sounded like an express train. By torchlight I waded through the rain and the water and went to investigate. It wasn't difficult to source the noise. It was the river. It had risen by several feet and was a blasting torrent of fury. I could even see waves – white caps, or brown caps – churning like an angry sea. Every now and then I saw large lumps flowing past at speed. By dawn I could see what these large lumps were: trees, bits of fencing, hay bales, slabs of wood and, at one point, a dead cow.

The papers are full of nothing but floods and rivers reaching record highs and the 200 mm of rain that has fallen within twenty-four hours in the part of New Zealand in which I happen to be. The *Wairarapa Times* is covered in headlines like: 'SWAMPED AGAIN'; 'ALL ROUTES OUT OF DISTRICT CUT OFF'; '31 WAIRARAPA ROADS BLOCKED BY FLOODWATER'; 'TWO MEN MISSING PRESUMED DROWNED'. Mauriceville (site of historically disappointing village hall), which I cycled through three days ago, has no power and has been cut off from everywhere else by 1.5 metres of floodwater covering the roads and what appear to be called 'slips'. I always thought slips were another word for pants or petticoats, but in this context it seems they are mudslides or rockslides. Here's a taster of what the *Wairarapa Times* is saying:

Many Mauriceville residents have had to be evacuated from their homes in the early hours of this morning . . . Farmers were up all night trying to move stock to higher ground in the darkness and rain . . . One man shifting pigs around 4 a.m. had to get his son to swim to a gate to open it because the water was so high in his paddock.

A state of civil emergency has been declared for some areas around here. Parts of the main railway between Wellington and Auckland are under water; bridges and houses have been washed away; whole roads have disappeared. Thousands of sheep and cattle have been swept away by rising rivers, along with vehicles, farm sheds and equipment. One evacuee, talking about water outside his front door, was quoted in the paper as saying, 'There's like two or three metres of water out here, with all sorts of stuff floating down. It's just amazing.' Another resident said, 'We have been told the road is gone and it will be six months before we can get back in.'

People are being airlifted off buildings by helicopter and rescued by jet boat. Other residents are making daring rescues themselves to save neighbours. Tuffy Churton, which sounds more like the name of a cartoon duck than a man, has become a local hero by breaking into a house and swimming through the floating furniture to rescue a frail old man.

In Wellington's paper, *The Dominion Post*, under what they are calling 'THE BIG WET', there are more stories of heroism. Under a headline 'Saved by lasso and a trusty hacksaw', I read of a farmer who had to climb on to the roof of his farmhouse with his wife and son and five dogs. They took with them food and a change of clothing, a piece of rope and a hacksaw – the hacksaw being the son's idea. 'You never know, Dad,' he said. 'It might come in handy.'

And so it proved to be. After several hours on the roof the farmer managed to lasso his boat, which was chained to a trailer, and pull it over to the house. Then he dived in and cut the chain with the hacksaw. The family and posse of dogs motored upstream to a neighbour's property, where they came across 300 lambs trapped in a paddock surrounded by water and opened a gate to let them out. 'The lambs saw the gate open and swam for it,' said the farmer, 'but they missed it and got hooked up on a fence. So I got out the old trusty hacksaw and cut the fence in two or three places and then we worked hard pushing and throwing them over the fence. We saved about 250. It was a small victory.'

The Rumahanga River, which runs just outside Masterton, has stopbanks designed to handle 1500 cubic metres of water a second, but at its peak it has been flowing at around 2000 cubic metres a second – the largest flow ever known for the river. The Manawatu River, which flows through the Manawatu Gorge (which was closed a week ago when I tried to cycle through it), has been flowing at a depth of 8.9 metres. That's about 30 feet deep. No wonder so many sheep and cattle are getting washed away. About thirty cattle, mostly cows and calves, have been found on their way to do a little window-shopping in Palmerston North. They were discovered wandering through the town's Esplanade area after being swept down the Manawatu River. A helpline has been set up for homeless cows. Something called The Livestock Improvement Corporation is asking town dwellers or 'lifestyle block owners' all over the region who find cows washed downstream in floodwaters to note their ear tag numbers and to ring the freephone hotline so that the cows can be reunited with their owners.

Although thousands of sheep and cattle are missing, feared drowned, some have had lucky escapes with some exciting stories to relay to their grandchildren. I heard a radio report describe how a flock of sheep were swept away to certain death only to be found several kilometres further on, contentedly grazing where they had washed up. But in general, cows have a higher chance of survival as they make the best buoyancy aids. As dairy farmer Michael McAloon put it to *The Dominion Post*, 'A cow is a 44-gallon drum on legs and they float pretty easily. Three hundred came through the Manawatu Gorge on Monday night and many of them survived the trip.'

Cows are even coming to the rescue of drowning humans. 'THROW ME A COW, I'M DROWNING' reads one headline. The paper described how a swimming cow saved the life of Kim Riley,

a Woodville dairy farmer, in raging floodwaters near the mouth of the Manawatu Gorge. Mrs Riley and her husband Keith were moving their 350 cows to high ground last Monday night but the cows, obviously keen to try out their doggy-paddle skills, headed into a swollen river. 'Kim tried to head them off on foot,' said Mr Riley, 'but the current swept her off her feet. She got swept along with the cows and couldn't get back to land. She missed a couple of chances to grab a tree and a post and then a couple of cows swam over the top of her. It wasn't looking too good, but then she grabbed a cow and managed to hang on. The cow swam 200 to 300 metres through the water till it got its footing and took her to safety.' She says she has taken a note of her rescuer's tag number and is going to repay her with a drum of molasses.

When Mr Riley was asked if he had been relieved to see his wife safe he said, 'Well, I asked her what she thought she was doing going for a swim when she was meant to be getting the cows in.'

The *Sunday Star Times* has charted the rainfall for the past week. Normally the average February rainfall for the ranges of the region I'm in now is 340 mm. But in only six days 550 mm has fallen. *The Dominion Post* has a list of what to do during an emergency in this flooded time. Along with doing obvious things like boiling rainwater and throwing away any food that has been submerged in floodwater, there's a tip for making a temporary toilet by 'lining a bucket or rubbish bin with a strong leak-proof plastic bag. Put half a cup of liquid bleach in the bag. Bury the bag when full, away from vegetable gardens and downhill from water sources.' I'd have thought it would be better for everyone, including the earth, simply to take a shovel and dig a hole and go in that every time the need arises.

The radio is advising people to 'get an emergency kit ready of food, water, batteries and birth certificate.' It also says 'Don't enter floodwater alone.' Which rather begs the question: what are you supposed to do – take a friend? Because sometimes you haven't got much choice – the water can take you before you've had a chance to ponder the dilemma of entering the floodwater alone.

There again you could take a cow, the perfect buoyancy aid to survival.

The final piece of advice: 'Don't go sightseeing flooded areas.'

But advice like this is just wasted on people who feel their only vocation in life is to stir up the muddy floodwaters of trouble. On the letter page of *The Dominion Post* there is 'A plea to 4WD drivers'. Brian Smaller wrote:

> With floodwaters in our street already getting into our house and garage, it was more than frustrating to see people sightseeing in 4WDs. The wake from their mostly high-speed dashes through the water sent waves washing into our already flooded property.
>
> I know the floods presented those with 4WDs with a golden opportunity to drive in difficult conditions within the confines of suburbia but I would say to them that their lack of compassion for those affected was surpassed only by their ignorance of the potential and actual damage they caused.
>
> I hope that, next time, they'll do what the authorities advised: stay at home.

Tuning into my radio I heard that today of all days (thrashing rain, hurricane winds, flooded roads) is National Bike to Work Day – motto: 'Get Bike Wise for National Bike Week'. There's an advert

on the radio that warns: 'When you cut corners you could cut up
a cyclist. Don't burst their bubble.'

Apart from German tourists on bikes, the odd mountain biker
and clump of racing cyclists, I haven't seen anyone riding a bike in
New Zealand at the best of times so I can't imagine today is going
to be a roaring success for encouraging commuters to mount their
dusty steeds and cycle off gaily to the office. Ploughing through my
pile of papers (well, I haven't got much else to do with myself
except get flooded or find a cow) I can only see a couple of references to bikes, one of which is a letter in *The Dominion Post* by Peter
Keller from Ngaio, who wrote:

> I suppose that while I am riding my bicycle, I am unlikely to be
> pinged by some policeman manning a speed trap. However, I
> would like to point out that if I am hit by a car at 60 km/h, there
> is 44 per cent more energy available to mangle me than if I were
> hit at 50 km/h.

Many 50-tonne logging trucks career along these roads at 100
km/h or more. Should they crash into me I have no idea what per-
centage of energy they have available to mangle me. All I know is
that it would be a messy result and a terrible waste of a very nice
bike.

The other reference to bikes I've come across is hardly going to
encourage a generation of cyclists to break free on their wheels.
Some 'Education Review Office' report on a Lower Hutt (one of
the 'dormitory' cities just outside Wellington) early childhood
centre has suggested it should introduce 'trikeless days' because
'tricycles encouraged not only competition and ownership, but
aggression. It is only natural for a parent to protect their children
from danger,' concludes this completely hare-brained report.
Whoever writes this nonsense should be hurled into the Manawatu
River – preferably when it's in full flood. And don't throw them
any life-saving cows. We don't want them back.

Wellington, 19 February

Well, here I am in Wellington – a currently very appropriately named city seeing as the headline on the front page of *The Dominion Post* is 'BRACE FOR NEW STORMS – GLOOMY FORE- CAST: 120 KMH GUSTS AND MORE RAIN TO COME'. Though I think more than wellies are needed – more like a storm bunker.

Yesterday I made the most of a brief lull in the weather to make my final assault to this windy capital. Apart from sudden bursts of forceful showers the morning was dry as I left Masterton, riding past trees poleaxed by the gales through the 'tons' and towns of Carterton, Greytown and Featherston. Actually I didn't so much ride as half drag and half fight with my bike in order to control it in the battering wind that slammed into me from all angles like a crate of concrete. By the time I arrived in Featherston ('Gateway to the Wairarapa!') the sky had collapsed in on itself and the rain was falling like the Battle of Agincourt's armies of arrows. It was impos- sible to walk down the street without being blown over. Instead you had to move along the pavement from one handhold (lamp post, railing, letterbox) to another as if clambering about the decks of an oscillating ship pounded by storming seas. Any pedestrians who were silly enough to be out in all this looked as if they were seri- ously drunk.

Featherston is the last town before the climb up over the Rimutaka Range – a mountainous road notoriously windy at the best of times, but completely ludicrous in the present gales. It came as no surprise to hear that this road was temporarily closed owing to the vigorous weather, a jack-knifed truck and a rockslide. There were also rumours of a motorhome having been blown clean off the side. So instead I paid £5 for a backpacker's bunk (on which I ended up camping – that way I kept warmer and drier as the window, taking the full force of the wind, was leaking like an underwater porthole) at the Leeway, which was part motel, part backpackers. I spent the rest of the day either eating, reading, put- ting a new chain on my bike or loitering in the Fell Locomotive Museum.

It's amazing how bad weather can suddenly make you take an uncharacteristic interest in something that you would otherwise pass off as steam-buff fodder. Five minutes after I walked into the museum, I had suddenly become worryingly fascinated by the NZR Fell locomotive H199 – the only remaining Fell engine in the world – which for seventy-seven years successfully made the 1:15 grade climb of the Rimutaka Incline on three rails over the Rimutaka Range until a tunnel was built in 1955. I climbed up into the cab of the gleamingly restored engine to peer at and take photographs of shiny levers and pulls called things like blower control, test cocks, main steam turret valve, whistle control lever, westinghouse pump. A most enjoyable experience – especially as I was the only one in the museum. Every one else was stuck in floods.

The road was still closed over the Rimutakas this morning so I took a train through that tunnel in the mountains and got out the other side to cycle through the flat urban sprawl of the Hutt Valley to Wellington. I had been hoping to jump straight on to the Interisland ferry to cross over to South Island, but not surprisingly all boats have been cancelled because of rough seas in the Cook Strait, that narrow passage of water which acts as a wind funnel for the constant westerlies that hammer through the area from the volatile temperaments of the Tasman Sea. On my way to using the toilets in a downtown Wellington cafe I walked past a television and watched a bit of the news. A handful of passengers who had caught the last ferry over to Wellington before they were all cancelled were recalling their 'voyage of hell'. The crossing, which normally takes three hours, took six because of high winds and an eleven-metre swell. Double-trailer trucks toppled over, others had their roofs ripped off, cars were crushed. One man said, 'It was a nightmare! I threw up three times – I want a refund!'

7

Picton, Marlborough, South Island, 20 February

I had to abandon any thoughts of diary writing last night as all hands were needed to man the decks. I ended up camping out in some of the severest weather I think I've ever camped in. Although I had an address of a friend of a friend of a friend, there was no answer when I tried ringing their number (maybe they've got water in the line) and there was no time to linger around wondering what to do next; the weather was closing in and I had to act fast.

After trying several hostels and finding them all full, I finally found a big building called Rowena's Lodge, crammed full of backpackers, where I could put my tent up alongside three other tents in a small, squashed-in, litter-strewn patch of worn-out land behind the hostel's car park.

The wind was blowing such a flapping gale that just the act of trying to feed in the poles and get the tent up without the whole thing taking off for Eketahuna, or even Elephant Island, was like playing a major feat of Twister, involving all manner of legs and limbs (mostly mine, I believe) and rocks and panniers pinning down every available corner. I hammered in all the pegs as far as they would go with a rock, but the billowing and ballooning tent still looked as if it could launch itself into the stratosphere at any moment. So I hurriedly threw in my heavy ballast of multiple panniers and gathered up every boulder in the vicinity and dropped them on top of every peg.

Then the rain started, pelting my tent like lead shot. Although it was only early evening (a supposed summer evening at that!), day turned immediately to night beneath a filthy lowering sky of glowering intensity. Headlights came on, streetlights came on, shop lights came on. The rain fell down and the wind blew with a frighteningly unnatural ferocity. The combination of the wind and the rain was completely deafening. I knew a man was in his Terra Nova tent only about six feet away from me, yet no matter how much we tried yelling to each other we couldn't hear anything other than the sound of the hammering rain and howling wind. The noise was so intense that I couldn't hear my radio even on full volume. My world had suddenly shrunk to the tiny confined space inside my tent. Nothing else beyond the torch beam of my fast-dampening abode existed.

Within moments of the storm starting the water came gushing down the slope, passing under my tent like a river. When I put my hand on my ground sheet there was so much water beneath me that it felt as if I was floating on a boating lake. And that's after I had put my tent on a part of the site with the highest chances of drainage. I hated to think of the state of the other three tents, situated in dipping wallows.

Then came the lightning, followed hot on its tail by the crashes of thunder. Soon the thunder cracked with such shuddering explosions I instinctively cowered even though I was already flat on the ground and had nowhere else lower to cower. The idea of seeking shelter in the hostel did occur to me. But then I thought: I can't abandon ship leaving all my dog-eared worldly possessions to fend for themselves. There was also something quite perversely enjoyable about the awfulness of the situation and seeing how much my tent (and I) could take before it (or my nerves) got ripped to shreds. Equipment-testing, I believe it's called in the trade.

At one point I unzipped my tent door an inch into the tumult of wind and, with rain drilling against my face, directed the beam of my headtorch outside for a quick monitoring of the situation, just time enough to glimpse the shredded remains of one dome tent flapping like a dervish attached to a couple of pegs. A second later

I caught sight of the other dome tent sailing clean off into the night (I'm not sure whether it contained human form or not). That left only me and the Terra Nova man – if he was still in there. Maybe I was the sole survivor, standing my ground to go down with the ship.

As water started to find its way into my tent the wind wound up the scale, intoning a terrifying whine, and I grew increasingly conscious that I was in a rising gale. I packed everything back into my panniers, including sleeping bag and diary and books, and then, still in my jacket and hat, climbed into my Gore-tex bivvy bag as the cold seeped into the tent, the dampness into my bones and spirits.

The storm lasted about seven hours in all. Finally, cold and exhausted, I listened with relief as outside the rain gradually decreased in intensity. It dropped haphazardly upon my tent and the thunder moved away.

This morning when I emerged tired and stiff from my sodden hovel it was only 10°C. There was no sign of Mr Terra Nova, but his tent was still there – just – hanging on by a thread of a guyline. The wind was still blowing a hooley, but slowly the sun started to appear and I spent the next few hours trying to dry everything out.

The Dominion Post's front page headline for today read: 'STORM CHAOS – CAPITAL CUT OFF AS RAIN SHUTS ROADS'.

It seems that several fronts swept across my tent last night, bringing 24 mm of rain, with 17 mm of it falling in the space of one hour. Lucky thing I camped on top of a hill, because Wellington has been hit by flash floods causing bridges to wash away and road closures all over, affecting water supplies and collapsing houses down mud-moving hillsides. Wind gusts in the city hit 120 km/h but the strongest gust recorded by the Met Service was 230 km/h at Angle Knob at the top of the Tararua Range – not *that* far away! The winds have lifted roofs, cut phones and brought down trees and power lines. Some are saying that this spate of ridiculous weather is the offshoot of the cyclone that is currently hitting Vanuatu. On the hostel TV I saw aerial views of the Wellington area – whole swathes of land resembling a vast watery landscape: a collection of lakes fuelled by raging torrents, swelling and bursting over fences, roads and hedges, surrounding hundreds of houses.

Scientists are saying the weather system that caused all this mayhem is different to the one behind the 'weather bomb' that hit the Coromandel nearly two years ago. Mr Met Service ambassador man, Bob McDavitt, said of the present weather, 'It is truly, truly abnormal.' Well, that's good to know. An editorial in the paper remarked that the Met Service was saying this event was 'abnormal' because it was ignorant of the cause. Scientist Dr Renwick warned against making a link with global warming. Instead New Zealand has apparently been hit by something called the Antarctic oscillation, a climate pattern that appears to be in reverse mode. I've no idea what this means. All I hope is that it oscillates away. Dr Renwick said he was 'pinning his hopes on a dry and settled March'. So am I.

Forecasters are admitting that 'weather engineering' (whatever *that* is – a team of cumulus and nimbostratus with spirit levels and socket-sets in hand perhaps?) is as much the cause of the disaster as climate change or Antarctic oscillation. So far the storms and flooding (which have been described as the worst natural disaster since the Napier earthquake) have caused around $100 million worth of damage in the lower North Island alone, and the Insurance Council says this cost is set to double. Uninsured losses are estimated to be three to six times the insured amount overall. Around half the total cost is expected to come from damage done in Wellington.

Cycling to the Inter-island ferry terminal this afternoon, my bike computer plinked from 999 miles into the triple zero mark. The direct route from Auckland to Wellington on SH1 is 658 km (roughly 400 miles) and takes about 9 hours to drive. In contrast my route had taken me exactly 1,000 miles and 50 days. A much more satisfactory amount.

As I waited for the 2 p.m. boat, the *Aratere* ('Quick Path'), two other women on bikes turned up, though they weren't travelling together. Laura Ottjes, a Dutch occupational therapist from

Haalem, did a double take when she saw me before admitting she had read some of my wafflings. She seemed on good chatty terms with me, so I took that as a good sign. She had only arrived from Holland the day before yesterday in between two massive storms. Still, she hadn't let the weather put her off and went out yesterday and bought a mountain bike for her planned two-month trip around the South Island. Trouble was, she'd arrived with her four Ortlieb panniers, but as her bike had front suspension there was no place to fix a front rack, which meant there was no place to attach her front panniers. So when I saw her, she had four panniers on the rear rack stacked up in a sort of interesting leaning-tower formation. She said she was going to devise a method for hanging one pannier off the handlebars.

As for Achintya Paez, she was a Venezuelan living in Hawaii where she worked as a 'Reiki Master' with Oriental and holistic medicine. She had spent the first twenty years of her life in Venezuela going nowhere until she finally acquired a passport and then she spent the next fourteen years backpacking and working around the world. 'I would do any job that came my way,' Achintya told me. 'I told people I would do anything for money – except sex!' She admitted that, when desperate, she would even go up to people waiting in vehicles at traffic lights and tell them she was travelling alone around the world before asking whether they had any money they could give her. 'No one ever refused me,' said Achintya. 'I think that's the benefit of being a lone woman and asking nicely!'

This was the first time Achintya had travelled by bike. 'Usually I backpack or walk,' she said. She was travelling extra light on a Specialized Stumpjumper with front suspension. 'I started out with a load of camping equipment but then I sent it all home because it never stops raining!' Before we rode on to the boat, I noticed that the quick-release lever on her front wheel was undone so I did it up for her. 'Thanks,' she said. 'I don't know how those things work.'

Travelling from the North Island to the South Island by boat you'd think you would be sailing from north to south. But as Wellington sits slightly south of Picton you move ever so slightly north in an east to west fashion. All very confusing for the likes of my meridians, I can tell you.

The *Aratere* ferry ride was completely fantastic across an angry sea swept into hissing and foaming windrows. Despite the sun shining bright all the way, most passengers chose to sit inside. This might have had something to do with the yowling wind that tore across the upper deck like a stampede of Kaiser Chiefs, blowing anyone without a firm handhold clean off their moorings. The highest recorded wind gust in the Cook Strait reached 267 km/h (166 mph) on 10 April 1968 during a shocking storm that sunk the Inter-island ferry *Wahine* ('Woman') after the gale-force winds drove it on to Barrett Reef at the entrance to Wellington Harbour.

Two people testing the waters of the wind with me were a man and woman in the hinterland of their sixties who for one brief moment positioned themselves nearby, clinging on tight to the railings. The man had white hair and purple legs. She, on the other hand, was a dark bundle of a woman with hair crushed and subdued by the wind. Over her forearm she carried a Pekinese, neatly folded like a waiter's napkin. I caught a snippet of their shouted conversation. She was saying something about how she would never be able to move house because her husband had over 3,000 books plus thousands of tapes and CDs and endless piles of papers. 'Some people are hoarders,' she said, 'while others like to clear every surface in sight. My husband is a hoarder. I can only throw things out when his back is turned!'

Once over the rough seas of the Cook Strait, the *Aratere* nosed its way into the narrow but calmer waters of the appropriately blue Tory Channel (site of early whaling station) and Queen Charlotte Sound. Rising abruptly on all sides of the ship stood the sharp escarpments of deep green mountainous hills, covered with a thick pelt of forest. The fjord-like indentations of the Marlborough Sounds are a labyrinthine fretwork of peninsulas, inlets, bays, islands and waterways that was formed when the rising sea invaded a series of river valleys at the northern tip of the South Island. While so much of New Zealand is still being lifted by tectonic

Welcome to New Zealand, where some things fall from the sky and others jump backwards out of the sea: a woman bungee-jumping off the Sky Tower, Auckland; Warbirds over Wanaka; Maori boy, Matakana Island

Unfurled fern
of the forest

Wind-tortured
trees, near Curio
Bay, the Catlins,
South Island

Wind-sculptured
cloud with a
difference.
Kurow, South
Island

The rich-coloured textures of New Zealand: view from the road to Herekino,
North Island; near Omarama, South Island; Lake Wanaka, South Island;
driftwood, East Cape, North Island

Have shack will travel – one of the many Kiwi-style DIY mobile homes seen on the road

A Maori-made 3-horse-power pallet

A cyclist's nightmare – 50 tonnes of logging truck thundering down the road

Gary propping up a lamp post in downtown Kaitaia, North Island

Twenty-two cubed cars dumped in the middle of nowhere. Herekino Forest, Northland, North Island

One of the many roadside shrines marking the spot of yet another car-crash victim. Wairau Valley, South Island

On the road to
Mount Cook,
South Island

Getting closer

Nearly there

Gesticulating towards the long-awaited downward swoop from atop Porter's Pass, South Island

Travelling light (for me) at Lake Hawea, South Island

Bearing down on my mini tripod. Near Lake Tekapo, South Island

Puffed up in seventeen layers of clothing to combat the icy conditions of Lake Wakatipu, South Island

Giving wonked ankle a rest on another vertical hill. Banks Peninsula, South Island

Demonstrating size of boulders sent ricocheting off bike and body from passing jeeps and trucks. Near Cape Reinga, North Island

forces, the Sounds revolve around a drowned landscape where the northern tip of the South Island is being tilted into the sea. The coastline of the Sounds has an intricacy unmatched elsewhere in the country – to the extent that this relatively small area contains 15 per cent of the national coastline.

Sandwiched between the hills and the sea lies the former whaling station of Picton. Because of its position set in the upper reaches of Queen Charlotte Sound, this small town is the South Island terminus for both the Cook Strait ferries and the main trunk railway, and the start (or finish) of State Highway 1, which carves its way for nearly 1,000 km to Bluff. The seafaring Maori were the first settlers of the Marlborough Sounds and in their day they kept to the coastal areas, living off the abundant fruits of the sea. In fact, many Maori were so expert in the water that they didn't even need a boat to cross the Cook Strait (its unpredictable weather conditions and powerful currents making it one of the most dangerous stretches of water in the world), which at its narrowest point is 20 km wide: they simply swam instead. It wasn't until 1962 that the first European, Barrie Davenport, achieved this swimming feat, taking just over eleven hours. I don't know if it's because of the number of people who may have drowned in this crossing, but the Maori name for the Cook Strait is Raukawa, 'leaves of the kawakawa' – a decoration worn by a chief in mourning. As for its English name, although the Dutch explorer Abel Tasman was the first European to encounter this lively sea in 1642, Captain Cook felt he had earned the right to name the strait after himself because he was the first to chart it accurately.

Te Rapa, Marlborough, 22 February

As Picton (pop. 4,500) is a mere eleven hours' swim away from Wellington, it was perhaps not surprising that it had not escaped the storms. A civil emergency was declared when up to a thousand residents had to be evacuated from their homes because of fears that the nearby Humphreys and Barnes dams would collapse after hours of torrential rain caused flash floods (40 mm of rain fell in forty minutes) that swept away campervans, flooded houses and caused mudslides and general mayhem and disruption.

Cycling north out of town past the Toot 'n' Whistle Inn and the Dog & Frog Cafe and Ye Olde English Barber Shoppe, I managed to find a slab of relatively drained land up at Waikawa Bay from where I could walk up to the end of a little peninsula, which in Maori is called Te Ihumoeone-ihu ('the nose of the sandworm'), but in Pakeha patois is simply The Snout.

Since my arrival in the north of the South, I've happened upon a local radio station on my mini radio called 'Easy FM'. The music has its ups and downs and there are plenty of weather forecasts (rain, rain and more rain. And wind. And then more rain). Trouble is, there's a woman presenter on it who tells me with every other word that I'm listening to Easy FM. 'Hi there, you're listening to Easy FM and this is Easy FM playing The Scissor Sisters. So here we go, from Easy FM, here's "Take your Mama".' Added to this intensely aggravating and constantly repetitive reminder of what I'm listening to, when I know what I'm listening to, is the way she pronounces Easy FM as 'Izzie If Imm'. I ask you!

Lying in my tent near The Snout, I tuned into National Radio and heard the Met Service issue yet another weather warning as yet another low pressure system was expected to hurl itself at the lower North Island and the upper South Island, with wind gusts of 150 km/h predicted. There was also talk of a possible cyclone coming our way, though no one was quite sure quite when.

The trouble with forecasts like this is that they initiate a dilemma in your head. You lie in your sleeping bag thinking: shall I go or should I stay? Shall I risk it or should I play safe? Though the wind was raging itself into a frothing great tizz, it wasn't yet raining, so grabbing hold of a positive in the face of a negative I upped pegs and took off south on SH1 towards Blenheim.

As tends to happen in this game, the minute you decide to do something and dismantle your home with all panniers open to the skies, the rain starts. Which it did. And it didn't stop. Nor did I.

Bracing myself for impact from the wind and the water, I rode a road that went up and then down, following a river valley through Koromiko ('Japanese Womble') and then a flatter expanse through Tuamarina ('elaborate docking facility for yachting tuna'). In fact Tuamarina is near the site of the 'Wairau Incident' (formerly known as the 'Wairau Massacre') of 1843, when a disputed land purchase (some things never change) led to a bloody clash between settlers hoping to muscle in on Maori land. It seems the whaling captain, John Blenkinsopp, had tried to pull a fast one on local Maori. In the ensuing affray, twenty-two Pakeha and six Maori were killed. The terms of the 'agreement' were renegotiated in 1847 when the new European owners handed over all of £3000.

Down the road lay Spring Creek (site of a backpackers called Swampy's – 'mind those underground tunnels and rattails around the Newbury Bypass!') by which stage the wind was so strong that I could hardly stand up, let alone cycle. I narrowly missed being turned to pulp when a tree crashed down across the road in front of me. The remaining 5 km to Blenheim took over an hour – it was that stupidly windy.

Blenheim was originally named Beavertown by a party of surveyors who apparently identified with the beaver when they became stranded in the area by floodwaters. I'm not quite sure why. Maybe they resorted to building a dam by cutting down some trees with their teeth. For some obscure reason the town was later renamed to commemorate the Bavarian battle won by the Duke of Marlborough when the English defeated the French and Bavarians. Quite what the connection is between this area and the Duke of Marlborough though is anybody's guess. Maybe he once came for a little recreational cycle-touring holiday down in these wind-blown parts.

Because the road south of Blenheim involved a couple of exposed passes, I decided I wouldn't tempt fate and be blown clean off the planet never to be seen again. So in a rushing flap of wind and rain (Blenheim, by the way, calls itself the 'Sunshine Capital of New Zealand' – ha!) I threw my tent up in a corner of the run-down

Duncannon Holiday Park. The owner, a hangdog man with a death-rattle cough, had told me in no uncertain terms to put my tent beneath a large cedar tree. But I didn't fancy camping under a tree in this wind so I stuck to my guns and kept to the corner.

And a good thing too. After a wild night of howling wind and gushing rain, I was awoken with a start this morning by a loud splintering sound followed by an almighty crack and thud. Taking a peek out of my tent door, I saw that a bough, the size of a large tree, had been torn from the cedar by the wind. I think it's safe to say that if I had placed my tent where Mr Happy had wanted me to put it, there wouldn't be too much left of me now.

The news came on and I heard how Marlborough had been hit by wind gusts up to 200 km/h last night. How very silly. They were also saying that the cyclone was now set to miss New Zealand but that there was heavy rain still coming this way. Hadn't we just had that? Or was that just medium-rare-to-heavy rain without the full-helmeted heavy?

Contrary to what the weather forecasters said, the rain cleared this morning and a slightly sodden-looking sun plopped out. As I was shaking the rain from my tent, a couple in a Maui motorhome walked over to tell me how they had started out cycling around part of the South Island. 'But we gave up on it because it never stopped raining,' said the woman. 'So now we're treating ourselves to a van. I recommend it. It's a lot easier this way!'

For the first two miles after setting off I scarcely had to pedal. The raging tailwind blew so strong that it hurled me along the flat road at over 25 mph. It was like being attached to a rocket. But then I turned the corner and the wind slammed into me from the side. Suddenly things had gone from fun and fast to slow and harrowingly hard.

It was while I had been bowling along at top knots that I caught sight of the much-locally advertised tourist lure – Riverlands cob cottage. This cottage, made from cut tussock grass mashed with puddled clay, is classified in Kiwi terms as a site of ancient historical importance. It was built in 1860.

As the road began its winding climb over Weld Pass, I suddenly entered a barren landscape of big and smooth and symmetrically rounded brassy-coloured hills. In the distance, towering high above the low-altitude hills, rose the harsh scree slopes of the Seaward Kaikoura Mountains still mantled with dog collars of snow. Sometimes I love cycling uphill and this pass was one of those moments. The gradient was good, the twists and turns were fun (apart from the moment when a double-trailer truck squinched me up tight against a cliffed wall of scree), the scenery almost startling. I then dived down and dashed up Dashwood Pass (hardly a pass, more a mere blip of a rise) before flopping into Seddon and filling up on liquid supplies at the Cosy Corner Cafe.

After that it was up and down, up and down over the shorn flanks of hills passing over ribbons of water with names like Hog Swamp River, Blind River Loop and Puka Puka River (obviously a Jamie Oliver favourite). Just past Blind River and Tetley Brook Road came the weird sight of the purple-pink and white crystallising ponds of Lake Grassmere – New Zealand's only evaporative solar salt works, formed by the almost constant winds and (supposedly) many sunny days that occur around here. Not far away lay Cape Campbell (South Island's most easterly point) and Boo Boo Stream. Once past Atacama (not a desert but a farm dwelling) I was in and out of Taimate ('tea-flavoured Coffee-mate') and upon the tiny roadside settlement of Ward, where I paused for a breather outside the Flaxbourne Tearoom MOBIL petrol and diesel stop. A tourist bus pulled up and one of the occupants who spilt out of the doors was a short-haired girl from Barrow-in-Furness in Cumbria. 'A dive of a place,' she said. 'That's why I'm here!' She was now trying to get a job in New Zealand as a physio, but last year she had attempted cycling around some of the country. At one point she'd cycled over Lewis Pass (where I hope to find myself in a few days time) into a headwind. 'It was so hard,' she said, 'I cried all the way!'

On I went past Gulch Road and Needles Point (ah, nearly home!) and Mirza (oh, maybe not). The road then hit the coast. Although the wind was still blowing like billy-o, the spectacular sight of big seas and high mountains that pressed in close to the coast fired my energy levels and I thought I'd push on down the coast for another three or more hours. This idea soon went to pot when, in the middle of nowhere, I came across a sign in the shape of a large bicycle saying 'Pedaller's Rest Cycle Stop' and pointing down a long gravel road that headed up a valley towards a nest of mountains. I clunked down over the single-track railway and up the jolty dirt track that my map told me was Ure Road – a dead-end road that wove its way deeper into the valley alongside Waima ('ask your mother') River to a pretty non-existent-looking place called Kilgram. On the southern edge of Kilgram rose Isolated Hill over-looking Headache Stream.

But well before this place of neuralgic remoteness, I came across an old farmhouse set amid a beautiful garden and trees, one of which was a cabbage tree. Trying to steady themselves with a loud flapping of wings while clambering about upon this tree's peculiar yucca-like leaves in search of its yellow-white flowers perched a couple of stout New Zealand pigeons. These were much bigger and plumper birds than the common vermin-spreading pigeons I'm used to at home. The New Zealand versions have a fine plumage sparkling with a green and purple sheen above a large pristeen white apron. Unlike their Trafalgar Square brethren, these two were quite shy and soon took off with heavy, thumping wingbeats.

The farmhouse belonged to Jim and Denise Rudd, sheep farm-ers who farmed an area that stretched into the hills as far as the eye could see. In other words a blinking long way. Farms round here aren't small patchworks of dainty fields. They are whole huge swathes of wilderness, enormous hills and mountains that appear to cover an area the size of Wales. Down here, the average farm is nearly a dozen times the size of those back home.

In a field behind the farmhouse stood a sturdy little stone build-ing. This was the bunkhouse – site of the Pedaller's Rest complete with five-star view. Denise said I could either camp or have a bunk, but as I'd slept in my tent every night since leaving Auckland (fifty-three nights to be precise – not that I'm counting) and as I prefer being outside to inside, I erected my Tadpole with tent door over-looking the boundless expanse of sun-crested hills.

Denise told me that visitors to the bunkhouse came and went. Sometimes it was full of a busy mob of sweaty cyclists, other times days and days and days could go by with not a soul. She said that at present I was the only one staying tonight. No one had phoned up to book a bed. 'So it looks like you've got the place to yourself. Enjoy!'

And enjoy it I did. With only the sound of the weird whooping birds and the wind whistling down the valley, the place was perfect.

I had just finished writing up my diary and was in the middle of a nice quiet read when suddenly all hell descended in the shape of six boisterous cyclists. Not all of them were travelling together. It was just by chance that they all arrived at the same time. First there was James, a good-looking, blond-haired, sun-tanned Kiwi, a teacher I think he said he was, from Auckland. Although he had a bike with him, he had walked the last few miles as he'd had a tyre blow out on him. I had a spare folding tyre with me that I would have gladly given him (I wasn't after anything in return – no, really!); the only trouble was my tyre was a 26-incher and he was after a 700 c. So we discussed various tricks of the trade about how to patch up the sizeable split (gaffer tape, wad of hard packed grass, a taped patch of spare inner tube etc).

Then there were Dutch Marten and Karin who apparently knew me, though I not them. Karin immediately donated some surgical tape to James which she said was much stronger than gaffer tape. Both Karin and Marten worked in Marten's family business – a bike shop, but had given up their jobs to cycle around the South Island for three months. They both had Gazelle frames and had built up the bikes themselves with what they thought were the best components for the job.

Next came the travelling threesome: Glaswegian Anne-Marie (a forty-year-old-looking fifty-year-old fitness instructor), Glaswegian Bridget (a twenty-six-year-old eco-architect-cum-Reiki Master) and Pete (a thirty-something plumber from Bacup, near Manchester). Bridget looked at me and said, 'Josie Dew!', which in her fetching Glaswegian accent came out as 'Jer-zzie Duue'.

No one slept inside. Everyone whipped up a tent, the only two to share one being Mr and Mrs Marten. The area around the bunkhouse had turned into a sudden tent show. As I am particularly partial to tents I was now in my element and accordingly did the rounds, trying them out for size and investigating pockets and air-vents and materials and zips like a true tent anorak. Anne-Marie's little 1½ kilo Vaude made up in weight what it lacked in size – it was like a glorified coffin with no space to entertain a friend or pile in a pack of panniers. Camping alongside me as she was, her Vaude made my abode look like a double-decker bus.

Bridget and Pete were both flying the flag with British-made Terra Nova Voyagers that were practically the same shape and style as my North Face Tadpole, just much better made. James had a big bright yellow dome that offered enough room to swing a sheep, but was not a practical colour if you wanted to sneak into the bushes and pass a night unseen. Not, that is, unless you could find a field full of dandelions or sunflowers to camp among. Marten and Karin also had a Vaude, only it was about ten times bigger than Anne-Marie's with all sorts of interesting sections and doors. I think they even had an upstairs and a front garden in there too.

When it got dark, we went into the bunkhouse and lit a log fire in the little pot-belly stove. We were minus Bridget at this stage because she had disappeared off to the farmhouse to do a session of Reiki on Denise. Although they all knew each other at home and were currently all travelling together, Bridget, Pete and Anne-Marie had flown to New Zealand separately. Bridget was away for the longest – about a year. Pete had about a month and Anne-Marie six weeks. Pete never used to cycle. He was a keen footballer and from the age of fifteen would play every weekend religiously. Then, during one match, he was passing the ball to another player who made no effort to run for it whatsoever. Pete looked at this player and thought: what's the point in playing football if the other player can't be bothered? So he gave up football and played more squash until around 1987 when, becoming fixated with the Tour de France and Bernaud Hinault and Greg Lemond, he saw the light and took up cycling. He had since done the End-to-End

(Land's End to John o' Groats) five times. On another occasion he embarked upon cycling across America and managed to get 1500 miles under his belt when he suddenly stopped in Oklahoma, about halfway across. 'I kept getting to places and there would be nothing there. So I gave up and flew home. As soon as I got back I went straight up to Scotland and cycled around there instead. It was far more interesting!'

There seemed to be a little bit of friction between the three-some – at least between Bridget and Anne-Marie. Today, when they were cycling up the Weld Pass, Pete (who was also a triathlete) and Bridget (who was just naturally competitive) starting racing each other to the top, leaving Anne-Marie standing. Anne-Marie was not impressed; she didn't see why everything should be a race and when she next saw Bridget she gave her a piece of her mind.

In the 'Millennium Edition' of the 'Pedaller's Rest Register' I read a few comments from various pedallers who had pedalled this way in the past. A certain Nao Nishinaga from Sendai, Japan, obviously had one very large lop-sided leg because he called by here while travelling the coast on a micro scooter. A fellow countryman, Sosaku Kawagoe, at least was on a bike, but the weather was not being conducive:

> Today I from Kaikoura. It was not so long but with head-wind. It was hard to cycling. I talked to myself 'wind is friend, I am plaiing with the earth'. But . . . it was hard. Anyway, I made it. This hostel is lovery place. I'm happy here. But no shops nere here. This is bad or good?

A bit of a philosophical conundrum there, Sosaku. Though I would say 'good' myself.

More philosophical musings came from MB Armstrong, Washington, USA, who noted, with an interesting use of capitals and tagged on statements of confusion: 'The only Cure for Lonliness is Solitude – someone from Broadmoor.'

Dave Russell from Canada was a little more down to earth.

'Pretty kick-ass place. A couple of crazy cunucks on tour give it the big thumbs up! Need a tailwind tomorrow. Please.'

When Bridget returned from her Reiki consignment complete with a brand new merino wool cycle jersey bought off Denise, she told me how four years ago she'd got some sort of agonising hereditary muscle-seizure disease and how for the past year she'd been living on a raw food diet. She also told me how a month before Christmas she'd had a bike built up for her 'big trip' (she was thinking of maybe trying to cycle home from New Zealand) and when she was standing at the side of the road with her bike at a junction, pausing to cross, a truck stopped at the junction, the driver apparently seeing her. But when he started up again he had obviously forgotten all about Bridget and drove right over her. She blacked out, broke a cheekbone, but somehow managed to survive. The bike was a complete right-off, though. Apart from the gear levers.

8

Kaikoura, Canterbury, 23 February

Although my Ortlieb panniers are waterproof, everything I have in my panniers is wrapped up in plastic bags (you can't be too safe in this game with weather like the weather in New Zealand). This means that whenever I move about the insides of my tent or extract something from my panniers, I rustle like a trapped rat in a bag. Anne-Marie camped so close to me last night that my inner tent activities were severely inhibited; I didn't want to wake her up from an excess of rampant rustlings.

This morning before breakfast Bridget sauntered off to a corner of a distant field to perform a dose of tae kwon do movements – an interesting-looking form of pushing-air-slowly martial art. Pete said in his deadpan northern accent, 'She don't half get some weird looks, yer know, like. I see people on campsites looking at her out the corners of their eyes!'

When Denise's husband Jim stopped by the tents in his farm pick-up for a chat, he looked over at Bridget and said, 'Is that girl all right?' Jim had five lively farm dogs on the tray of his truck. He said that the job of the two English sheepdogs was to push the sheep, whereas the three brown specially bred New Zealand dogs pushed them back again.

Quite what the sheep were to make of this pushing, I don't know.

I was the first off this morning. Although the forecast had been for rain there was no sign of it yet so I decided to sally forth south. The forecast had also said a strong southerly would blow, but instead I had a frisky northerly, which sent me shooting off along the coast through Wharanui ('I'm fine wearing my shorts, thanks') and past Willawa Point to Kekerengu ('Japanese kangaroo') where, despite the road continuing in exactly the same direction, the wind suddenly decided to run round from my tail and slam into me head-on. How very devilish of it. Still, no matter how hard the wind tried to push me packing off back to Picton, it couldn't mar the enjoyment factor of cycling along this most spectacular of coasts that kept offering tantalising glimpses of the Seaward Kaikoura Range still mantled in snow. The road lay pinned between the high, eroded hills and mountains on the right and the wide, ruffled sea on the left. Between me and the waves, which crashed with a continuous swooshing crunch on to long and lonely shingle beaches, stretched the narrow railway. Only once did a train rattle past. A passenger train at that (one of only three services that run in the whole of the South Island) with an open viewing carriage where the passengers could get a taster of enthusiastic wind and bracing sea air. The rails ran so close to the road that had a passenger stretched out an arm, I could have shaken their hand.

Wild fennel and cabbage trees seem to do well round here. As do fords. Washdyke and Deadman Stream had a small trickle to them, but, during the spring melt, these dry beds would become raging torrents that would force traffic to use the adjacent one-lane bridges. I continued skirting the hem of the mountains and then, once over the shingle-braided Clarence River, the winding road was squeezed even tighter between the coves and bays of the rocky shore and the tall, steep cliffs. At times SH1's wrap of tarmac balanced on a narrow ledge together with the railway – the tracks occasionally being swallowed by the black, gaping mouth of a tunnel.

Just south of Okiwi Bay ('watery Chinese gooseberries') and Waipapa ('Ask your father!') Bay and Paparoa ('paternal oarsman') Point, the rocks were covered with basking and frolicking and bellowing seals. This was Ohau ('Oh how what?') Point seal colony and proved a most amusing sight to be seen and heard. If you were travelling down this road on anything other than bike or foot (or in that Japanese man's case, microscooter) you would miss most of the delights and antics of the seal cubs at play. There is the odd lay-by and designated viewing point for a vehicle to pause in, but it's not quite the same as being out there with these sluggish and bawling great beasts, flopped out on the boulders like large whiskered slabs of putty with glistening squash-ball eyes.

At Rakautara I passed a fishing boat called *Liquidator* pulled up on to the shore and then I was upon CAY'S CRAYS and NIN'S BIN 4 COOKED – two roadside stalls selling freshly cooked crayfish (rock lobster). The Kaikoura coast is famous for its crayfish; the area was named by Tamatea, an ancient Maori chief, when he stopped by to eat some crayfish while pursuing his runaway wives (who were eventually transformed into greenstone in Westland). Tamatea was so impressed with the quality of the crayfish that he called the place *kai* ('food') *koura* ('crayfish').

A car and a motorhome were parked in the gravel lay-by, their occupants sitting at picnic tables sucking on some of Cay's and Nin's large pink-clawed legs and picking out the flesh. The car's licence plate asked in text speak HW U DN, while the motorhome simply advised all to CUT LOOSE.

Blue Valley Duck Road came and went as did the Puhi Puhi River. Just on the outskirts of Kaikoura I saw a church with a big plastic noticeboard outside claiming that 'JESUS DIED 4 U'. Seems the holy scriptures had turned to text talk to ram their message home.

I had just pulled up outside Kaikoura's new New World supermarket when a woman with harum-scarum hair climbed into a fat SUV and promptly reversed into a slab of concrete that dislodged a part of her rear bumper. She drove off. I don't think she was even aware of what she had done. That's one of the advantages of driving an urban tank – you can crash into things, or even mow down a cyclist, and not even notice. Means you can still pick up the kids on time.

Kaikoura, Canterbury, 24 February

Last night I camped beside a stream complete with drifting ducks at 69 Beach Road Holiday Park – an immaculate site with a big shiny kitchen run by Katrina and Colin Legg. Colin told me he used to be a sheep farmer. 'So I've gone from fleecing sheep to fleecing people!' he said. Despite the site being on Beach Road, there was no beach to this site – just a huge valley view dominated by snow-topped mountains. I pointed my tent door down the valley as the wind had burnt itself out by now. But then as I watched the sun drop out of sight and the sky grow in colour, the pastures turned up their undersides in a sudden flap of breeze.

This morning that breeze is more like a small hurricane and is completely distorting the shape of some tents and flattening others. My neighbours hurriedly collapsed their tent and threw it into the back of their hire car. The woman is Glaswegian and is wearing one of those Action Man khaki-coloured sleeveless jerkins you see photographers wearing that contain about eighty-seven pockets. Her partner has long grey hair tied back in a ponytail. He had met his Action Woman when he was working in Glasgow at something highfalutin to do with tax. Then they downshifted and moved to the Isle of Wight where, because they loved collecting things, they owned the Blue Slipper Fossil Shop in Sandown. One day they thought they would do some exercise and cycled across the island to Cowes, where they had coffee and read the papers in a cafe. And then they cycled back again. 'That was our training ride and after that we decided to shut the shop for a year and cycle around the world.'

So they had arrived in South Island with bikes and panniers and off they went with round-the-world tickets in their pockets. But they immediately hit hills and wind and rain. 'We lasted four days – four days of hell! So we sold the bikes and panniers and hired this car. Travelling by car is far more enjoyable! Now whenever we pass a cyclist on the road we look at them and wonder how they do it!'

Kaikoura, 26 February

Even though I didn't mean to be here, it seems I still am. But that's one of the nice things about having no schedules to schedule myself into. Means I can come across a top spot like Kaikoura and lounge and linger without any pressing need to race and rush. Unlike the travelling threesome. I caught a quick sight of them the first night I arrived, stocking up on supplies at New World super-market. The following morning I met Bridget as she was on her way to post a postcard before departing for Hanmer Springs with the other two. But she wasn't very happy. Seems there was some-thing of a rumpus going on between them all.

Kaikoura sits on a small rocky protrusion of limestone and silt-stone that pokes out into the Pacific, overlooked by the mountainous upthrust of the Seaward Kaikoura Range, a spur of the Southern Alps. The Maori regard the area as a place of mythi-cally historical significance as this was where the earliest Maori ancestors of the South Island tribes apparently arrived on the back of a huge whale. Also, the Kaikoura Peninsula was the foothold that the fearless warrior and demigod Maui used when he fished the North Island up from the depths of the sea. Unlike the European settlers who, observing that New Zealand was a country of two halves, stated the obvious by calling the more northerly island North Island and the more southerly one South Island, the Maori used a little more imagination. The North Island became known as *Te Ika a Maui* – The Fish of Maui (Wellington Harbour is the fish's mouth, the Taranaki and East Coast protrusions are its fins, the Northland peninsula its tail). The South Island was named *Te Waka o Maui* – The Canoe of Maui, the one he was sitting in when he hauled up the North Island fish. But the canoe is appar-ently a stricken canoe (I'm not sure what it crashed into – maybe a cross-Channel ferry that took a wrong turning at Dieppe) with the crew on one side forming the mountains, and its shattered sunken prow in the north forming the Marlborough Sounds.

The first Europeans to settle in Kaikoura were whalers. The waters just off the peninsula are unusually deep with a complex submarine canyon system forming a network of trenches and troughs where icy cold waters from Antarctica mix with warm waters from the north and east. All this creates an incredibly rich food chain for fish, marine mammals and seabirds. Swimming about in the krill-rich waters or moving about in the trench just off the continental shelf, barely half a mile from Kaikoura, live an abundance of squid (including the infamous giant squid of sea-faring lore with eyes the size of cannon balls). Sperm whales, the largest toothed mammal on earth, are particularly partial to krill – and to squid. As a result sperm whales frequent the Kaikoura coast in greater numbers than anywhere else in the world. But where the whales were once exploited and hunted and harpooned and slaughtered in their thousands for the oil in their blubber, they are now protected and sought for an entirely different reason: eco-tourism.

Should the fancy take you, you can go on a whale-watching boat tour with WhaleWatch Kaikoura. Or you could take to the air with Wings over Whales or WhaleWatch Kaikoura Helicopters (how very eco) to try to catch an aerial view of a broaching whale – both sperm and pilot. And sometimes orcas. But it's not just whales that draw the teeming tourists to Kaikoura. Also on the agenda to view or to swim or dive with are the particularly playful and acrobatic dusky dolphins, the bottle-nosed dolphins and Hector's dolphins (the smallest and rarest and most threatened of dolphins). Then there are sharks to be viewed from an underwater cage (which is surely cheating), blue penguins and New Zealand fur seals, not to mention the largest number of pelagic bird species within such a small area of New Zealand coastline: shearwaters, gannets, terns, fulmars, petrels, royal and wandering albatross and mollymawks.

As I'm not very good at joining tour groups to go in search of something surrounded by excitable people exclaiming excitable remarks, I gave all the plentiful tour outfits like Shark Dive Kaikoura, Seal Swim Kaikoura, NZ Sea Adventures, Kaikoura Executive Sea Tours, Dolphin Encounter, Ocean Wings Albatross Encounters, Life on the Reef, Graeme's Seal Swim and Topspot

Seal Swim a miss. Instead I went exploring on my bike and walking all over the peninsula, marvelling at the size of the bull kelp (monster tube-like intestines built like trees) that washes up on the beach around these rocky shores.

Some who did go whale-watching and quad-bike sightseeing were Debs and Simon. I met Debs in the campsite reception and she looked at me as I was paying for my tent spot and said, 'Have I read your book?' This was a bit of a difficult question to answer because, as this was the first time I had ever met Debs in my life, I didn't know how I was supposed to know whether I knew whether she had known whether she had read my book or not. As you can probably tell, when you spend so much time alone in the saddle, life can get immensely confusing. Especially when it comes to simple questions.

Anyway, Debs was an affable soul and invited me back to warm my cockles (the nights have been decidedly chilly of late and it was now night) in her hired Pacific Horizon motorhome. The motorhome was the size of a small removal lorry and contained beds and bunks, lighting and heating, toilet and shower, cooker, fridge and microwave and a dining table the size of a tennis court. It was a long time since I had sat in a seat at a table and it was a most enjoyable experience – no tent-induced backache or dead-limb pins and needles.

The other occupant of the Pacific Horizon was Simon, Debs' boyfriend, or maybe even fiancé but I don't think they had got quite that far quite so fast yet as they only met eighteen months ago on an organized End-to-End bike ride. Seems they took an immediate shine to each other. 'We stuck together solidly almost to the exclusion of talking to anyone else on the tour!' said Debs.

Debs, by the way, lived in Putney and worked in the city. She used to be a lawyer but was now a high-flying banker. 'What do bankers actually *do*?' I asked. Debs looked at me as if I've spent too much time alone on my bike. Which I probably have. But that still didn't answer the question. It's like hedge fund managers and actuaries. Apart from actuaries dabbling with a few statistics and sums, and hedge fund managers dabbling with (presumably) roadside bushes full of hawthorn, field maple and dog rose, I have terrible difficulty grabbing a grasp of what it is they do to make such a pile of money. But before I could get any further down this road of cul-de-sac querying conundrums, Debs was telling me how she had been living a high-flying life all her working life and felt that now she had reached her mid-thirties it was time to do something else. 'I've been picking up DoC leaflets since we've been in New Zealand,' she said. 'Maybe we'll move here and I'll work in conservation.'

Simon, who was a website designer from the North-East (somewhere around Sunderland, I believe), was quite keen on this idea because he thought New Zealand was a good country to maybe start up a cycle-tour company. He wouldn't do too much of the cycling, mind you. Just the organising. He and Debs had gone on a two-week cycle tour of Cuba a little while back. It was an enjoyable time, by all accounts, apart from the cycling (hard work) and the roughing-it part. 'I like my comforts,' said Simon. 'I much prefer motorhomes to tents!'

He and Debs were now away for a month because Debs was 'in between jobs'. Banking jobs, that is. Whatever banking means. They both got on a treat. 'We hardly ever argue,' Debs said, 'apart from when Simon's reversing and I'm standing behind, seeing him back and apparently making all the wrong hand signals!'

Debs' mum lived on the Lincolnshire coast. She had recently split up with her husband after thirty-six years of marriage. 'Which I think was thirty-four years too long,' said Debs. So her mum left her dad for a man called Mike. 'She didn't tell Dad,' said Debs, 'she just left him a note to say that she had left. She also left lots of meals she had prepared in the freezer with little notes attached to them with instructions on how long to microwave them all for. There were notes everywhere. Even the washing machine had a note on it to say how it worked and which setting to use and how much powder to put in.'

Debs' mum met Mike on a beach in Lincolnshire when either he, or she, or both of them had been out collecting pieces of coal. As you do. Anyway, last year her mum and Mike had met up with her dad and they all spent Christmas together. 'It went very well,' said Debs. 'Mum and Dad get on so much better now. Dad likes Mike and Mum is miles happier. So is Dad because he's got his independence and is doing his own thing.'

Headlines today: 'WEATHER LASHES VEGGIE BUYERS'. As a result of the floods, people would be paying more than double for their greens because of a major shortage in vegetables. As of yesterday, the price of most vegetables increased by more than 200 per cent. Here's a taster of the price hikes: a cauliflower up from $1.60 to $4.30; spinach $3 a bunch, now $7; broccoli at around $1, now $4. 'The shortage could last a further two months as growers struggle to clear their patches and renew their plants,' says Vegfed chief executive Peter Silcock. Bananas are unaffected, so that's a relief.

And here's the weather news: the *New Zealand Herald* warned me that 'foul weather will thump New Zealand from both sides this weekend. From the west, a low will arrive, lashing the whole country tomorrow. The South Island and the lower North Island will be hit hardest, with strong winds and up to 150 mm of rain. Come Sunday and Monday' (it is now Thursday) 'the country will feel the effects of the remnants of tropical cyclone Ivy. Met Service weather ambassador Bob McDavitt said it looked like a "tempestuous" end to summer.'

Another headline says: '*Read and Weep*. Come Saturday, comes torrential rain across the country. Come Sunday, a monster, slow-moving, low system with rain and wind from Invercargill to Cape Reinga. And then to top it off – come Monday, comes cyclone Ivy.'

Fin-tis-tic! I can't wait. In fact, I can barely contain myself.

Waiau, Hurunui, Canterbury, 27 February

If you let a little rain put you off (even a little cyclone), then you'd never get anywhere in this cycling-around-New-Zealand game. So I left behind all the Pacific Horizons, Britz, Apollo and Kea Campers, not to mention a posse of Hardtop Pop-Up caravans and Kiwi

Experience, Flying Kiwi and Magic Travellers bus tours, cramming up the car parks and double-parking in Kaikoura, and set out for Hanmer Springs with the idea that I would ride inland over the Lewis Pass to the west coast before zigzagging back to the east coast over Arthur's Pass and Porter's Pass. Of course it would be a lot easier to continue south down the coast across the flat plains of Canterbury, but there's something about mountains, especially the Southern Alps that extend in an unbroken northeast–southwest line for 450 km from Lewis Pass to Key Summit Divide on the Milford Road, which are just asking to be ridden over. Cyclone or no cyclone.

A cold night was followed by a streaky red-sky dawn that turned the snow-tipped mountains to pink. Heavy dew quadrupled the

weight of my tent this morning. I shook the better part of it off before rolling it up and taking off past Maori Leap Cave. I then turned my back on the sea and headed on to SH70 that for some touristy-branding reason had changed its name from the Inland Kaikoura Road to the Alpine Pacific Triangle. Apart from the fierce headwind and the air-sucking stock trucks that went barrelling past, this route proved hugely enjoyable for cycling – despite the steep climbs and continual roller-coaster gradients. It was a fantastically lonely road with no shops or communities for about 85 km, just the odd deer farm and sheep station and rock fall and lots of single-lane bridges. It was a good route for roadside grazing: the bushes were loaded with blackberries and there were plenty of trees weighted with wild apples. All I needed was some crumble topping and custard to complete the find.

Talking of stock trucks, they travel at such a rollicking speed that I wasn't surprised when I read in the paper the other day of two stock truck drivers who were trapped in their cabs and hundreds of dead and dying sheep were strewn for 100 metres after a smash near Dunedin. One of the double-trailer stock trucks lost control on a bend and a following truck full of ewes struck the crashed truck. The clean-up took more than seven hours.

I trundled onward past and through such places as Kowhai ('tall cattle'), Mount Furneaux, Green Burn, Hawk Hills, Surrey Hills (though no sign of Woking or Guildford), Mount Horrible, Black Stream, Humbug Stream, Stag and Spey Road, Cloudy Range Road, Mount Lyford ski resort (no snow, just deserted slopes of grey scree topping a thicket of forest that looked as if it had slipped down the mountain), Mount Tinline, Lottery River and Stackhouses Road. I was hauling myself over a particularly steep hill when I caught sight of a blur of cyclist streaking down the road in the opposite direction. It was the electrically long-haired Austrian wizard whom I had briefly met at the cicada-infested campsite at East Cape. I was still inching my way upwards when I spotted him again far below following the thread of road along the bottom of the river valley. He saw me and waved, so I waved back

and then I had something happen to me that never had before: I
was yodelled to. A proper mountain-echoing Austrian yodel that
bounced back and forth from one hillside to another. How touching.

And then he stopped. So I stopped. And he shouted, 'Are you
vell?'

So I shouted back, 'All well, thank you!'

It was like a sort of Shackleton exchange when Ernest finally
returned to Elephant Island to rescue his men and had shouted
out across the water a greeting along similar lines.

At last I rolled into Waiau, which means 'swirling river', though it
sounds more to me like a Geordie greeting. After passing not one
store all day, Waiau was a hive of commercial activity. There was a
dairy, a takeaway, a tearoom, a hotel, a small Four Square and a
Hammer Hardware store. And a dump of a motorcamp. Which is
where I am now, camping as far away as I can from three big
snarlingly delirious dogs attached by chain to a kennel. Apart from
two caravans, the place is deserted. One caravan is coated in a
mossy slime and doesn't look as if it has gone anywhere for the past
forty years. It belongs to a bearded and long-haired man with a hat
who slouches about in the shadows. I came across him in the tip of
a kitchen eating a big fry-up, fag hanging limply from lips. He told
me he'd been doing odd jobs around here for a while, working on
the roads, that kind of thing, but was thinking of going north to
pick fruit because he'd heard they were looking for pickers and
packers.

The other caravan belongs to George and Elaine. George was
originally from Southport, just north of Liverpool. 'I came out
here in 'seventy-five – before your time,' said George (incorrectly).
'During the miner's strike. I got a job as a motor mechanic.'

When I asked him if he had ever gone back to Southport he
said, 'Only once. I'm not a snob, but I looked around me at the
downcast faces and shabbiness and I thought: well, at least I've
made something of my life.'

We had a bit more chat and when George found out I was

cycling around the country he advised me to be careful, especially with my possessions. 'New Zealand's not what it used to be. I'm not being prejudiced, but it's mostly the Maoris you got to watch.' He turned to Elaine and said, 'Remember up north that Maori guy who got chatting to us and then ran off with our mate's wallet?'

Then the rain started so we retreated to our respective abodes. As the water cascaded down the sides of my tent, I turned on my radio and heard a man telling me, 'This country's at a crossroads. We've had the Maori Renaissance; we've had the burgeoning Asian population. We have the possibility of all this upset and hatred tearing us apart.'

Hanmer Springs, Hurunui, Canterbury, 28 February

It rained all night. And it rained all morning. Finally at about two o'clock this afternoon it decided to take a break. So I threw the whole sopping lot of my nylon abode into my panniers and took off for Hanmer Springs before the weather decided to do the dirty on me again. I sped off along the flat of the Emu Plains to Rotherham, then veered off on to Flintoft–Mouse Point Road until I hit the busy SH7, with its fast cars sporting licence plates trumpeting things like COCKY and logging trucks with plates saying things like LOGGER 1. The road went up and down and up and down as I crossed over the likes of Brown Stream, Deadman's Stream and Stinking Stream. One bridge was accompanied by a small forest of white crosses. Yet more road deaths.

On one of the hills two Lycra-sheathed men on road bikes sped past me. The rear rider called, 'Hang in there!' as he flashed by. 'I'm hanging,' I called back, though I wasn't quite sure to what.

At Waiau Ferry Bridge I turned off for Hanmer and crossed a spectacular bridge, 115 feet high and 117 years old, from which a couple of scared-looking people were forking out $100 each to jump from a special bungee-jumping gantry. Across the way at the Thrillseekers Canyon Centre, others were gearing themselves up for a session of jet-boating or white-water rafting. I can't say the idea of spending large amounts of money for a wet, heart-attack-inducing ride appeals to me. I find it quite exciting enough simply trying to cycle to wherever it is I'm trying to go before a cyclone hits me.

Deer Valley, Hurunui, Canterbury, 29 February

I've just realized that it's leap year day today. Where's Gary so I can ask him whether he'd care to take my hand in marriage as his wedded nagging wife? Oh, I've just remembered – he'll be up to the rafters with his undersquinted abutments and compact stub tie truss posts in his wood-filled workshop 15,000 miles away. That's the trouble with me – always in the wrong place at the wrong time. I must learn to position myself more carefully.

Last night, which was wet and windy, I camped overlooking Dog Creek beside a Nomad Nifty Pop-Up Hard-Top – one of those soft-sided caravans that resurrect themselves from a trailer. This morning my neighbouring Nifty Pop-Up resembled more a small swimming pool than a place of shelter. It seemed one of the sides had blown in.

Most people come to Hanmer Springs to wallow in the mineral pools of Hanmer Springs Thermal Reserve (motto: 'The Natural Place to Unwind') while gazing up with an appreciative unwinding sigh at the surrounding snowy peaks. But the pools all looked a bit busy and anyway I'd had quite enough of getting wet lately, on top of which I had a mountain pass to be tackling before the weather caved in on me again. So once I'd mended a rip in my flysheet (I'd hung my tent over a fence to dry but a small protrusion of wire slashed a foot-long tear in the material) I set off into a thumping great headwind for the Lewis Pass. I thought this would be quite a popular route for touring cyclists but not one bicycle passed me all day. Maybe they knew something that I didn't.

In fact there was scarcely any traffic of any kind, so maybe everyone knew something that I didn't. But I carried on anyway, inching my way steadily up the gradual gradient alongside the great Waiau

River that rushed downwards in the opposite direction. The scenery proved dramatic and rugged, riding as I was between the Hanmer Mountains dominating the views on my right and the Organ Range and Doubtful Range on my left. I passed over Cow Stream, Calf Stream and Wee Stream and then the swirling River Waiau transmuted into the Boyle. The higher I rode, the more the wind felt like cycling into a jet-engine testing tunnel. Churning cloud swirled all around. Occasionally the cloud emptied its contents heavily on top of me. Towards early afternoon a storm that must have been lying in wait behind the Spencer Mountains, or possibly even the Victoria Range, launched its attack when I was at my most vulnerable – out in the open with not a hint of shelter. As the sky detonated with a thunderous roar and jagged cracks of lightning flashed all around, I raced onwards through a blinding deluge of horizontal rain. With senses heightened and skin tingling from the electrical ions charging the atmosphere, I felt slightly concerned that I might be incinerated at any moment by a direct bolt of fire.

Several miles up the road I spotted the remnants of a shanty shed, which looked just the job for diving into for a bit of half-hearted sheltering from the storm. So in I lunged out of the rain only to discover rain coming through the roof, pouring down in a black funnel. But by standing up tight against one of the dank corrugated corners I could keep my head out of the flow, only my body getting wet by the ricocheting splash-back off the sodden ground. Then suddenly the downpour stopped and the roof dripped and the rain moved on, with the lightning quivering on its flanks like a protective barrage.

More rivers came and went, displaying conflicting ideas of optimism such as Hope River and Doubtful River. Then came the rivers of Nina and Lewis. I also passed a mountain called Mons Sex Millia, which rather begs the question of just exactly what it was that Nina and Lewis got up to when they came this way.

The scenery continued wild and remote, the road continued free of traffic and the wind continued to be no help whatsoever. Then somewhere around Windy Point, a flattish stretch of open wind-battered road, I came across a car that had slewed across the road, slammed into some small rocks and was now in a sorry state at rest in a ditch. The car was a hired car, appropriately a Rent-a-Dent (though I don't think it was part of the contract to rent it to dent it), driven by an American couple. They had both clambered out of the dented door and were now standing in various tragic attitudes about the car. I asked them if they were all right. Yes, no injuries, but owing to them having whacked the undercarriage of the vehicle against a football-sized boulder and dislodging the oil department, which was now leaching oil into the ground, the car understandably did not want to start. The woman, a long ratty-haired, pale dishcloth of a person with a splintery voice, had been at the wheel at the time of the incident. She had been driving along, travelling in the opposite direction to me, and then for no apparent reason lost control, skidded and flew off across the other lane and into a ditch. I find it rather worrying how someone can be driving along a wide, flat straight road in good visibility with no other vehicles around and no animals running out under the wheels, and then suddenly just go ploughing off the road. If I had been a minute or two earlier, she could quite easily have crashed into me and sent me for a sorry Burton.

The man, who clearly didn't know his arse from his elbow, stood looking at the car with dazed befuddlement. Had Gary been here, I bet he would have rolled up his sleeves and been under the car like a shot, knife clamped between teeth and various assortments of spanners and strips of wire and zip-ties clasped in hand. A few minutes of whistling later, he would emerge with black hands and a splattering of oil streaks on his face, then throw up the bonnet and fiddle with something in the murky inner depths of the engine before declaring the job done and the car ready to go. Gary loves engines, anything from car engines to steam engines (both external and internal) to traction engines to early plane engines (like the Tiger Moth's radial engines). I've learnt a lot more about engines from Gary than I ever really wanted to know (or deem necessary), from flame-ignition Crossley's (gas engines) to 8-stroke aeromotors (once used for driving water pumps on remote farms in America) to sleeve-valve engines (as found on old Buicks where instead of overhead poppit valves the actual cyclinder liner shifts and rotates) to Wankel rotary engines (a dubious-sounding but apparently wild device conceptually evolved from an internal combustion engine usually found lurking beneath the bonnet of a Mazda). And for some reason he knows how they all work. The other day when I gave him his bi-weekly phone call from a phone box, you'd think we might talk about something vaguely romantic or even topically interesting, but instead I heard myself having a conversation about Stephenson's Links and fly ball governors. To the uninitiated this may sound like an euphemism for a spot of below-the-belt talk, but rest assured, a fly ball governor is nothing more dodgy than a device that regulates engine speed in a revolution-per-minute type of way.

Anyway, all the Rent-a-Dent man had to say was, 'You gotta cell phone?' Indeed I did (I use it to text Gary about four times daily to talk about the delights of the lifecycle of a fly ball governor). The man wanted to ring for help but could get no signal on his cell phone, so why he thought my phone would have a signal was a little mystifying. The reason he could get no signal on his phone was simple: we were in the middle of the empty mountains about fifty miles from any signs of habitation. If you're a telecom company, you don't just stick up a telecommunications mast willy-nilly in the middle of nowhere for the fun of it. But the man insisted I turn my mobile on and then expressed surprise, followed by despair, at how I too failed to receive a signal.

I asked the Rent-a-Dent couple if they were in need of any sustenance (I am after all a travelling larder on wheels) but no, they were quite happy in their unhappy way with their bottle of Coke, so, assuring them that some form of vehicle would be along before too long, I took off into the wind.

A long time later I entered a thicket of forest of green dripping beech trees and the road got steeper and steeper as it climbed upwards in a stepped sort of way. The rain returned and it poured and poured. Everything was looking very subalpine. Mini waterfalls tumbled down the hillsides and the light was washed from the sky as a thick mist descended. Despite being wet, it was all rather lovely. On one corner I passed a white cross upon which were scribed the simple letters: DAD R.I.P. Then out of nowhere a motorbike came hurtling down the hill, braked hard when it shouldn't have braked hard and flew into a big fish-tailing skid heading directly for me, which gave my heart an invigorating moment. The rider managed to gain control just before slamming into my side and carried on his way. I wish people wouldn't do things like that. It's not good for my welfare.

The mist grew thicker and the gradient steeper and the slower I cycled the denser the clouds of sandflies became. Unlike Australia, where most of the country's wildlife tries its darnedest to sting you, eat you, poison you or burrow into your flesh and start raising a family, the only predators on human life in New Zealand are a timid spider with a puny bite (non-fatal) and the sandfly. Sandflies are as extremely irritating as Scottish midges, only they are bigger and more ferocious in their bites, drawing blood and welts that can make a victim look as if they've come down with some horrible pock-marked disease. And unlike their name suggests, they don't just dwell in sandy regions. As was evident from the number that were crawling up the sleeves of my jacket and down my neck and under my shirt, they particularly like sweaty cyclists struggling up thickly forested mountains in the rain.

As it was growing dark and as I didn't know exactly how far away the top of the pass would be (though I sensed not far), I made the most of a little camp spot down beside a gushing stream called Deer River. This was a Department of Conservation site. The DoC operates over 120 camping grounds around the country in national parks and reserves, and in maritime, forest and farm parks. More often than not these tend to be set deep in the bush, on distant sweeping beaches or beside isolated lakes. Most are just an expanse of stony ground reached by a track. Some provide water, some don't. Ditto toilets. Deer River was not much more than a lay-by, set away from the road down a dip. The choice of ground on which to pitch a tent was either hard and rocky or wet and mossy. There was a pit toilet set in a whiffy hut. The only water supply was the river. There is something very enjoyably back to nature about washing your hands and face in a cold mountain river in the rain and then scooping up the cold clear water and slurping it down your throat.

Deer River was deserted so I flung my tent up on one of the mossy wet patches as fast as possible before a cloud of sandflies could make themselves at home on my skin. But I wasn't fast enough. When I threw myself inside I found the inner walls of my tent wallpapered with the bastards. The next half an hour was spent on a murderous mission taking great pleasure in slaughtering every sandfly I could either see or find with the beam of my headtorch. Some fell into the hotpot I was making in my pan, but I didn't bother hoicking them out. I was too tired and hungry for that. And anyway I considered their presence as an extra protein count.

As night fell an odd stillness dropped over the forest and welled up in the mist from the ground. There are people who live in cities who couldn't sleep in a place like this because of the silence: silence can be like noise, dinning against the eardrums. But I love the lonely remoteness of it all – just so long as an axe murderer doesn't decide to turn up on the scene.

9

Moana, Lake Brunner, West Coast, 3 March

Late during the night two headlights appeared out of the mist, boring a tunnel of light into my tent. I lay as still as a corpse hoping it wasn't an axe murderer on the loose. This morning I discovered it was an innocent motorhome belonging to a retired couple of Kiwis travelling about the country. The husband, a bearded whippet, said to me as I was packing up my tent, 'Have you found the natives friendly?' Which made it sound as if the country was running amok with naked forms in loincloths wielding blunt instruments.

It was still raining when I set off into the cold foggy mist. The top of the pass came sooner than I expected – about 5 km from Deer River – but with the heavy mist making it impossible to see a thing I only knew I had reached the top when the road suddenly started falling away. The trees were still thick and green and dripping and I could hear the roar of the Maruia River crashing downwards through the forests of red and silver beech.

The last three days have been wet and hilly, but because I felt bursting with energy I went veering off course and have got nearly two hundred unplanned kilometres under my belt. From the Lewis Pass I rolled west, then north, then east, then south and then west again. In other words I'd gone round in one big hilly circle. All in the name of fun, you understand. I sprang through Springs Junction, rose up over Rahu Saddle (much puffing), skirted

Mount Haast and glided down through dense bushy woods set among steep hillsides laced with fetching babbling brooks and small waterfalls. Then came Inangahua Gorge and the old gold-mining cowboy town of Reefton. An information board in the town told me that Reefton is famous for having been the first place in the southern hemisphere to generate and reticulate its own electricity for public use, back in 1888. Well, I never.

The other thing I learnt about Reefton (apart from the fact that it had a shop called Rags to Retro and that the town is named after the gold-bearing quartz reefs and was once nicknamed Quartzopolis) is that the summers in Reefton are hot and dry (funny, it's still summer now and I've never seen so much rain) and that when it does rain, the locals don't consider it rain, but champagne for the rainforest.

From Reefton I soared north alongside the Inangahua River through Waitahu ('I'm waiting here, thanks') and Inangahua Landing and Inangahua Junction to Inangahua ('questionably cross person') passing en route Larry's Creek and Mount Copernicus ('horse-riding policeman who arrested us'). Next it was east along the broad Buller River, which carves the deep Buller Gorge from the jagged mountain peaks and which once carried a phenomenal amount of gold, turning places like Lyell into bustling mining towns. I rode over the Alpine Fault Line that shook the area to extreme in the 1929 Murchison and 1968 Inangahua earthquakes. At O'Sullivan Bridge it was south to follow an undulating road (though it proved a lot more dulating than un) through the coniferous podocarp ('fishy feet?') forests as I climbed upwards following a downward-flowing Maruia River over Shenandoah Saddle. Next came Frog Flat with views of Rappahannock Saddle ('hammocky-style wrapping of bicycle seat'). Before I knew it I was back in Springs Junction and Reefton and then I was cycling south down the road that I had meant to cycle south down before I had turned north then east then south then west.

A sweeping road bordered by fields of cows and sheep saw me shooting along beside the railway and the Grey River through

Ikamatua and Ahaura, where the *New Zealand Truth* headline sandwich board informed me that there was a 'DRUG HELL IN GANG BROTHEL'. At Stillwater I looked around the graveyard where thirty-three men and boys killed in 1896 in the country's worst mining disaster are buried in a mass grave. Sixty-five men and boys were killed in total (which was virtually everybody underground at the time) by a methane explosion when they were working down the nearby Brunner Mine.

I'm now camping at Moana, overlooking Lake Brunner and surrounded by magnificent hills and mountains. I had hoped to cycle further inland towards the Alps and Arthur's Pass, but my ankle (Achilles tendon department) has suddenly wonked on me and doesn't want to push me any further. So there I was calling it a day, with tent just put up, when who should arrive on the scene but the travelling threesome – Bridget, Anne-Marie and Pete. Back on the Kaikoura coast, Pete had told me in his northern way that what would make him 'rhaat happy' about being in New Zealand would be seeing an Austin A35 with sticking-out indicators. (Until quite recently, before most New Zealand cars were imported cheaply second-hand from Japan, the country's roads were full of Ford Anglias, Triumph Heralds, Morris Oxfords, Austin Cambridges. There are still quite a lot around, but they mostly now sit in quiet retirement in fields and backyards.) And somewhere between Kaikoura and Moana he spotted one so was well pleased. Anne-Marie, in that strong Glaswegian accent, told me that making herself understood in New Zealand was not easy. Last night she was in the pub and asked the barman for two packets of crisps. He just stared at her with a look of complete incomprehension. So she repeated her request and got two pints of lager.

Bridget, being heavily into Reiki and crystals and meditation and dousing, took it upon herself to heal my ankle. Under her instruction, I crawled into her tent and lay flat on my back on her Therm-a-Rest sleeping mat. She crawled alongside and started hovering her hands above my clapped-out ankle. After a while she asked whether I could feel a healing heat pass into my body. Err, no, Bridge. Can't say I can. In fact, never mind heat, I'm feeling a little chilly.

Bridget, undaunted by my unreceptive body, continued to float her hands above it in a floaty manner. Things then turned so floaty that I fell asleep. When I woke up, Bridget was still there trying to do things with my meridians and inner energy canals and narrowboat passages. She then told me to smile at my ankle. Bridge, you loopy nutter. It's an ankle – not a person! I can't smile at my ankle. Especially when it's stopping me from cycling!

Undeterred by my non-believer's outburst, Bridget continued with her hovering-handed pursuit. I had to admire her staying power. Anyone else would have given up on me long ago. Finally I managed to get her to give herself a break and acknowledge that my unresponsive body must simply be dead to the world in certain areas. So, after rummaging around for a while in the depths of her substantial homeopathic medical kit and feeding me with a mixture of ruta and rhus tox, she flopped down beside me and for the next couple of hours we lay in the tent talking. Or maybe I should rephrase that – we both lay, but she talked. Bridget was a great talker and in between dozing off several times (well, it was getting on for midnight and I'd had a busy day getting nowhere fast) I heard quite a bit about her life, like how in 1998 the pains in her joints got so bad that she could scarcely walk. Sometimes her whole body would go into intense spasms and seizures. The doctor was no help whatsoever so that was when she turned heavily alternative. One day she was doing Reiki on herself and she suddenly felt all the pain wash out of her through her feet. Later the pain returned, though I'm not sure if it entered through her feet or via other means. Because of all the pain, Bridget had to give up her work as an eco-architect. But last year she had started working again whereby she became involved in an eco-project, which (if I've got this right) concerned her designing some sort of means to generate power for Scotland using nothing more than icicles and frozen water. Seems she won all sorts of awards for it. But then she's pretty bright, is Bridget.

Next, she told me about her family (a complicated saga) before progressing to how she had met Anne-Marie in a walking-cum-climbing club and then they went cycling together. When Bridget got the idea to cycle in New Zealand and asked Anne-Marie to come with her, Anne-Marie said she couldn't afford it, so for Anne-Marie's fiftieth birthday party they had a ceilidh for 150 people and Bridget told everyone to give Anne-Marie money instead of a present and about £800 in total was given, which meant Anne-Marie could afford the flight to New Zealand after all. Phew! Bridget said she was very competitive by nature, but it was good for her having Anne-Marie here as it prevented her from racing ahead at top speed. Though I'm not sure Anne-Marie would agree with that.

Moana, Lake Breuner, West Coast, 4 March

This morning I was up early. So was Anne-Marie. In fact, she had eaten breakfast and was all packed up and ready to go, unlike Bridget and Pete who were still fast asleep in their respective tents. In the campsite kitchen Anne-Marie vented her frustration about Bridget with me, explaining she was just too intense and that she had decided she was going to go her own way. Not wanting to get too involved in the domestics of a threesome, I kept a neutral position. But I could see what Anne-Marie meant. Bridget could do your head in – in the nicest possible way.

When Bridget and Pete woke up and discovered Anne-Marie's plans to go it alone, Pete was his usual laid-back self. As for Bridget, she joked to me on the quiet that Anne-Marie's huffiness was all my fault. 'The first time we met you,' said Bridget, 'was just after Anne-Marie had blown her top at me for the first time when we'd got to the top of that hill outside Blenheim and she said to me, "It's not a fucking competition you know!" And now we see you here and she's gone off her rocker again. You must be a bad influence!'

The owners of the campground are Jackie and Graham. Jackie, a short-haired no-messing woman, was a senior nurse in her time.

She told me in no uncertain terms that I was not to cycle for at least three days on account of my malfunctioning ankle. As the nearest store around here is a good 40 km away in Greymouth, she offered to give me a lift into town so I could experience the joys of shopping at the Supervalue supermarket. So I left the travelling threesome to work out whether they were going to stick together or not and climbed into Jackie's car. This was the first car I had been in for months and I can't say it was a particularly pleasant experience. She drove like the devil incarnate.

'Jackie, what is it about Kiwis that make them drive like lunatics?' I asked.

'There are only four million of us in this country – three million in the North Island, one million here in the South – and we're used to our space,' she explained. 'We hate someone in front of us. Makes us go bananas. When I see someone up ahead of me I think: WHAT ARE YOU DOING IN MY WAY!'

Crikey. How very het-uppishly dramatic.

We then got caught behind a bus, which Jackie tailgated in an agitated fashion. She kept trying to squirt past and when the bus suddenly braked we nearly rammed it up its rear. This made Jackie even more irked and she pulled out and performed a supremely dangerous overtaking manoeuvre into the path of an oncoming vehicle. With an open view of the road we could see why the bus driver had suddenly braked: an Australian harrier was slowly flapping away from tugging at a lump of carrion in the middle of the road. Jackie yelled at the bus driver, 'What did you brake for a bloody bird for? Jesus!'

As if you should just mow down a big and beautiful bird that was in your way.

Maybe it was just Jackie. She seemed to be a particularly impatient person. She told me she had spent two winters working as a nurse in a hospital in Bath. 'Your National Health Service drove me nuts!' she said. 'It's so antiquated! So badly managed! Us Kiwis and Aussies who go over there to work soon discover what a backward system it is. We say to you lot, "There are better ways to do this and we're prepared to show you," but you Brits just don't want to know and say, "But we've always done it this way and won't change now." I mean, how frustrating is that?'

Jackie also said that the first time she went to work in the hospital in Bath a woman told her to make tea. 'It was like an order!' said Jackie. 'So I told the woman I was a senior nurse and that in New Zealand senior nurses do *not* make tea. That they have hospital helpers to do that sort of thing!'

It wasn't just the NHS that got Jackie's goat. She said, 'Unlike us Kiwis, who are by nature really quite aggressive, you Brits are so passive it drove me insane!' She went on to tell me how when she first went to work in England she went to the bank to open an account. 'In New Zealand we can walk into a bank and open an account on the same day and get all the necessary bank cards etc. But in the UK it took forever. Weeks! And you Brits put up with that sort of service!'

On another occasion Jackie went to the Post Office to buy some stamps and the woman behind the counter said very sternly to her, 'Did you wait for my bell to ring?' It was only then that Jackie noticed a long queue of people waiting in a special corralled area behind her. 'They were all silently glaring at me for queue barging,' she laughed. 'My mum and dad say: *we don't do queues!* If there's a queue anywhere they want to go, they won't wait.'

Later Jackie said, 'Another thing that drives me nuts is Helen Clark and her bright brainwave to close down scores of rural schools. Brash says keep them open, but Helen Clark is hell-bent on closing as many down as possible. Up at Arthur's Pass there used to be a school with eight children but it has been closed, which means the children now have to travel seventy kilometres each way to the nearest school – sometimes along icy and dangerous mountain roads. It's completely insane!'

Jackie had a son who was working in England and a daughter who was training to be a nurse over here. This got Jackie on to Maori and Pakeha – another subject that got her hot under the collar. 'When Labour got in with Helen Clark as prime minister, suddenly Maoris were given lots of advantages over Pakeha,' said Jackie. 'For instance, my daughter has had to pay to take herself through nursing college and is now in debt, while a friend of hers at college who is one-eighth Maori has had it all paid for her. That Helen Clark really drives me mad. I can't stand the woman! She can't seem to understand that we're all New Zealanders now. There aren't any pure-blood Maori left as they are all so interbred. That's why Brash is suddenly so popular because he recognises we are all New Zealanders and should all be treated the same.'

This 'One people, one law' thing was something that a lot of die-hard Maori were quite wary about. They said it disguised the reality that Pakeha would, because of their greater numbers, define what that would mean by reinforcing 'white privilege'. They said that ever since their first contact, Pakeha feared that Maori would dominate and frustrate their plans to colonise Aotearoa. Every day I heard on the radio or read something in the papers about the Land Wars or the 1840 signing of the Treaty of Waitangi, the accord between the British Crown and the Maori that is the official founding document of New Zealand. Just the other night I heard on the radio a Maori man talking about the 'era of colonisation, assimilation, deception, lies and rampant expropriation of indigenous resources, which has been corrupt, corrosive and must not continue.'

Moana, Lake Brunner, West Coast, 5 March

I've just found a four-day-old *New Zealand Herald* in the kitchen. The headline says: 'AND THAT, BELIEVE IT OR NOT, WAS SUMMER'. Although I've been pelted by heavy rain in South Island over the last few days, it apparently hasn't been half as bad as the rain in North Island. The *Herald* described how 'summer ended in dramatic fashion' when more heavy rain in the North Island yet again forced people from their homes and closed main highways. The army was on standby as rivers came close to bursting their banks, threatening areas already devastated by flooding. The highest recorded rainfall was at Mount Taranaki, which received more than 400 mm in twenty-four hours. Nearly one-and-a-half feet! As if that isn't quite enough to take on board for one summer,

New Zealand, which is renowned for being a windy place at the best of times, has just had its windiest February ever recorded.

When I came back from my Supervalue near-death drive yesterday with Jackie, I found no signs of the travelling threesome so I didn't know whether they had patched up their differences and left en masse, or went their separate ways.

Today a rare thing happened: the sun shone. The lake shimmered and the mountains beckoned in the bright, clarified light. The air here was cool and had the same scrubbed clarity as that of Iceland. There was no way I could lounge around wasting a day like this so I decided to test my ankle by cycling 100 km (there and back) up the 3,032-foot Arthur's Pass – which if you cycle from west to east is the hardest, steepest pass in the country. Jackie said the last five kilometres were virtually vertical and suggested I take the train. Taking the train may be a sensible move for preserving twanged ankles, but it's not the same as cycling. But to appease the wrath of Jackie I compromised by cycling up the pass pannier-free. Well, pannier-free apart from my two front panniers. You can't leave home without emergency rations of bananas and unnecessary clothing, you know.

All started off fairly fast and easy as I rode past Kangaroo Lake and Crooked River and Inchbonnie and the old tavern at Jacksons, which had once provided accommodation and fresh horses for the horse-drawn Cobb and Co. coach parties who made the arduous 270 km trip from Christchurch to the West Coast over the alps in the days of the Westland gold rush. As I joined the Otira River things started going upwards through the nigh-on deserted and ramshackle settlement of Otira with its derelict playground. By the time I hit the Otira Gorge and the newly built Otira Viaduct that traverses the alpine faultline and treacherous rock falls and shingle slides which stretch hundreds of metres from mountain top to the river at the foot of the gorge, I had reached the part on my map that says 'Not suitable for caravans'. This was where things turned a bit stupidly steep, albeit in a spectacularly sort of stupidly steep way.

I struggled and I lopsidedly cycled but I made it to the top (with lungs and ankles still intact), where there stands a monument to Arthur Dudley Dobson. He is the Arthur of Arthur's Pass and in 1864 he rediscovered the former Maori Route (the Maori crossed to the West Coast in search of greenstone – a form of jade which they made into tools and weapons and jewellery) while seeking a way to supply West Coast gold-diggers from Christchurch. The names on the road leading up here recall the calamities and torment that those gold-miners and road-builders suffered before the road was built: Starvation Point, Lake Misery, Death Corner. Arthur's Pass marks the boundary between Canterbury and Westland, a boundary often reinforced by distinctive weather patterns. During an infamous nor'wester, you can leave on a hot and dry day on the Canterbury side of the pass only to descend into heavy rain in the West Coast's Otira Gorge. But during a southerly or easterly, you can be West Coast-bound and leave the rain and the cold behind in Canterbury for a dramatic landscape of mountains and sea bathed in dazzling sun. Getting the winds right round here means a lot. Especially to cyclists.

Cycling up Arthur's Pass is one thing. But cycling down it is quite another. It was the most ridiculous fast fun I'd had in a long time. The road immediately after the pass was so steep that I felt like my back wheel was going to flip up over my head. Everything apart from the road in front of me turned into a blur. At one point I caught up with a car with a bumper sticker that read: 'I'M DRIVING THIS WAY TO PISS YOU OFF'. But I didn't let it piss me off for long because I undertook a spectacular overtaking manoeuvre that sent my adrenalin levels almost into overdrive. By the time I arrived back at my Lake Brunner basecamp I was on a happy endorphin-bursting high. What a day!

10

Lake Pearson, Selwyn, Canterbury, 6 March

There were two cyclists in the campsite last night. Young Aussie lads called Robbie and Cameron. Robbie was on a mountain bike pulling a Bob Yak trailer so he only had a handlebar bag on his bike. Cameron had a road bike with two rear panniers and a top rack bag. They made it look as if I was carting around a couple of cows in my panniers.

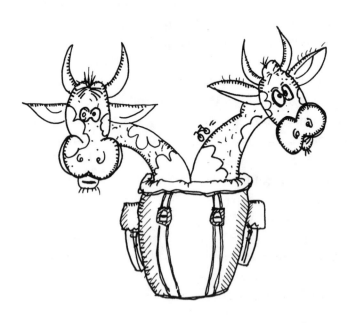

This morning was well and truly murky with a thick rainy mist. When I walked up to the toilets in the night, the mist was so thick it felt like walking through water. Sitting in my tent having breakfast, I overheard Robbie tell Cameron how he had heard Cameron swearing at him in his sleep during the night. Cameron denied the accusations.

Robbie said, 'You were, mate. You were saying, "You fucking bastard!"'

Cameron said, 'Did I wake you up?'

Robbie laughed. 'Of course you did, you bastard, coz I heard you, didn't I?'

I went up and over Arthur's Pass again today, but this time by train. My ankle felt fine (-ish) but I was not so sure it could take the strain with fifty kilos of kit on board. And anyway, I was a bit scared of Nurse Jackie's reaction if she knew I was going to tackle cycling over this pass two days in a row. You didn't want to get on the wrong side of Jackie – otherwise it could hurt.

There was only one train a day that passed through Moana from Greymouth. The trouble was that it didn't stop unless you rang ahead and told the driver that you wanted to be picked up. It seemed that not many people did.

As the touristy TransAlpine Express (as it was known, though I don't think it went much faster than running speed) didn't leave Moana until 14.42, I spent the morning admiring the particularly ugly houses that were springing up on the lakeside – big and modernly boxy million-dollar monstrosities of corrugated iron and concrete. It's amazing planning permission was ever granted to build such diabolical eyesores in such a scenic area. A nice bit of wood would have gone down a lot better.

After sauntering across a wobbly suspension bridge and going for a long walk in the jungle-woods, where I was attacked by clouds of flying ants, I wandered back to my bike along the lakefront. Here the Lake Brunner Yacht Club was based, containing boats with names like *Barnacle*, *Nirvana*, *Ratbags* and *Glydeawave*. As I was walking along, an upmarket boy-racer revved up unnecessarily fast in a souped-up car with go-fast stripes. The car's licence plate was VENOM 8 and it pulled a trailer with an expensively sleek speedboat on the back called *Extreme.* Funny the lengths some people go to in order to try and toughen their image. The driver who got out was a puny mite with I suspect not a lot down his trousers. Thus the need to make up for what he lacked in size by the attachment of a couple of throaty engine roars.

The 14.42 arrived at 14.55. Only trouble was the guard's van overshot the short platform because, the guard said, the driver nearly forgot to stop. The height of the floor of the guard's van stood at least five feet above the track, so trying to lift an unwieldy overloaded bike above my head felt like trying to lift an elephant. Fortunately the guard gave me a hand, but even he struggled. 'Jesus, mate,' he said, 'you got a couple of Maori in here, or what?'

The guard, a stout fella in his fifties with a large nose, round and pitted like a golf ball, was a friendly and jocular chap. Together with a stewardess called Vanessa, he made all the announcements on the train. But his announcements were quite unlike anything I've ever heard emanating from the tannoys of GNER or Southwest Trains back home. Here's the nub of his first announcement: 'Now it's of some concern to me that many of you have been taken in by the seductive tones of Vanessa, but I'm happy to announce that she still has copious supplies of fruit cakes and cup cakes at her disposal.' Then the next thing you heard him say was a sort of cry for help in strangled tones. 'Help me, Sparky! Help me!'

It's always good to know you've got a nutter on board.

As the train approached Otira and the mountains closed in, I caught snatched views of the road on which my legs had emitted a cry for help yesterday afternoon. Otira was where the disembodied voice of our guard reappeared, informing us that in its heyday Otira was a busy railway town with a population of 600. 'Now it's nothing more than a ghost town with a population of forty-five with a lot of vacant sections,' he said. 'This is the place to live if you like rain. It gets six metres a year compared to half a metre in Canterbury. Storms here are as intense as they are sudden, dropping as much as 250 mm of rain in twenty-four hours. Back in the seventies when I was a young man, I was overcome by the foolish notion that I wanted to be a stationmaster in Otira. So I brought my wife up here to show her where we might live. She looked at me real stern and she said, "You listen here, boy. You want to be a stationmaster in Otira, and you'll be a single boy!'"

It was the coal and timber trade that first demanded a railway over the Alps and work began on the rail crossing soon after the road across Arthur's Pass was completed. The major obstacle was the completion of the 8.5 km long Otira Tunnel, which, by the time it was finished in 1923, was the longest in the southern hemisphere and the seventh longest in the world. The narrow-gauge single-track line drops from 620 metres above sea level on the Canterbury side to 483 metres on the Westland side of the tunnel, a gradient of 1:33.

When the TransAlpine Express entered the tunnel from Otira we left behind an anguished sky of broiling storm clouds. But by the time the train had emerged from the tunnel eighteen minutes later we were in bright crisp sunshine.

As I knew I would be arriving in Arthur's Pass Village late afternoon, I thought I would probably camp the night there – hopefully not getting pecked to pieces by the inquisitively mischievous keas (large native mountain parrot – the only alpine parrot in the world), which, along with their traditional diet of leaves, fruit, buds, insects and carrion, have a fetish for rubber, particularly windscreen rubber and bicycle seats, which they tear apart with gusto with their big hooked bills. (Farmers aren't so much concerned about rubber as they are their sheep, which they claim are killed by kea who grip the sheep's backs and peck them to death.) But as sun seemed to be at a premium in this fair, storm-ravaged land, I thought it best not to waste the opportunity of cycling down the mountain in good weather, because tomorrow could well be a day of rain and gale-force winds. Before I cycled down, though, I cycled up – just the four or so kilometres to the top of the pass. Then I cycled back down, filling up on some over-priced supplies at the Arthur's Pass store.

When you cycle down a mountain pass you imagine you're going to go down, so it comes as a bit of a shock to find yourself going up. Well, this is not entirely true: I did go down but not as much as I'd been expecting and not half as much as the falling sensation I got when I plummeted off Arthur's Pass in the opposite direction. And it always seems very inconsiderate of a mountain to put in a few little ups when you're expecting a big down. The wind wasn't helping either, blowing such a humdinging gale that even when I was cycling downwards it felt like I was going uphill. And when a down bit did come, it was accompanied with a sign that warned TEMPORARY ROAD SURFACE and plunged me into skiddy deep loose gravel – not a pleasant surface to be taken at speed, as it feels akin to ice.

This road took me into bigger, wilder country, similar to parts of the west side, but now in Imax – sparky snow-peaked mountains, dense all-enveloping forests of mountain beech, gaunt eroded hills, high open country of golden tussock and swaying toetoe grass and plentiful rivers all set in a dramatic, desolate landscape. I passed Klondyke Corner and Bealey Spur and Mingha River, which joined forces with the Bealey River, which itself joined forces with the broad Waimakariri River. It was these rivers that once posed such a challenge for the Cobb and Co. coach parties; they would frequently flood, causing either days of delay or a raft of drowned passengers when some drivers dared to force a way through. All over Canterbury the wide rivers proved major obstacles to nineteenth-century travel and settlement, as they did to much of New Zealand. Between 1840 and 1870 so many people drowned in rivers that Parliament went so far as to suggest that drowning be classified a natural death.

As I climbed Goldney Saddle the sun sank and the light flattened, the shadows stretching across the open land as the mountains receded. Soon I was upon Lake Pearson, set against erosion-torn hillsides, where I put up my tent in the basic DoC site beside the perfect mountain-reflecting water. The dark came quite suddenly with a sky of low and brilliant stars.

Springfield, Selwyn, Canterbury, 8 March

You might have thought that I'd have learnt my lesson yesterday – that I shouldn't expect any downhill until a downhill came my way and then be very grateful that it came at all – but all morning I was cycling a mostly uphill battle when I imagined I would be having a downhill bonanza. I knew Porter's Pass lay ahead, but I also knew I was already high in the mountains so I didn't think passing by this Porter would be too much of an ordeal, even though at 944 metres it is a smidgen higher than Arthur's Pass. After all, I was at an altitude of about 2,500 feet and I was heading for Christchurch at sea level. Again, the socking great headwind didn't help. And again, the scenery made up for any strugglesome misgivings. I inched onwards past Flock Hill and the Craigieburn Ski Field and Broken River Ski Field and Mount Olympus Ski Field and Mount Cheeseman Ski Field (see, I must be high), all up in the Craigieburn mountains. Then on past the Torlesse mountains and Staircase on my left, with the fortress-like limestone outcrop of Castle Hill on my right.

Somewhere around here a man driving towards me stuck his head out of the window and shouted, 'You got one fat hill ahead!' This was of no help whatsoever because he didn't say whether it went up or down. But when I finally reached the top of Porter's Pass, I realised he meant down. I stood on the brink of the pass surveying the fun that lay ahead: one steep descent of multiple switchbacks dropping 400 metres in 4 kilometres.

Two girls turned up in a hired car, one with cropped bright red hair, the other in floaty clothing. They spent the first five minutes standing near me in a state of (how shall I put this?) wandering hand-and-tongue interlockment, before expressing amazement that I was travelling alone *on a bike*! As I mounted my steed in preparation for an eye-streaming downhill, the red-haired girl said, 'Have a real cool time, man!'

And a cool time I had – it wasn't exactly hot up here in these mountains – leaning into the switchbacks and overtaking a beached whale of a motorhome that braked on every corner. I shot

past Kowhai ('Hawaiian cow') River and through the Waimakariri
Valley, where the land went backwards at a low even roll to
Springfield, once a staging-post for the Cobb and Co. coach parties. In the early 1900s more than 5,000 people used to live here,
due to the railway and tunnel construction. Today there are but a
mere measly 400. Short in number Springfieldites may have been,
but big on friendliness they seem. Especially the owner of the small
store here who threw in a few extra bananas for nothing.

I'm camping tonight on a nice little mown patch of grass down
at Springfield's domain campground. In New Zealand the
'domain' is an open grassed areas of public land in towns or cities.
Usually you can put a tent up on it for free. There's generally a
public toilet somewhere around. Where the local council operates
a more organised domain camping with basic facilities, you sometimes have to pay a bob or two.

Templeton, just outside Christchurch, Canterbury, 9 March

Good thing I stick to my tent for accommodation purposes. News
this morning is of a man who was staying last night at a youth
hostel in Punakaiki (just north of Greymouth) being rushed to
Grey hospital with a knife embedded in his head. Seems the man,
who's about my age, was stabbed in the chest as well as the head.
The paper says his injuries have been described as 'moderate'. If
having a knife embedded in your head is a moderate injury, what
would, say, having your head cut right off be classified as? A fair to
middling injury, perhaps?

When I arrived at the Springfield domain last night, I only had a
deluge of magpies for company – the Australasian variety, that is,
which are a far cry from European ones. Magpies in New Zealand
look about twice the size with a plethora of pied plumage. At nesting time they can get very aggressive and go on dive-bombing
missions – smacking into people's heads. But by far the most distinctive thing about these birds is the rippling flute noise they

make, a sort of gurgling burble of babbles as if someone is holding their heads under water.

Just before dark an elderly couple from Nelson turned up in a campervan, shortly followed by two cyclists. This morning I had a little chat outside the toilets with the cyclists. They were John and Pip from Nottingham and they knew I was Josie from a similar neck of the woods. Pip did something in computers, whereas John used to be a professional mechanic for a bike team though said he now did anything to get work. 'Everyone comes to me with bikes to fix and wheels to make, but I don't make any money that way. If I charged £500 for a set of wheels, then maybe I would.'

Both John and Pip had been to New Zealand before. In fact, they had spent so much time down here that they must surely have cycled almost every road in South Island. They were last here about three years ago and told me that, even in that time, the amount of traffic on the roads had increased hugely. Last September, when back in Nottingham, Pip had a head-on collision with a car and broke her wrist as well as acquiring lots of other pains and her new Mercian was completely smashed. So she was now on her mountain bike. They had both toured in other countries, but strangely, they didn't enjoy cycling in Italy at all. 'The Italians are just nasty people,' said John. 'We'd have been better off being German!'

Later this morning I bowled along the flat roads of Canterbury, through Sheffield and Darfield and Kirwee and Sandy Knolls. Darfield was notable for its surplus of farm supply merchants, specialising in a very high-quality line of stock boots. Darfield was also notable for a small happening that occurred outside the small Four Square supermarket. A big stocky farmer, built like a bulldozer in a china shop, walked towards the Four Square, but before entering he removed his great clod-hopping boots – stock boots, just like the ones in all the stores, and almost as clean – and left them beside the door outside. He then walked around the supermarket in his socks as if he had entered some Holy Shrine.

To give the busy main road a miss, I veered off along a rumpled road of potholes and gravel to Rolleston. This was when my ankle suddenly twanged again. Only worse than last time. It felt as if my Achilles tendon was being spiked with barbed wire and bee stings. I pressed on in a mostly one-legged fashion passing farms that finally gave way to patches of commercial land – a mountain of bald tyres, a stepped angular cliff of scrap-metal car wrecks, several aircraft hangar-sized warehouses – and into an area of car dealerships, fast-food outlets and shopping plazas. Here I rang the number that Nurse Jackie had given me for the sports injury clinic in Christchurch and I booked an appointment for tomorrow with a man called Dr Tony Page.

Tonight I'm camping in a shabby suburb of Christchurch alongside a travelling circus that includes a woman in orange braided bunches walking about in a top hat and dangly clothing. I'm sandwiched between a burger van man and a lot of Maori. Strutting among this melee is a big vain rooster admiring its reflection in various vehicles' hubcaps. At least it was until I heard a large squawking commotion and saw a brute of a dog tearing the rooster apart. An old Maori woman came flying out of a caravan and launched into an enraged attack on the dog's owner, who was hurriedly trying to scoop the remnants of the rooster into a plastic carrier bag. When the dog and owner had disappeared she came over to me and said, 'That bastard dog should have a bloody muzzle, it should. I fed that rooster, I did. And I fed its wife – or whatever they have. Bastard dog. I'm going to report that bastard owner, eh?'

Akaroa, Banks Peninsula, Canterbury, 12 March

A few days ago I limped into Christchurch – second largest city in New Zealand, founded as a well-to-do Anglican enterprise, intended to recreate a little slice of England in the South Pacific. People call Christchurch the most English city outside of England.

There may be punting on the River Avon and a hundred-year-old cathedral, but the whole place still looks and smells very Kiwi to me. Christchurch is also known as 'the world's aerial gateway to Antarctica' – which is not a boast that the likes of Manchester or Margate can make.

Dr Tony Page was a very fast-talking Kiwi who had me flat on his couch as he poked and prodded while bending this and tweaking that. He didn't think I'd done anything too serious to my Achilles. He seemed pleased that the tendons were thin ones and knobbly-free as opposed to fat ones with lumps. He said the ankle was more irritated than anything else and gave me some dropping-heel-off-step exercises to do and advised me to give cycling a rest for a few days.

So that's what I'm doing now, camped high on a hill overlooking the volcanic crater-cupped harbour and French-flavoured town of Akaroa. Akaroa sits out on a limb on the Banks Peninsula, which itself stands out like a giant clenched fist just south of Christchurch. When Captain Cook sailed this way in 1770, he initially mistook the peninsula for an island, which it had been several millennia ago, so he wasn't too far out.

To abide by Dr Tony's advice, I reached Akaroa by bus – a memorable experience of air-conditioned awfulness. Claustrophobically sealed in, I became progressively more crotchety that I wasn't out in all that wind, cycling up the large number of incredibly strenuous-looking hills which seemed to cover the Banks Peninsula from top to toe. There were about fourteen passengers on the bus. The man in the seat in front of me had a plastic-wrapped straw tucked behind his ear like a smoker might have a cigarette or a carpenter a pencil. He was from Virginia and was over here to visit his daughter, who lived just outside Christchurch in Lyttelton. 'I've booked myself on to one of these organised hiking treks,' he told me. 'Only a two-day one, starting in Akaroa. Any more than that and I'm not sure my old body could take it.'

A blonde girl sitting across the aisle with a Windtunnel rucksack, and sunglasses pushed back on her head keeping her hair out of her eyes like an Alice band, overheard our conversation and said to the ear-straw man, 'I'm going on that same trip. I'm now wishing I'd chosen the four-day trek.'

'Same scenery,' said the straw man.

'I know,' said the Windtunnel girl, a city worker from London, 'but four days would give you more time to appreciate the views without rushing through it.'

'By the look of the size of these hills,' said the man, 'I'm not so sure I'll be in any state to appreciate anything, let alone the scenery.'

Our bus driver was a bearded man called Bob. He was attached to a microphone over which he insisted on giving us a light-hearted commentary whether we wanted it or not. He also gave us a bit of flora and fauna talk. Driving past Lake Ellesmere, he told us that the area around here is akin to a desert and that if we looked carefully, the scrub of bushes we were passing sprouted leaves on the inside while being prickly on the outside in order to conserve water. Careful examination of roadside bushes is not possible when travelling past them at 100 km/h, so as they were but a mere blur we had to take Bob's word for it.

Lake Ellesmere is a large but shallow expanse of water – more a lagoon than a lake – covered with more than 70,000 black swans (these are Australian black swans, introduced in the 1860s to control the watercress – itself introduced – that was choking Christchurch's Avon River). Bob told us how the lake was full of floundering fish (or should that be flounder fish?) and that the area was used for para-chute practise during the Second World War. 'Some of the men landed in the lake and one of them couldn't swim and started thrashing around in a panic. Then he noticed some of the others standing up in the water and realised he was only in waist-deep water. So he just walked out and was fine.'

My neighbour on the campsite here in Akaroa was Greg from Thatcham, Berkshire. He was cycling in New Zealand for about six months (with two months left), only he was travelling by bus at the moment because he'd left his bike and Bob Yak trailer back at a bike shop in Christchurch to get some new bearings put in. This was his first ever cycle tour. He had backpacked around New Zealand in

2001 and kept seeing people on bikes so thought he'd give it a go. 'In only three years there's been big changes,' he said. 'More traffic and I don't remember campsites like these resembling car parks.'

Greg was right. At most of the main campsites here hardly anyone turned up under their own steam. Those in tents mostly arrived in a hire car or a 4WD. But mostly it was retired couples travelling around the country in caravans, campervans, motorhomes or big buses, like America's recreational vehicles.

Greg was a bit of a deep person, and always looked slightly troubled. When I asked him what he did at home, he said, 'Be unhappy mostly.'

I got him to elaborate. 'I'm not happy in Britain at all,' said Greg. 'The TV's crap. So's the radio. And I see people around me and all they want is a little house with a little car with little children and a little two-week holiday. Is that all there is to life in Britain? I've owned my house for twenty years and I thought: I'm going to move. Get away from the area. Start afresh. But then I thought that after a few weeks' frenetic activity you are back in another little house and it starts all over again. You go to work, you go to the supermarket, you go on your two-week holiday. I hate the things in the UK that people there consider important. It makes basic human existence so meaningless.'

Not so long ago Greg had gone on a trip to Alaska. 'It had been a childhood dream,' he said. 'A wild animal thing. I had to pinch myself when I saw my first moose.'

Then he came home and got involved in a long-term relationship with Sally, a divorcee with two small children. 'It was all going well, I was happy and thinking this is everything I ever wanted. I thought I'd get the house together – maybe even get married. We used to have this big ritual where after breakfast we would all go upstairs to the bathroom to clean our teeth. Sally would sit on the edge of the bath and her little boy would stand beside the basin while her daughter stood up on a box to reach and I would brush my teeth making silly faces at them to make them laugh. One time we were doing this and it was summer. The window in the bathroom had frosted glass, but the top window was open and I looked out and I saw this incredibly vivid image of the Alaskan mountains. I didn't say anything at the time, but afterwards I would see the mountains quite often from this window so I took that as a sign that I wasn't supposed to get involved in this relationship and ended it. It was a messy ending. Sally didn't deserve that.'

Greg was now happy he had made the move to come away. 'I love the simple lifestyle of travelling by bike,' he said. 'It puts everything in perspective.'

Although Greg had put money aside for his trip to New Zealand, the rent from his house in Thatcham would see him though Australia – his next port of call. 'When I last came to New Zealand I did the same thing – got an agent to rent out my house. When I got home the tenants had left without cleaning the toilet. Which was no big deal so I just got on and cleaned it. But the agent said he had asked the tenants to clean the toilet before they left and didn't think it was good enough that they had left without cleaning it. So he asked me how long I had spent cleaning it, and I said about two minutes. "Let's make that half an hour," said the agent. Then he asked me how much I had spent on cleaning products so I said, "I don't know – a couple of quid." So the agent said, "Let's make that £5." In the end I made £25 for cleaning my own toilet. It was the easiest money I've ever made!'

Greg said he wanted to get qualified in something when he got home. When he was younger he had always thought he wanted to be a farmer. 'But then I decided farmers were boring people because all they ever do is talk about farming.' Instead he got a job working for Panasonic – putting together the electronics of mobile phones, working in a shift of four days on, four days off. He now had other ideas for making money. 'I fancy being a masseuse,' he said. 'It's something I could do anywhere. And I'm told I'm good with my hands.'

Akaroa, Banks Peninsula, Canterbury, 17 March

The news today in Christchurch's *The Press* was of the Queen swearing at a police constable patrolling the gardens of Buckingham

Palace armed with a machine pistol of the kind used by diplomatic protection officers. The Queen had just returned to London after a break on her Sandringham estate and was unimpressed to find the new beefed-up security at the palace. When she set eyes on the officer and his MP5 Heckler and Koch she turned on him saying, 'You can take that bloody thing away!'

It's always good to hear the Queen going a little potty-mouthed. Brings her down to earth a peg or two.

One of the pluses about staying at this rather fancy campsite (apart from the view) is the outdoor swimming pool. Despite it feeling like plunging into the Channel in winter, I've been swimming twice a day going up and down and up and down doing one-legged crawl. Means I can still do exercise while giving my ankle a rest. By the time I get out I'm so cold that my whole body is shaking and it takes me about fifteen minutes in a hot shower to get any sense of feeling back.

Today, though, as my ankle has felt ready to go, I've been on an injury-testing cycle. Trouble is, I really need to be ankle-testing in a flat place like the Fens or The Netherlands and not the Banks Peninsula, which is one of the hilliest places I've ever cycled. The peninsula was formed following violent eruptions by three volcanoes and its coastline resembles stumpy fingers of land between which the Pacific laps into high-cliffed bays and long deep harbours. Summit Road is the only road that crosses the middle of the peninsula and, as its name suggests, it traverses the highest ridges of this massively crumpled area. On a good day, the views from Summit Road are almost too good to be true, surrounded as you are by a 360-degree view of slopes tumbling away from you to the slender necks of water ringed by creased and rugged hills with rock faces bursting from the crests.

Cycling up and down and in and out of the bays of Pigeon, Okains, Le Bons and Little Akaloa tested my ankle above and beyond the call of duty. I knew I probably shouldn't be putting my flimsy limb under such strain, but I just couldn't resist. Sitting around waiting for injuries to mend is not my strong point, especially when the sun's out and I'm surrounded by a wrinkled and rumpled land of the most amazing beauty.

Greg has long gone, taking the bus back to Christchurch to pick up his wheels and resume his trailer-pulling journey north. The interesting thing about staying somewhere a while is to watch people coming and going. One woman I met in the campsite kitchen was a Scot, now living in Australia. She told me that as a student she went to work in Butlin's in Bognor and progressed from a Blue Coat to a Red Coat. 'I moved to Oz because I could earn twice as much money than staying at home,' she told me, 'though that's not the case any more.' When I asked her if she ever went back to Scotland she said, 'Occasionally. But I would never live there again. The people have tunnel vision.'

Talking of Scots, who should arrive on the scene but Anne-Marie? She was no longer part of the travelling threesome – and hadn't been since I last saw her, when she really did go her own way after splitting up from Pete and Bridget. She hadn't regretted one minute of being by herself. She cycled down the West Coast to Queenstown where, because she was running out of time (she was due to fly home to Glasgow), she took the bus to Christchurch. She told me she found the competitive side of Bridget too hard to deal with. 'I was always cycling behind and I couldn't enjoy the scenery because I was always trying to catch up.' She also said that, although she thought that turning to alternative therapies had helped Bridget a lot, she had told Bridget she thought she was taking things a step too far when, as instructed by her Reiki Master, she threw some crystals into the sea in New Zealand in the name of inner healing sanctity. 'She didnae take kindly to tha'!'

A most peculiar English couple travelling around in a little jeep put up a tent almost on top of me last night despite there being a huge space the other side of the tree. The man was as thin as a toothpick with eyes netted with wrinkles, while the woman was built like a hippo – her ample size accentuated by wearing a crinoline skirt which stood out like a frilled lampshade. How they squeezed into a tent the size of a coffin, I don't know. It was hardly a surprise to hear them not getting on too well (words travel through tent walls as easily and audibly as through thin air). It was about ten o'clock when all the crackling of crinoline and shuffling of sleeping bags finally settled down. Despite it being a cold night (the last few nights have necessitated sleeping with socks on) I heard Mrs Lampshade release a huge discontented sigh before unhappily muttering, 'It's hot in here!'

'It won't be at two o' clock in the morning,' replied the long-suffering husband in a tetchy tone. There then followed a five-minute argument which reignited the fuel from a previous argument – a subject that Mrs Lampshade obviously wanted nothing else to do with because she said, 'As far as I'm concerned that's all done and dusted!'

The husband replied in something of a similar nature, but she wasn't standing for that because she said, 'Well it's obviously still narking you as you're still slating me for it!'

The arguing went on and on. The woman's favourite phrase was: 'For your information . . . !' She would prefix every shouted sentence with, 'For your information . . .' before going on to say that she had said this or said that. Finally I plugged into my radio and went to sleep. In the morning the bickering couplet packed up without saying a word to each other. Their body language was not good.

More comings and goings in the camp kitchen. A boy on a bike with long blond curls arrived on the scene. He was cycling around South Island in what sounded like about two weeks flat. He told me he was from Belgium so I asked if he was a Walloon – a fine air-inflated word to describe a part of Belgium's population who speak a French dialect, as opposed to the Flanders-dwelling Flemish who speak Dutch. Unfortunately I never quite grabbed whether he was a Walloon or not because we immediately got on to the subject of Belgian people in general who have bricks in their stomachs. The Belgian boy told me that in Belgium the expression 'to have a brick in your stomach' meant that you didn't want to travel, you just wanted to stay at home. 'Most Belgians have bricks in their stomachs,' he said.

Later on two girls who put their tent up beside me parked their 4WD Toyota Hilux Surf bang in front of my tent, obscuring my sweeping panorama of the harbour and hills. Their bumper sticker declared: 'Fishing is not a matter of life or death. It is more serious than that.' The girls didn't look like fishers. They looked more like clubbers. As soon as their tent was up, one of the girls, who was rushing around trying to find her 'smokes', tripped over a guyline and nearly knocked herself out on the back bumper of her Hilux Surf. She was wearing a tight pink T-shirt that said, 'REQUIRES CONSTANT SUPERVISION'. I could see why.

Little River, Banks Peninsula, Canterbury, 18 March

For hundreds of years the Banks Peninsula had been settled by Maoris and all was going well for them (specially the Ngai Tahu tribe) until they got into a right old hullabaloo of bloody intertribal wars which contributed indirectly to the decision taken by the British government to install a governor and sign the Treaty of Waitangi in 1840. The French missed their chance to establish sovereignty on the peninsula by a few days. Akaroa had been the site of a French whaling station prior to the establishment of the town. In 1838 Jean Langlois, a captain of one of the whaling ships, deciding he rather liked the look of the place, negotiated with a local Maori chief to buy the peninsula. He returned to France to gather together about sixty emigrants, but by the time they had sailed back to Akaroa they found the British flag flying. Still, there's lots of French influence remaining in the town (plenty of croissants and French fare served everywhere in places like Jaques Cafe, the Turenne Coffee Shop, Chez Marc and Cafe Eiffel). Everywhere you walk there are streets with names like Rue Jolie, Rue Benoit and Rue Renard. The architecture, an eclectic mix of French and British, is what makes Akaroa the most attractive place I've come across yet. It certainly beats the uninspirational standard format of most Kiwi towns.

Just before I left Akaroa, I was shopping in the small Four Square when I was intercepted by a couple from Romsey in Hampshire who told me they had come to a Japanese cycling talk I'd given in London a few years ago. ('*Ah so, desu-ka?*') Although

Kathy and Gordon weren't currently travelling by bike, they had done some cycling in New Zealand in the past so we compared notes for a while, as you do. At one point Gordon told me how not that long ago he was cycling from Land's End to John o' Groats when he fell off his bike in Wolverhampton, around the halfway mark, and broke his hip. 'Spent two months flat on my back in hospital,' he said. 'The doctors looked at my notes and said I might as well throw my bike away.' Five months later he was back on his bike and went off to Wolverhampton to finish the ride.

Unless you turn your bike into a pedalo, it's impossible to pedal off the Banks Peninsula without meeting several substantial hills. One route is easier than the other and climbs up from sea level to about 1,500 feet. I went the other way, the way that leads you up a vertical back road to almost 2,000 feet. This road was so steep and my ankle so weak and my panniers so heavy that it took me just under two hours to ride 6 km. Though it rained all last night, this morning was sunny and quite hot. But as I hauled myself up to 2,000 feet the sky filled and sagged and reached down to envelop me in barricades of mist, turning my sweat to shivers. I had chosen this route up to Summit Road, not to ruin my ankle completely, but because it was empty of traffic compared with the coast road and offered top-notch views. Well, it did last time I was up here. Still, it was rather lovely being encased in a cotton-wool world. It made the apparitions of the skeletal windblown trees and the moaning wind in the power lines all the more atmospheric. Things turned even more moody when the mist occasionally parted, revealing a miniature cove or bay or harbour far below bathed in sun. On either side of the Summit Road, the mist-cracked land fell away, turning from grey to green to blue, then evolved into a crazed fretwork of foggy islands and sea lakes and strange peaks.

What a difference a gradient makes! Falling back down off Summit Road from the fittingly named Hilltop took just seven minutes to cover the same distance of 6 km. I'm now down at Little River, camping in a bird sanctuary surrounded by Chinese quail, golden pheasants, paradise ducks and shining cuckoos.

There are various hens and bantams roosting in the toilets and showers too. Lends a rather alternative edge to the performing of one's ablutions.

Mount Somers, Ashburton, Canterbury, 21 March

Until I came to New Zealand I had never heard of braided rivers. Maybe I didn't pay enough attention to Mrs Outlaw, my Geography teacher at school. Cycling into Rakaia I rode 1.8 km over what the tourist leaflet says is 'the longest bridge over the widest braided river in the southern hemisphere'. It certainly looked quite impressive – multiple channels of water divided by sandy alluvial deposits. Seems people come to Rakaia not so much for the braided variety of this river as for its salmon. 'The Salmon Capital of New Zealand' is how Rakaia likes to brand itself, emphasised by an eyesore in the shape of a roadside model of a large leaping salmon the size of a small whale mounted high in the air on a pole stuck uncomfortably up its bottom.

It is flat cycling around here. The wide Canterbury plains feel as if they stretch into infinity. Far over to the west they stretch as far as the scalloped crinkle of distant Southern Alps, where the land doesn't so much roll up to meet the mountains as rudely cough them straight up. Down on the plains the green and ochre-coloured land is a vast patchwork of giant fields, covering an area of more than 12,000 square kilometres.

This area had once been cloaked with forest, with a sizeable Maori population living in coastal areas. These early Maori roamed the plains hunting the giant flightless moa, using fire to flush their prey from the forests. Over time, the trees as well as the birds were destroyed, leaving a barren, windblown waste. The first Europeans to arrive saw the plains as a desert, tussocky and gravelly and often lacking fresh water. Today they are a criss-cross of horizontals, divided by long spearing Roman-straight roads and shelter belts – thirty-foot-tall hedges of cypress-smelling macrocarpa that act as windbreaks to the howling nor'westers and are vital in protecting the plains (and cyclists) from damage and erosion. Left to their own devices, the plains would be arid and parched. But when ex-Indian army officer Colonel De Renzie Brett came this way, he initiated a water-race system that brought life-giving water for irrigation. Cycling across this iron-flat land, I kept hearing and catching sight of the restless waters of the irrigation channels busily gushing behind a complex maze of mini dykes.

Somewhere near the junction of Tramway Road and Spoors Forks Road, a 4WD with a GO FISH licence plate and a car sticker that said YES YOU CAN-TERBURY stopped up ahead and a woman jumped out and a gave me two carrier bags full of home-grown runner beans and peaches. She said that what I was doing was 'awesome' and that she thought I looked like I could do with a good load of runner beans and peaches. How anyone looks like they need a good runner bean and peach, I don't know, but I accepted them gratefully anyway.

*

The wind was blowing hard from just the sort of direction that I didn't want it to blow: head-on off the mountains. It made cycling along an endlessly straight road that tilted gradually uphill feel as if I was dragging a concrete girder behind my wheels. The telegraph poles crept by in slow motion. At last I arrived in Mount Somers, a small smattering of houses just south of Windwhistle and Pudding Hill. There was not a lot at Mount Somers: a motel, a motor camp, a pub and a small wooden general store complete with an ancient petrol pump standing to attention outside like a stiff-upper-lip red British pillar box. There were a lot more trees up here, but although autumn was beginning to tighten its chilling grip in the evening air, I'd noticed that the leaves weren't changing colour yet, though they did have that slightly off look that meant they were just about to do so.

Weather in New Zealand can change in a flash. When I put up my tent in the Mount Somers campsite the sun was hot and the wind still warm and strong from the northwest. Good clothes-drying weather. So I hurriedly washed everything washable I possessed apart from the minimal clothing I was wearing. Five minutes after I had hung everything out on the line, the wind swung round to the south, the temperature dropped by ten degrees and the sun was something of distant memory. A muffling Antarctic fog rolled in, shortly followed by a glacial rain. I had to throw on my hat and jacket over my flimsy shorts and T-shirt and climb into my sleeping bag to prevent a sudden onset of hypothermia.

After a while I went to sit in the small kitchen to drink a pint of tea and write my diary and some letters. An hour later, the only other person staying on the site (in one of the on-site cabins) walked through the door. For the next two hours I chatted non-stop with Kathy Rogers, a garrulous and vivacious Irishwoman originally from Dublin. Home for Kathy was a forty-two-foot gaff rigger steel boat called *Leto* (daughter of Apollo, said Kathy, when I looked a bit blank) on which she sailed the world with her partner Peter. Peter was South African, but he had left the country when he was nineteen to live on boats. On their latest leg, they'd sailed to New Zealand from Panama, taking in a plethora of South

Pacific islands on the way with Tonga coming out top. About three weeks between land had been their longest sea passage so far. While at sea they tended to live on tins of beans and tomatoes, pasta, powdered milk, bread that Kathy made every couple of days if the sea allowed, and fish caught over the side. For fresh fruit and vegetables, Kathy said potatoes, onions, carrots and green tomatoes all kept fine. 'Most fruit keeps pretty well,' said Kathy, 'as long as I buy it from a market. Any supermarket fruit that has been refrigerated is useless.'

Kathy had been walking around Mount Somers and, before that, Stewart Island for two weeks, leaving Peter back in Whangarei, north of Auckland, which was where they were currently based while living and working on the boat in dry dock for about a year before they set sail for Chile or Indonesia and Sri Lanka. 'Peter's a carpenter, so he does all the work himself, which is handy,' said Kathy.

She called the shiny and expensive fibre-glass yachts that yachties flounce around on in marinas 'plastic fantastics'. And she likened marinas to caravan parks. 'I admit there is a lot of snobbery that goes on between those of us who like to think we properly use and sail our boats, and those who simply keep a yacht as another expensive status symbol!'

She and Peter certainly sounded like 'real' sailors. They had no radar ('though we ought to get one') and they had nothing electrical on the boat. No electric heating, no electric lighting, no nothing. But Kathy thought that as they got older (she was probably hovering around the fifty mark now) they might have to splash out on some electric winches to help them on their way. 'As for navigation,' said Kathy, 'we have always used a sextant, though we do now have a little handheld GPS, which is very useful when approaching a port in thick fog.'

I told her I had sailed to New Zealand on a Russian freighter and that when I'd been on board I'd been quite concerned about the possibility of our vast lump of metal running down any single- (or double-) handed sailors sailing around the world in small boats. 'That was one of our big concerns,' said Kathy. 'A lot of the container ships don't have radars manned twenty-four hours.

Often we would ring up a ship on the VHF and no one would even answer.'

Kathy was an English literature teacher so was thinking of trying to get a job teaching here in New Zealand. For a while we talked books. She said she didn't like Jonathan Raban's *Passage to Juneau* at all. 'It was self-indulgent nonsense!' said Kathy very certainly when I admitted I really quite enjoyed it – despite it being a bit heavy going in parts. She also thought Ellen MacArthur was too young to write an autobiography. For sailing books, she recommended that I should read Eric Hiscock's books, such as *Around the World in Wanderer III*. Away from sailing, we both seemed to think highly of Dervla Murphy and Rose Tremain and we both agreed Annie Proulx's *The Shipping News* was a top book.

After this literary chat, Kathy asked me whether I was doing all my cycling alone or had anyone who was going to join me. I told her Gary might be coming out with his bike sometime, though it wasn't that likely as he was a bit tied up with building and restoring oak-frame buildings. This got us on to the subject of Peter and Gary, both carpenters, who both seem to be able to mend or make anything they put their hand to, whether it be wood or metal or engines or whatever. I told Kathy that Gary can lose me very easily when he tries to explain to me how something like a centrifugal ball governor or a Wankel rotary engine might work, or even the finer details of a length jointing principal rafter where there is a chance of lower arris plate rotation. 'If I start looking dazed,' I said, 'Gary says, "I'll draw you a diagram, Jose," which doesn't really help, though I pretend it does and nod knowingly while I'm thinking: I must wash the kitchen floor later.'

Kathy laughed and said just the same thing happens with her and Peter. 'They just need encouragement, these men,' she said. 'When Peter goes into great detail about something I nod and say "What a good idea!" Like if Peter says, "I've got a new idea for a rigging set-up on the top mast," and then starts explaining his idea, I have to be quick on the uptake because if I pause for a minute as if I don't understand then it's fatal and I get the "coloured pen" treatment for ease of understanding.'

Geraldine, South Canterbury, 23 March

News today was of an eighty-year-old woman visiting relatives in a Nelson hospital who herself had to be admitted into the hospital when the automatic doors closed on her and broke her leg. A hospital spokesman said, 'It's a freak accident.' I'd say more like dodgy doors, myself.

After a teeth-chattering night of icy rain, it was sunny, clear and hot this morning and the mountains looked resplendent with their dazzling snow-topped crowns. I shot along what is known in tourist leaflet speak as The Inland Scenic 72 Route. Myself, I would just call it a most enjoyably flat road with the hills on my right rolling skyward. The only place of any size I passed through (all of four-and-a-half houses – plus the ubiquitous community swimming pool) was Mayfield. As I entered Mayfield I saw a sign at the side of the road in the shape of a nightcap-topped Santa. Santa said, 'WELCOME TO MAYFIELD – blink and you will miss out.' I blinked but I didn't miss out: the public conveniences were spotless with a clean stripy roller towel and fresh soap and soft toilet paper imprinted with butterflies.

Then, before I knew it, I was in the town formerly known as Talbot Forest, then Fitzgerald before finally becoming known as Geraldine, which is a bit like calling a town Derek or Kevin. I was planning on ploughing onwards from here into the hills, but because my ankle seemed to have gone up the spout again I decided to call it a day. This decision was helped by the fact that there was a handy park-like campground right in town and situated directly opposite the Geraldine Medical Centre. I wandered in, thinking I would never get an appointment (I have NHS waiting lists in my bones), so was surprised when Rob Hill, the in-house physio, whisked me off there and then to his consulting room for an investigation of malfunctioning parts. Rob was a Yorkshireman, originally from Barnsley, and had been in New Zealand about nine years. He had no intention of living in England ever again. I said, 'Don't you miss the dales and the good, sturdy forthright folk, Rob?' And he said, sweeping an arc of arm towards the window and the all-embracing but hidden-from-view mountains, 'What, when I've got all this on my doorstep?'

Rob reiterated the importance of stretching before and after cycling. He couldn't find anything too wrong and told me to simply listen to my ankle (I try but I often can't hear). 'If one day your ankle tells you it's fine with cycling fifty miles uphill, then that's all well and good. But if on another occasion it says "Whoa there!" after a mere ten, then do what it says and stop.'

'But it's not that easy on a bike. I might be in the middle of nowhere with no food or water,' I said.

'Then cross that bridge when you get to it,' said Rob with a wink. And I left thinking: would that be a bridge over braided waters?

Fairlie, Mackenzie, Canterbury, 24 March

Not very far today. Only about fifty kilometres under my wheels. This is because I couldn't decide whether I should give my floppy ankle another day off, or press on and risk snapping it off.

Everywhere I've been in New Zealand, from city to town to smallest village, there have been vast swimming pools (both inside and outside varieties), devoid of crowds, just asking to be swum in. And unlike back home where even a short dip in a public pool can make you feel as if you've been swimming in bleach, making your skin feel three sizes too small, Kiwi pools were more akin to swimming in spring water. In New Zealand I've stopped to swim in most of the pools I've come across. In fact, at this rate, I think I might have swum further in New Zealand than I have cycled. Geraldine had a very come-hither outdoor pool, sparklingly clean in the sun. I spent hours in it, one-leggedly crawling up and down, thinking: *This is the life!* Mostly I had the place to myself, but this morning, which after a night of chilly rain dawned bright and cool, I was mid-length when a group of local women, all on the well-built side and pushing sixty plus, with white legs that had come out in goose-bumps and purple splotches, entered the pool for a class of aqua aerobics. *And ONE leg in and ONE leg out. And ONE leg up and ONE leg down*. Occasionally they would embark on a length, swimming with their chins held high so they wouldn't wet their hairdos. The aerobics teacher, who also doubled up as the receptionist, was an attractive, big-smiling, fair-haired Dutch woman. When I was in a state of undress in the changing room, she came in to invite me to her home (she had emigrated to New Zealand) as she was a keen cyclist and said she felt she knew me after reading my translated *De Wind in mejn Wielen*. I would have gone had I not decided to hit the fairly hilly road to Fairlie, which is where I am now with a thin film of frost covering my tent. I sense a cold night ahoy.

Lake Tekapo, Mackenzie, Canterbury, 25 March

There's been much in the news recently about how Fuarosa Tamati and her daughter Saralia were given $26,000 of taxpayers' money to travel the world on a hip hop investigative tour. The two women from Christchurch, who described themselves as 'established youth workers', spent seventy days travelling between New York, Los Angeles, Hawaii, Fiji and Samoa to trace the origins of New Zealand hip hop. Or, as one of the women (who was given the money by something called the Social Entrepreneur Fund) put it, so that they could 'do a whole lot of travelling for hip-hop'. The mother had just admitted to having a stopover in Paris and spending some of the cash 'chilling out' in Hawaii, but she was adamant that any investigation into her spending would prove she had not wasted money. 'I think people are being really bitchy and horrible,' she said. 'They don't understand I apply for lots of grants and haven't had them all approved.'

The best letter about all this was by Mike Harris, printed in *The Press*:

Having read your article re the hip hop overseas trip (and the undoubted value of this to New Zealand as a whole), I feel sure that taxpayers will be only too willing to fund another of a similar nature.

For many years I have been an avid wearer of jandals and as such I intend seeking funding for a world tour to trace the origins of flip flop. Progress will be slow, however, as I will be stopping off for a few weddings and chilling out on the Riviera.

Readers wishing me well can email to ripoff.com.

Much had been made of this hip hop extravaganza on the radio, especially talkback Radio Pacific. But I kept losing the train of conversation because the programme was constantly interrupted by the annoyingly urgent voice of someone called something like Magnus Benrow who insisted on cutting the presenter or caller off in their prime to scream his live horseracing commentary: *And as Fly Away Babe overtakes Baycity Blue Jeans, Life Stock and Barrel is closing in fast . . . and what's this . . . ? Jacket Turbine is tripping over Bow Anvil . . . and now Temple Franco falls right across the whole heap of them with Life for Living adding to the chaos . . . and as Classy Calendar takes the final fence . . . only to find Cheery Cola and Guilt Trip collapsed in a tangle of hoofs . . .*

Or something like that.

National Radio (a bit like the BBC's Radio 4, but more lighthearted) tends to be a little more relaxing on the ear. And it's where I became quite familiar with the tones of Dick Wheeler. Dick doubled up as both chatty newsreader and continuity announcer. Unlike Radio 4 announcers, who usually just read their lines in a mostly demure and sensible manner, Dick was a little more excitable and actively involved. After a documentary programme that he'd particularly enjoyed, he could be heard saying in a sort of Queen's English form of Kiwi accent, 'Well, well, well. That really was very interesting, wasn't it? I wouldn't mind hearing that all over again!'

Nor me neither, Dick!

Yesterday, I listened to a play on the radio. The minute it had finished, Dick said, 'My goodness! What a mysterious ending! That will keep us all guessing no doubt for a long time to come.' *I should say it will, Dickie old chap.*

*

I seem to be cycling through lots of gateways in New Zealand. The latest one is right here in Fairlie, a small Wild West type of country town that heralds itself as the 'Gateway to Mackenzie Country'. Mackenzie Country begins just west of town at Burke Pass – a gap through the foothills that leads to a vast tussocky basin of moonscapes, rivers, lakes and wild lupins. After stocking up on food at the Four Square and passing one of Fairlie's few shops (a craft and clothes shop called Fairlie Interesting), that was just the direction I headed in, up and over the surprisingly easy Burke Pass sandwiched between the Rollesbury, Albury and Two Thumb Ranges. The change in scenery was dramatic. Suddenly I was riding among the high barren hills, an anchored remote land of intense country shades and storms and snow and sun and crystals and desert. Tuffets of native tussock grass, growing in golden clumps like excitable heads of wind-tossed hair, shook their locks wildly in the strong northwest wind. Ahead of me in the far distance rose the indomitable ridge of jagged Southern Alps – the wedding-cake icing blowing off a few of their peaks like a blurring streak of cloud. Apart from the odd tourist bus with its processed contents of jet-lagged, dozing passengers, and the occasional motorhome with names like 'MEANDERIN' ALONG' and 'LET'S GO HOMEY', I had the whole wonderful wide expanse to myself.

So here I am at Lake Tekapo. Tekapo is Maori for 'sleeping mat night', quite an appropriate interpretation as I'm camping on my sleeping mat at the lakeside, overlooking the extraordinary brilliance of its icy turquoise waters. This magnificent colour is caused by 'rock flour' – finely ground particles of rock brought down by the glaciers at the head of the lake and held in suspension in the meltwater, which, in combination with the sunlight, creates the unique bright blue.

Nearby stands an unusual memorial commemorating the hard work of the trustworthy sheepdogs of the area. The bronze sheepdog statue, sculpted in England by a certain Mrs I Elliott, stands proud on a stack of rocks and was built in memory of all high-country mustering dogs 'without the help of which the grazing of this mountainous country would be impossible'.

Mackenzie, Canterbury, 26 March

This morning I awoke to a bright blue lake and a rich red dawn.
Oh, and a northwest wind blowing like a devil possessed. As I followed the straight dyke-like service road alongside the Tekapo
Hydro-Electricity Canal, this wind slammed into me from the side
with such force that I had to cycle on the opposite side of the road,
keeled over at an acute angle into the wind like a spinnaker-racing
yacht to prevent the gusts from hurling me down the steep
embankment into the water. Fortunately I was the only one following this canal road. All the other traffic stuck to SH8.

And so to Twizel, site of the black stilt (one of the rarest wading
birds in the world) and precious little else. This highly uninspiring
town, resembling an army barracks minus the high fences of razor
wire, only came into existence thirty-five years ago to service the
nearby hydroelectric power scheme, and was supposed to have
been bulldozed flat once the project was finished. Shame it wasn't,
although I have to admit that at the moment it's quite a useful
place to have in the middle of nowhere as my ankle has conked out
on me again.

Twizel, Mackenzie Country, 31 March

The only good thing about Twizel is its proximity to Mount Cook.
After three days of ankle-resting amid the high winds, intermittent
storms and freezing nights (lowest temperature so far has been
minus 7°C, turning bones stiff and tent rigid and air as cold as
steel), a brilliant crisp morning saw me taking off with just front
panniers on the 130 km ride along the dead-end road that skirts
the choppy milky blue waters of Lake Pukaki. As I headed deeper
up the valley in brittle autumn sunshine, a continuous conveyor
belt of dazzling views and colours unravelled all around, headed by
Mount Cook – a 3,755 metre monolith of rock, ice and snow. The
Maori call Australasia's highest mountain Aoraki – 'cloud
piercer' – but the day was so pristine perfect that there were no

clouds to pierce. Instead a saintly circle of wispy wind-blown snow seemed to hover above its head like a celestial halo.

There's always something slightly shivery about standing at the foot of great mountains – the height, the scale, the grandness, the aloofness, never minding the power of the earth to shoot these magnificent monoliths skywards. The Alpine Fault, a huge rent in the earth's crust, lies at the snub end of the Southern Alps about 20 km west of the range's crest. Here not only are the Pacific and Indian–Australian tectonic plates grinding past each other along the fault, but the Pacific Plate is also being pushed up over the other one to form the Southern Alps. A spectacular illustration of this uplift equilibrium (plus the following erosion) was the Mount Cook rock avalanche in December 1991. During the night the summit rock and icecap collapsed, plummeting an estimated 14 million cubic metres of debris down to the surface of the Tasman Glacier nearly 3,000 metres below, at speeds approaching 600 km/h, and instantly reducing the height of Mount Cook by 10 metres.

Cycling to Mount Cook proved good for spirit but bad for ankle. So I've spent the last few days in Twizel, going nowhere. Saying that, I have fitted in a couple of appointments with a physio called Katharine. Katharine is from Bristol. Out of all the people I've seen so far about my ankle, she is by far the youngest but seems the most thorough. She says I've got tendonitis in my Achilles and she can feel that the muscles in my calf and hamstrings have gone all hard and knotty and into spasm to try to protect my ankle. So she's given my leg a good pummelling massage. She's also given me ultrasound on my malfunctioning Achilles and acupuncture in my calf. She even set light to the needles. Five minutes later my leg was emitting smoke signals.

During my stimulating travels around the concrete bunker of Twizel, I came across a Buddhist monk called Jampa Khandro. She was seventy and originally from Worthing on the sunny Sussex coast. She had left Worthing when she was twenty and became a nurse. Then she worked with the aborigines for a while in

Australia. She'd worked her way through three husbands, one of whom was a helicopter pilot at Mount Cook so she lived up there for years. All Khandro's husbands had been violent. 'I'm just no good at picking husbands,' she admitted. So the best thing for it was to become a monk and she seemed quite content now in her Mackenzie Drive white-walled home that doubled up as the Shaey-Drub Buddhist Centre, with its colourful Himalayan prayer flags flapping in the wind out the front.

Khandro, like Katharine, was good with her hands – only with Khandro she went for the full body massage, using lots of heady-smelling oils. Before I knew it, I was in my altogether and lying face down on the slab of her towel-covered massage table in a darkened room surrounded by the sounds of New Age floaty music.

Halfway through this palm-pummelled delight, one of Khandro's friend dropped by. Win, or Winipera Maoi to give her her full name, was a big and buoyant Maori who also knew a thing or two about massage. One of the fine things about New Zealanders is that they are very uninhibited, so the next I knew Win had set to on me as well. Suddenly I had hands everywhere. I was not quite sure if all these hands running themselves all over my body was going to make any great shakes on my ankle. But I can't say I minded. Four-handed massages aren't something that come along my street every day of the week and I feel it's best to grab them while you can.

11

Wanaka, Otago, 1 April

I phoned a friend of a friend in Auckland the other day, and when she discovered I was immobilised in Twizel she said, 'Can we get you helicoptered out?' That's the sort of reputation Twizel has. It's definitely not a town to inspire.

But instead of being helicoptered out, I was jeeped out, care of Katharine. She only worked a couple of days in Twizel. Sensibly she had chosen to make her home not in Twizel but in Wanaka, where she also worked as a physio in the modern practice there. She was in the middle of setting me on fire again when she offered me a lift in her jeep to Wanaka. 'Wanaka,' she said, 'is a lot more exciting than Twizel. And I could also work on your ankle there for you.'

I pondered on this for a minute while watching the smoke from the mini bonfires pouring from my leg.

'And then if you want I could give you a lift back here again because I drive back and forth once a week.'

So here I am in Wanaka, camping just across from the willow and golden poplar-lined shores of the wave-flopping lake, 311 metres deep and 45.5 km long – New Zealand's fourth largest lake, and one that according to Maori legend was carved out of the bedrock by a great tribal chief with his mighty *ko* (digging stick), piling up the debris to form the towering mountain ranges that surround the whole of Wanaka.

Wanaka, Otago, 12 April

Two weeks later and I'm still here. It's a good time to be in Wanaka: cold clear nights of weighty frosts and sub-zero temperatures; brilliant days that start out numbingly cold until sunlight gently warms my outer layers and then my inner layers. In New Zealand, Easter is autumn. And here, more than anywhere else I've ever been, autumn bends the lights of summer and spreads morning and evening skies with reds and golds. In the still of the early frost-sheeted mornings, I've watched birds hop on the hardened grass outside my tent door and heard the grass blades snap. The sound of birds hopping has never been so audible.

I've spent every night camping in the small fenced-off tents-only area of the Poplar Heights section of the sprawling Lakeview Holiday Park and watched backpackers (mostly carpackers) and cyclists come and go. Someone outstaying even my stay was Andrew Pye from Australia. He was travelling around on a yellow mountain bike attached to a trailer. Before I arrived here, he had already been in Wanaka two weeks waiting for the Warbirds over Wanaka – the largest international airshow ever held in the southern hemisphere, featuring planes like de Havilland Vampires, Harvards, Hercules, Mustangs, Spitfires, water-landing Catalinas, Sopwith Camels and Fokker Dr1 triplanes. For years Andrew had had his own radio communications business, which he'd now sold along with his house and most of his possessions to move to New Zealand. He'd always been keen on planes, he had his pilot's licence and in his spare time he built a plane back home in Perth and flew it three times across Australia. He now wanted to get a job flying tourist planes over Mount Cook.

One afternoon I was walking from the campground into town when I saw an Atomic Shuttle bus go past with a bike attached to the rack on the rear. I thought: I've seen that bike before. A minute later the bus stopped and I saw ex-threesome travelling Bridget staggering down the steps. After Pete had flown home she continued cycling south alone, but then decided to pack it in due to all the cold and the wet. For a few days Bridget was another addition to the Poplar Heights camp and she was surprised to find me still injured. I think Bridget felt I was in need of a little spiritual enlightenment: she gave me one of her books to read called *Body Electrics – Life's Turn On*, plus a magazine she bought from the crystal shop in town. The magazine, *Rainbow News – 'Feed Your Soul'*, had some unusual articles on offer like: 'Taoist Abdominal Massage'; 'Beyond Feng Shui'; 'Soul Psychology'; 'After Death Communication'; 'Whispers from your Angels'; 'Crystal Healing'; 'The Chakras – A Practical Guide'; 'Discover your Blocks with a Pendulum'. And I don't think they're talking about brake blocks you've lost down the back of the sofa. The magazine was also liberally furnished with adverts for things like 'Soul Psychology Workshops' and 'Aurora – Colour Magnetic Crystal Sound Healing'. There was even a 'DO-IT-YOURSELF SPACE CLEARING KIT – Picks up where Feng Shui leaves off! Learn to clear the energies of your space like a pro.'

Another passing inhabitant of the Poplar Heights camp spot was an Irishman with entangled hair – a ravelment of dreadlocks topped in a rainbow Rastafarian hat. He was trying to find work WOOFing (Working On an Organic Farm) and was travelling about South Island with a guitar and a backpack and a South Korean girlfriend. He told me how the West Coast was 'feckin' awful, man, for hitching'. One afternoon, up at Fox Glacier, they had packed up their tent and stood outside the campground at the side of the road for five hours. Not one person stopped to offer them a lift. Then it got dark, so they walked back into the campground and put up their tent again.

Katharine has been busy pummelling my ankle on a fairly regular basis. Lots of smoking needles have been stuck into it too. Seems to be working, though, as I've been swimming and walking and cycling every day – I even made it up the road to Mount Aspiring as well as the Treble Cone Ski Field without giving the twanged bits a set back.

Bridget became very friendly with Jenny, the owner of the crystal shop in town. In fact she became so friendly with her that she packed up her tent and was going to live with her for a while. One afternoon I was wandering past Jenny's shop and stopped to read the small hand-decorated messages attached to the noticeboard outside. Messages like: '*Inner peace creates world peace*'; '*I meditate everyday to nurture my soul*'; '*Once you have learned how to enter your Inner Kingdom, you have a special retreat within that is always available to you*'; '*You create your thoughts, your thoughts create your intentions, and your intentions create your reality.*'

I was just pondering whereabouts within my anatomy I might find my Inner Kingdom (just south of my superior vena cava and north of my duodenum, perhaps?) when Jenny stepped out of the shop and invited me over for dinner that evening. Jenny lived in Albert Town on the other side of Mount Iron. It was about a five-minute drive or a two-hour walk. I decided to walk along the banks of the Clutha River, the largest river (by volume) in New Zealand, following a narrow path flanked with poplars and willows bathed in a halo of autumnal gold. There were maples too, looking on fire. They glowed red at the tips, then faded into orange and yellow.

By the time I arrived in Albert Town it was dark and I was navigating my route by headtorch. Jenny's house was like a cosy cabin veiled with strings of prayer flags and painted in big bold colours. There was a big tent in the garden filled with a double bed. There was also a caravan, which was where Bridget was currently sleeping. I found Bridget inside the house, looking very at home with the dog and cats in front of a magnificent blazing log fire. When I asked Bridget how she was, she responded, 'Physically or mentally?'

'Just a general all-over synopsis would do,' I said, while thinking how you often got more than you bargained for with Bridget.

Jenny offered me free rein to have a bath (my first in six months), but in the event I only had half a bath because I didn't want to use up too much hot water. On my way out of the bathroom, and feeling hot for the first time in weeks (this was the longest I had been inside for three-and-a-half months), I noticed a shelf of books. One was called *Succulent Wild Women – Dancing with your wonder-full self*. Another was entitled *Mapping Your Birthchart*, which made me wonder whether such a process might involve contour lines and a scale of 1:350 000 along with a key indicating historic buildings and scenic reserves.

Jenny hailed from Dunedin and had spent quite a bit of time in both Canada and America. She had lived in Wanaka for twenty years and took over the shop last year. She now wanted to build a meditation centre. Since she'd been in Wanaka she'd seen big changes. 'It was a small, quiet place when I first arrived,' she said. 'Now it seems as if all Wanaka is a vast building site.'

She was right. Wandering and cycling around Wanaka you couldn't go anywhere within a short distance of the town without coming across an army of bulldozers carving out the hillside, marker tape delineating new building sites and subdivisions consisting of 300 or more 'sections', as they call plots over here. Some prices for houses had doubled or even trebled in just three years. Buyers were throwing money at the chance to buy a section for $500,000 to $1 million; a house with a lakeside view for $2 million to $3 million. Fancy gated communities were mushrooming out of the land with names like Sunrise Bay and Edgewater Resort. On the western side of the lake, Far Horizon Park was described as being 'themed on an English village' (what, with gangs of hoodies setting fire to the local bus shelter?). Most of the houses cost around $1 million and residents got a heated swimming pool, spa, gym, tennis courts, putting green, volleyball, petanque, and avenues of perfect trees and what was described as 'schist landscaping'.

Before I left Jenny's at midnight, she had invited me to stay the night. Although I could have fallen asleep quite easily in front of the fire, I didn't want to break the chain of sleeping in my tent so I went back to the campground.

The night was crystal clear and hard-edged – the temperature in my tent an exhilarating minus 6°C complete with layer of ice on the inside of the fly. I wriggled down into my sleeping bag dressed in as many clothes as I possessed, including hat and gloves. To combat the cold nights I'd bought a hot-water bottle (essential survival polar-exploring equipment, I believe) and utilised vast wodges of old newspapers I found about the campsite, stuffing my whole tent full of the crumpled-up pages to act as insulation. My tent was now so full of balls of newspaper that when I unzipped the door in the morning all a passer-by could see when they looked in was a mountain of newspaper. The other morning I crawled out of my tent to see an elderly man leaning on the fence looking at me a little concerned as balls of newspaper avalanched out of the opening. When I had straightened myself upright and casually kicked a few balls back through the goal mouth of my door, he asked warily, 'Do you have such a thing as a sleeping bag?'

'No,' I said. 'I just wrap myself in newspaper.'

And I think the man believed me.

Kurow, North Otago, 18 April

After the better part of a month getting nowhere, I'm suddenly steamrolling ahead at great guns, albeit in a backwards sort of direction. From Wanaka I was planning on heading north back to Twizel before heading south to the south of South Island, before heading north to the north of South Island and then north to the north of North Island, before heading south again. I'm still hoping to do all this cycling north and south of both North and South Islands, but not quite in the sequence that I had originally planned. This is because Gary has gone and put a spanner in my works, though a welcome spanner at that. When I last phoned Gary from Wanaka I discovered that all my trans-global naggings must have paid off, because he has suddenly decided to take the plunge and fly out with his steed to meet me. For Gary, this is quite a leap into the unknown as he is not the type to stray far from the familiarities of the highly tooled workshop of his comfort zone. Not that I think he hasn't ever wanted to stray far. It's just that working as a carpenter since the age of fifteen (he is now thirty-three) he has never had the opportunity or the money.

So from the end of May he is putting the building of buildings on hold and fleeing to what he's been looking forward to all winter, which is summer, by flying to the opposite side of the world to have winter all over again. Not that I'm making too much of this point. Don't want to put him off before he's even begun. Anyway, I hear winter here can be really quite nice – as long as you like lots of rain, wind and cold. Sounds like summer all over again to me. What fun.

As I've only got a month to cycle back up to Auckland, I've been hurtling along at a lickety spit. Fortunately my conked-out ankle is now only semi-conked (just minor prickly twinges) so in the past week I've been making up for lost ground.

From Wanaka, Katharine gave me a lift in her clunking jeep-truck back over the Lindis Pass to Twizel. I'm surprised we made it that far as the heater wasn't working, nor the temperature gauge, speedometer or rear door. The engine produced several last-leg splutters too. The Lindis Pass links northern Central Otago with Mount Cook and the Waitaki Basin of Mackenzie Country. As I had been trucked up and over it twice feeling highly fidgety I wasn't out there cycling among the stark beauty of this remote hill country, I was determined I wasn't going to pass by this pass except on my bike. So late one afternoon, as the sun burnished the golden hills, over I went, skirting Ewe Range, Wether Range and Snowy Top while dipping down over Dip Creek, Breast Creek, Camp Creek, Long Spur Creek, Short Spur Creek and Coal Creek. At Crippletown I joined up with the Clutha River again and over the next few days I forged my way through the desolate, treeless tussock country of Central Otago, which tends to be desert-like in summer and shrouded in snow in winter. I had a bit of both: desert sun during the day and a dusting of hill snow at night. The towns of Clyde, Alexandra and St Bathans once attracted thousands of gold-diggers, who rushed to uncover the treasure hidden beneath the bleak landscape. The towns are now at the hub of New Zealand's stone-fruit and Merino wool industries.

Merino sheep were the first sheep in New Zealand and are the most amusing sheep I've ever seen. With rippling folds of wool hanging from their necks like dewlaps, they look as if they have climbed into a coat ten sizes too big. All rams and some ewes sport horns that protrude like handlebars from halfway down their heads, giving the appearance that their faces are suffering from subsidence.

There's been much made in the news of late of nine-year-old Shrek, a Merino ram who had evaded the musterers for six years on Central Otago's Bendigo Station. While living 1500 metres above sea level, Shrek's fleece grew to 38 cm long. Then he was spotted hiding in a cave. He was relieved of his 20.5 kilo fleece in a televised twenty-five-minute shearing operation that took place just down the road in Cromwell and was broadcast around the world. Shrek has been in all the papers too – the headline in *The Press* reading: 'WOOLY YARNS SPUN AS HEFTY SHREK LOSES LOCKS'. But Shrek faces competition from North Island pretenders for the handle of world's woolliest sheep. The greater Waikato is laying claim to having three Shreks – dubbed the Taharoa Trio. One of the trio, caught in March, had wool 43 cm long, smashing claims that Shrek, at 38 cm, was the world's woolliest sheep. Billy Black, one of the sheep farmers who tracked down the trio, said he was dubious as to the authenticity of Shrek. 'I think it's a pet one,' he said. 'The South Island one was just a tourist sheep. This is real North Island King Country sheep.'

Still roaming in Shrek land, I spent a couple of days cycling along the vehicle-free gravel track of the Central Otago Rail Trail that sidled alongside the Raggedy Range and through places like Chatto Creek, Omakau ('Oh motherly cow'), Ranfurly, Daisybank, Rock and Pillar and Middlemarch. In summer this 150 km track, crossing nearly seventy bridges (including a couple of wooden trestle bridges), would be busy with bikers and hikers. But the whole route was now deserted – hardly surprising as the wind hurtling through the ravines careered into me from almost every direction, wrapping itself in a rage around my body and forcing me to push my bike to avoid being blown clean down the gullies.

Sometimes being alone and banged about by wind for so many hours can wreak havoc with your mind. For some reason, as I fought to control my bike in the maniacal gales, the only words I had going round and round my head were the stock phrases of Kiwis that have ingrained themselves into my brain: good as gold; sweet as; awesome. At one point along the Rail Trail, I stopped at the Omakau Four Square and heard all three much bandied-about phrases within the space of two minutes. A man with hair sitting close on top of his head like a small, tight-fitting stocking-stitch beanie walked past me in the store and said, 'Hi! How's it going?'

I was about to say, 'Not very easily. It's flippin' windy! I've nearly been blown for a Burton once too often!' But then I thought that was probably not what he wanted to hear, so I just said, 'Fine thanks!'

When I paid for my food, the woman at the till said, 'Good as gold.'

Then she handed the beanie-haired man a pack of cigarettes and he said, 'Sweet as.'

Outside the store, the beanie-haired man asked me where I was cycling and when I told him he said, 'Awesome!' He walked back to his pick-up, in which he had left the engine running. Lots of people do that round here. It makes me want to lean through the window and switch the ignition off. But I haven't been that brazen yet.

Another thing I've noticed about Kiwis is that, like the British, they tend to talk about the weather a lot. But unlike the British, who tend just to pass comment on the current conditions ('Chilly today!' 'Bit wet!' 'Could do with some sun!'), Kiwis appear to be amateur meteorologists – much more involved with their isobars and approaching highs and lows. They all seem to know when a cold southerly is approaching and what's going to happen when it slams into a more tropical front racing down from the north. Countless times I've been warned, 'Ya bitter watch out, mate – ya don't want to be stuck out there when a nor'wester is blowing!'

And whereas, say, *The Times* at home simply lists on its weather page the hours of sun, millimetres of rain and maximum temperature of various locations around the UK over the last twenty-four hours, New Zealand newspapers go to quite the other extreme. The *New Zealand Herald*, for example, lists the maximum temperature, the minimum temperature, the grass minimum, the 24-hour rainfall, the rainfall to date for the current month, the mean month rainfall, the rainfall to date this year, the mean annual rainfall, the humidity (%), the pressure (hPa), the maximum wind gust, the sunshine on the day before yesterday, the month's sun until the day before yesterday, the average sun for the month, the sun for the year to date, the sun average for the year, the evapotranspiration (mm) and the soil temperature at 10 cm. All of which, I'm sorry to say, I find quite riveting reading.

Then there's our friendly National Radio. Every evening they broadcast a farming programme containing lots of weather talk interspersed among all the crop talk. Back home, the BBC tucks its *Farming Today* programme well out of the way at half past five in the morning. And only once a week on Monday mornings does it give a quick précis of what the weather has up its sleeve for the forthcoming week. National Radio's farming programme, on the other hand, is broadcast at prime time listening. And it doesn't just discuss the weather in intricate detail during every programme; it describes certain effects of the weather with an intricacy that almost borders on the fanatical. Take the hailstorm, for instance, that struck Hawke's Bay yesterday afternoon. Instead of just saying a hailstorm hit the apple crop in Hawke's Bay, the two presenters deliberated on the size and shape of the hailstones. 'Fortunately the hailstones were small and round as opposed to large and jagged,' remarked one of the men. 'So the apples only suffered minimal damage.' There then followed much discussion concerning the various shapes and sizes of hailstone that have wreaked havoc on crops in the past. I'd never heard a simple hailstone being given such extended airplay before. It was quite heartening.

Another thing about New Zealand weather: it doesn't half produce some very uncloud-like clouds. Some are shaped like mushrooms or cones or rolls and rounded clumps, or are lens-shaped, looking as if aliens are coming in to land their spaceship. I've discovered these alien clouds go by the rather wonderful name of altocumulus lenticularis and are something which not that many people are lucky enough to see. I think New Zealand produces such chaotic weather and uncanny clouds due to its position in the world – out on a limb sandwiched between the volatile Tasman and the whimsical Pacific. Added to this mixture, cold air rushes up from Antarctica to collide with warm tropical air spilling in from the north. Thus meteorological anarchy ensues.

From the Rail Trail I started weaving my way north before cycling the road from Kurow ('argumentative queuing system') to Omarama ('Bananarama's mother') twice. As far as roads are concerned, New Zealand is still in its infancy. Compared with home, where roads have been built for thousands of years resulting in an intricate and historical web of highways and byways that criss-cross the country in a magnificent entangled network (enough to satisfy a dedicated cyclist for several lifetimes), New Zealand only started getting a grip on its road-building a mere 150 years ago. In the South Island there's a road down the west coast, a road down the east coast with a momentary strip in the middle and the odd squiggle across from side to side. And that's more or less it, which means if you spend any time on the move, you're bound to travel along the same road more than a few times.

I cycled the Kurow to Omarama road twice, not because I was lacking in choice but because, despite hitting an afternoon headwind that blew up the valley as regular as clockwork known locally as the Waitaki Doctor, it was such an enjoyable ride I wanted to elongate the pleasure and so rode it all over again in the opposite direction. This little-used road, which follows the Waitaki Valley, skirts Lake Benmore (the largest artificial lake in the country, holding a greater volume of water than the entire Wellington Harbour) and Mount Horrible (very nice looking, actually). There are lakes and mountains everywhere, because no sooner have you shot through Sailors Cutting and passed Pass Peak than you find yourself riding beside the banks of Lake Aviemore and Lake Waitaki – which in 1938 was the scene of the last hydroelectric dam in New Zealand to be built using labour-intensive picks and shovels. Autumn proved perfect timing to be cycling this road – the deciduous trees were flaming gold.

In Kurow I stopped at the tourist office, which was shut. But an unusual notice on the door advertised:

'THE SPIDERMAN – Glen Wylie ... the guy who is good at killing spiders. You will be truly amazed at the results that Spiderman can come up with! (And it doesn't cost much either!) RING TODAY! 0800 SPIDEY.'

I don't think I will be ringing this spider-killing Spiderman. Spiders in my tent are good news. They eat the sandflies that I feed them.

I cycled back up the street to the motorcamp, passing a house with a sign attached to the front gate warning: 'FORGET THE DOG – BEWARE OF THE OWNER'. The motorcamp was strategically located near the confluence of the Waitaki and Hakataramea Rivers, both renowned for their trout and salmon fishing. The only caravans on the site now were rows of permanent ones, vacated for the winter, but obviously belonging to fishing sorts judging from the fishy-flavoured stickers attached to their rears. Stickers saying things like: GONE FISHIN' AGAIN and WORK IS FOR PEOPLE WHO DON'T KNOW HOW TO FISH. Another one was more an advertisement:

WANTED: GOOD WOMAN. MUST BE ABLE TO COOK, CLEAN, SEW, DIG WORMS AND CLEAN FISH. MUST HAVE BOAT AND MOTOR.
PLEASE SEND PHOTO OF BOAT AND MOTOR.

The night I camped at Kurow was cold and wet. The only other person I saw at the motorcamp was Ian McKie, an elderly Scotsman with a fine shock of white wavy hair. He invited me into his caravan to warm up beside his electric bar heater. Ian had had his caravan here since 'seventy-five. He was proud of it too, not least because it fitted a double bed in it whereby you could still have room to walk round both sides of the bed. 'Most caravans have the bed up against the wall,' explained Ian. 'But here, look, I can walk up and doon both sides of the bed!'

Ian still sounded as Scottish as if he had stepped straight from the moors, though he'd been in New Zealand since 1958. He lived in Dunedin. 'Before I arrived in New Zealand I'd heard Dunedin was the Edinburgh of the South. I'd also heard that Auckland can get humid in summer and that Dunedin was said to be more like the weather in Scotland – cold and damp – so I thought tha' would suit me fine!'

Ian rose from his chair and shuffled down one side of the bed before turning round and shuffling down the other side – as if to demonstrate that, yes, both sides of the bed were indeed very accessible. Then he eased himself back down into his chair and ran a creased hand through his wavy hair.

'I was in the Navy,' he said, 'when I got chatting to some Kiwi fellas on the ship. That's when I decided to come to New Zealand on an immigration programme where if you kept the same job for two years, they would pay for your passage.'

Ian was originally from Dumfries, but he hadn't been back there since the day he left. 'When the Common Market started up, we suddenly had all these juggernauts rumbling through the toon. And in order for them to do that, they had to tear down half of Dumfries. That's why I never wanted to go back – I want to remember Dumfries how it always was.'

12

Timaru, South Canterbury, 20 April

Yesterday, cycling along the north bank of the Waitaki River, I was held up by first a sheep-jam and then a cow-block. I had never seen such an amassed wall of cattle. Approaching from the rear, all I could see of the road for a good half a mile ahead was a scene of total bovine gridlock. Several excitable dogs busied themselves acting all lordly, slinking, eyeing, steering and snapping at the hooves, especially when a clump of the herd would stop to observe me, moonily chomping and staring. A young girl on a quad bike was assisting the dogs by bringing up the rear. She wore a T-shirt emblazoned with the words 'I CAN'T SO I WON'T'. But despite that, she seemed to be doing very well. She told me there were 687 cows in front of me and to cycle straight through them. 'They'll make way for you!' she called. And they did, albeit a bit grudgingly. As I slowly carved a path among the sea of clumping rumps, it felt like sinking into a horizontal quicksand of cows – small air pockets would open up and then just as suddenly close up tight all around. I'm not sure if it is possible to drown among a surfeit of cattle, but I feel I came quite close.

After riding by fields with huge wheeled irrigation booms like horizontal pylons, I headed over Elephant Hill and through oak woods and eucalyptus groves and rocky outcrops until the sun disappeared and a grubby washcloth mist uncurled across the rolling pastures. Slowly another day was drawn across the sky like a grey slate. I plunged down through an unexpected gorge and then I

was upon the small country town of Waimate where a sign warns you to watch out for the wallabies. Instead of wallabies all I saw was a Chinese takeaway called Ping Ying and an elderly woman on a mobility scooter weaving about the road doing a grand job at trying to get run over by a logging truck.

There's been quite a lot in the news of late about mobility scooters. One woman called simply 'Mary' was reported in *The Press* as wanting to thank those who came to her aid on 10 April. A wind gust (don't tell me it was that devilish Waitaki Doctor) caught her mobility scooter and caused a minor accident. *The Press* said that, 'apart from bruising and minor cuts, Mary is fine and back on her scooter.'

What a relief.

Poor Mary couldn't help her wind gust, but other mobility scooter users have been acting more and more irresponsibly. In fact the situation is so bad that there's to be something called a 'scooter safety forum' in Nelson next month. 'Scooter users have been seen riding on the road instead of the footpath and bar-relling along supermarket aisles, knocking things off the shelves,' said Margaret Parfitt, the Nelson City road safety co-ordinator.

Mount Somers, South Canterbury, 22 April

For a brief few unpleasant kilometres (about fifty in all), I had to join SH1 – the main state highway that bulldozes its way down the east coast. The stretch between Christchurch and Dunedin was particularly busy and full of articulated lorries and double-trailer trucks thundering along at full throttle. Cycling along the edge of the straight, flat road in a frisky side wind as two trucks (particularly logging trucks) meet in opposing directions is always a reliably invigorating experience. Especially that bit where you hit an explosive whoomph of displaced air.

Added to the trucks was the steady stream of buses and motorhomes. I noticed, in a generally generalised manner, that the private tour buses were mostly full of parties of Japanese or Americans – most of whom looked very asleep. Younger students were the ones filling the seats of the organised backpacker-style tour buses like the Flying Kiwi, the pea-green Kiwi Experience and the black Magic Bus. Rented motorhomes and campervans were the domain of Europeans, while the impoverished long-term travellers went for buying beaten-up campercars and much-used vans with the makeshift double bed mattress crammed in the back. Retired Kiwis continued to travel the country in their personally named motor caravans (EAZEMOTION, PURR FECT, B' AWAY AWHILE, LET'S GO HOMEY, LUV-INN, DOOFA US, DUN-WORKIN', CRUIZIN', MAKIN TRAX, NOSE N AROUND, BIG-ENUFF, BED-FOR(D) US, SCAMPA CAMPA, SNOOZA DOOZA, AMPLE KARMA, TAR TREKA, TOULOOSE MOOSE, CRUZIN' BYE, CRUISE 'N' SNOOZE, 4 LAZ 'N' ABOUT; CUM 'N' GO, NO HANKY PANKY, HANK'S TANK, SHAG'N AROUND, BEDDY BUS, JUS PURRFIC, SWEET AZZ, BUG ER WORKIN', WELL BUGGA ME DAZE, CORK FORK & PILLOW, THE OLD FARTS, PEACED TOGETHER and CEE-YA). Then there were the Kiwis of an affluent nature who liked to own a no-expense-spared tour bus with full flip-up satellite dishes, home-from-home kitchens and bathrooms, small gardens and golf courses. Bussing Bill, an elderly widower I'd met in Wanaka, had just bought himself a new

Civilia bus, which he told me cost him $75,000. 'The woodwork alone of the kitchen units and cupboards cost me $45,000,' said Bill. And Bill's bus was quite a small bus compared with some of the monsters on the road.

Once through busy Timaru with its surplus of eateries with names like The Hairy Lemon, The Loaded Hog, The Red Rocket and Bold as Brasserie, I turned off at Washdyke for Pleasant Point. And before I knew it I was back in Kevin . . . I mean Geraldine. Far better to be back in a place I'd already been, than end up as road kill on SH1.

In the small behind-store car park of the local Supervalue supermarket, I had an interesting experience. Apart from three slope-shouldered adolescents sitting on an overlooking wall cowled like monks in their hoodies, there was no one else around. Then a young mum pushing a small boy in a trolley came out of the supermarket's rear door. She looked at me and said, 'You're not that girl who writes cycling books, are you?'

I was just about to deny all responsibility for past misdemeanours when she suddenly asked, 'Can I give you a hug?' But it was more a statement than a question because, still semi-attached to her trolley, she leant over to give me a hug. So there we were, two complete strangers, interlocked in a hug in the Supervalue car park, watched over by three perplexed boys in hoods. Then it was all over as quickly as it had begun and I walked into Supervalue to do my shopping.

When I returned to my bike I found a brown paper bag attached on a pannier. Written on the bag was a note. 'Josie,' it said, 'at the risk of sounding mad please come and stay if you come back to Geraldine. We are at— Thanks for the inspiration. Julie Blair.'

Made my return visit to Kevin all worth while.

Hawkeswood Pass, Canterbury, 30 April

Another 'been there, done that' place I stopped at was Mount Somers. When the very Kiwi-sounding woman owner of the motorcamp saw me she said, 'What are you doing back here again?' I told her I was doing a U-turn to meet Gary. When she heard that I wanted a place to put my tent she said, 'You don't want to be in a tint! You should git a kibin – it's going to be tin below zero tonight.'

But I held my ground, explaining that I wanted to see how long I could hold out in my tent before I gave in to warm, dry comforts.

'I bit you're going to git a kibin when you meet your boyfriend!' said Mrs Motorcamp with a nod and a wink.

Saucy devil.

Back past Pudding Hill I went. Then came Mount Hutt and the big rip of a dip down into Rakaia Gorge. Once past Zigzag Road, Windwhistle whipped by together with a bright yellow hillside covered with the rich musty smell of gorse. And then I was in Coalgate, Sheffield, Oxford, Omihi ('to greet oneself') and Greta Valley, a blip of a community with a 'Junk and Funk' store and a pub-cum-restaurant offering motorists a free 'Driver Reviver' cup of coffee.

I'm now camping in the freezing mist at the top of Hawkeswood Pass. I think I'm on a sort of farm, possibly called The Staging Post, but it's a bit hard to see anything because of the mist. I can just hear the lowing, bleating and barking of cattle, sheep and deer all around. There are wooden cabins here with big gaps in the doors, but the elderly woman owner who is occasionally sighted scuttling in and out of various doors has let me camp. The only other person here is Ken, a possum hunter from the West Coast working for Scope Hunting Ltd. He's putting poison down and setting traps all over the area 'to kill the little bastards!' Seems he's been over this way a lot. Knows the old woman well. She calls him Young Man. 'Evening Young Man,' she called as she bustled through the camp kitchen at one point. Over the kitchen sink is a black and white photograph of a woman reclining in a chair. The picture bears the words 'How beautiful it is to do nothing and then to rest afterwards!'

Ken saw me looking at this picture and, nodding his head in the direction of Mrs Staging Post, said, 'I wouldn't say those are the words to describe her!' He told me that although she was married, there was never any sign of the husband. 'She's the one who runs the place. The night before last I was woken up by a loud bang. When I went outside, I found her standing in the dark with a shotgun. She told me she'd just shot a possum in a tree. She hates the bastards too!'

A little later on, after Ken had retired for the night to polish his traps, Mrs Staging Post did a very rare thing and slumped in a chair for a moment or two. 'When I married my husband,' she told me, 'he said to me, "I just want to let you know I'm not going to be one of those husbands who keeps telling you I love you!" We've always done our own thing, but every Wednesday is our time together and we always go out for the day.'

Kaikoura (again), 1 May

I've just realised that I've now cycled 3,000 miles and I haven't had a puncture. Yet. It's also just occurred to me that I haven't seen another loaded cyclist for weeks. Must have all gone home as the weather, if not cold, is wet. Or both. There again, maybe they've got more sensible things to be doing than cycling around South Island in the winter.

Outside the Four Square in town I met a couple called Derek and Jenny who told me that they had once seen me waffling on about bicycles at a travel show in Bristol. They had both left their jobs a while back in an insurance company where they worked, to travel from Rome to Australia. They'd recently cycled from Adelaide to Sydney and preferred Australia to New Zealand. 'It's a much whackier place,' said Derek. 'New Zealand is too much like the UK – a similar culture with similar people.' They were currently bikeless, driving around just the South Island in a hire car before heading back to Oz in a week or two. Tonight they were treating themselves to a motel. 'We've just bought ourselves some comfort food,' said Derek, hoisting up the Four Square carrier bag in his hand. 'Fishfingers, baked beans and mashed potatoes!'

There's still much talk about the shearing of Shrek doing the rounds, not least because it's been revealed that Shrek's televised shearing attracted some of the highest viewing figures ever recorded. Tonight on Radio Pacific (station motto: 'Free speech is only a phone call away!') a man said how Kiwis liked to think of themselves as sophisticated these days. 'Remember it wasn't so long ago that towns only consisted of a Four Square and a milk bar – now we have street-cred cafes offering fifty different types of coffee, yet we still tune in to watch a sheep being shorn!'

13

Blenheim, Marlborough, 6 May

I've just cycled up the coast from Kaikoura in hammering rain and hurtling winds gusting at 120 km/h. The headwind was so strong that no matter how much effort I put into it, I couldn't cycle much more than 4 mph. Dispiriting stuff, yet strangely exciting wondering if I was actually going to survive the ordeal.

I met a woman in Blenheim today who was driving a friend's campervan down from Auckland to Christchurch. She left Auckland the day before yesterday. She was not enjoying it as she found the van far too cramped for comfort, despite the fact that the van had big bunks, a table, squashy seats, a kitchen and room to stand up. 'It's so cramped,' she said, gesticulating through the open sliding door of the van into what looks to me like a capacious expanse to manoeuvre, 'that I never make a meal in there. Not even breakfast. I go to Macdonalds instead. I look at motels and think *luxury*!'

Funny that, because I look at campervans and think *luxury*!

Richmond, Marlborough, 10 May

From Blenheim I had a choice of cycling the direct way back to Picton (about 30 km) or the non-direct way via the Nelson Lakes (about 350 km). I went the non-direct route which, for the first day at least, involved cycling slowly upwards through the mountain-edged wilderness of the Wairau Valley. Not for the first time, a headwind was blowing like blazes. When I left Blenheim in the morning, the wind had actually felt tinged with warmth, but by the time I approached the alpine meadows of St Arnaud, the wind, blasting in a wintry curve down the funnel of the valley, was knobblingly cold. That night, camping beside the splendours of the glacier-formed lake of Rotoiti, the thick blanket of frost that settled on my tent looked as heavy as snow. The only vehicles to pass me all day were three double-trailer stock trucks and the odd farmer's pick-up, all with wire-thin working dogs barking mindlessly on the tray behind the cab.

Last night I camped on a small patch of sodden grass at Hu-Ha Bikepackers, a fine bunkhouse overlooking the Lookout Range and the Hope Range. In the visitor's book, I saw that Karin and Marten Yurman, the Dutch cyclists I met at The Pedallers Rest with the travelling threesome, had passed this way not so long ago. 'What a view!' they wrote. 'Good records, nice paintings, loved the hot tub. Thanks.' The owners, Sam (who had a box load of his old LPs for hostellers to listen to – Bob Dylan, Roxy Music, Grace Jones, Talking Heads, the Police, the Rolling Stones) and Jo (a chef and artist), lived upstairs. No one else was staying, but Sam lit the woodburner for me. When he'd gone back upstairs, I turned off the light and watched the fire flaring and crackling, all the shadows in the room retreating to the corners.

Two scenic saddles lay in my way this morning. The first was Hope Saddle that, once I was over top, plunged me down a steep, twisty gradient alongside the Pinchback Range through forestland and then farmland. Spooners Saddle gave me a good vantage point for distant views over Nelson and for acting as temporary weathervane: a menacing curtain of black cloud was rolling in off the Tasman. With no time to dally, I sped off the saddle, hurtling downwards along with the logging trucks. After a fast spin I was back in what could be called civilisation – though it didn't appear very civilised, with cars and jams and traffic lights and road rage among the busy bottlenecks of the Nelson suburbs.

Cycling through Hope as the first fat raindrops began to explode on the tarmac in front of my wheels, I spotted a bunch of keys in the gutter. A photofit driving licence attached to the keys told me they belonged to Catherine Anne Newport. Her Video Ezy membership card was also attached. When I handed the keys in at Richmond police station, the officer on duty took one look at the photo on the licence and said of the woman who peered out at him with long straight hair, a double chin and glasses the size of television screens, 'Well, she's a bit gawky-looking! She could do with losing weight and getting some new specs!' This from an officer who was nothing if not ovoid himself.

Pelorus Bridge, Marlborough, 13 May

More rain. More floods. Tent, clothes, body resembled large sponge. You could wring several bucket loads of water out of my skin alone. Hang me upside down and I'd pass as a very effective gargoyle.

I aquaplaned through Nelson (big and busy) feeling too wet to explore and continued over Annie Saddle into the mountains. After I'd crawled up and round the multiple logging-truck-crushing hairpins of Whangamoa Saddle (a surprisingly enjoyable ride despite the near-death-sucking trucks and thrashing winds and surplus of sandflies) the rain finally petered out, though the low, unrelieved pewter of the sky remained. The tortured shapes of dead trees stood like gallows in the dark misty gloom of the day. Mount Duppa came and went, as did Rai Saddle.

Outside The Brick Oven Cafe in Rai, I read on *The Press*'s headline board: 'PATIENTS TOO FAT FOR HOSPITAL TREATMENT'. A tough-looking bloke, built like a centre prop forward, noticed me peering at the board as he emerged from the cafe and said, 'Serves them right, mate. They should do some icksercise. For bist effect they should do some ear roebucks! My dad found ear roebucks iggserlint for losing weight.' By the time I realised he meant aerobics, the Kiwi bloke was halfway through telling me how his sixty-five-year-old dad had got on his bike to lose weight and last year had managed to cycle up Whangamoa Saddle without expiring. Before the Kiwi rugby bloke (who was actually a vineyard engineer and commuted daily between Nelson and Blenheim) climbed back into his vehicle, he offered me a beer from his sucks peck (six pack).

I found more personal 'iffics' today. This time: a handbag hanging on a hook in a public toilet in Pelorus Bridge. If this were London or Paris or New York you'd probably be automatically programmed to think 'bomb!' But in New Zealand, where the height of all excitement is the televised shearing of a sheep, you see an unattended handbag and you simply think 'lost handbag'. I was walking across the car park to hand in the handbag at the tearooms when a fraught woman intercepted me. She had stopped for tea in the tearooms with her elderly mother and then driven about fifty kilometres up the road before her mother realised she'd left her handbag in the toilets. I'm not really sure why they were fraught, because being Kiwis you'd have thought they would know that most people in New Zealand are more interested in watching sheep being shorn and drinking sucks pecks than wandering around stealing handbags.

It is so wet, dripping and cold in Pelorus Bridge and the ground is so squelchy and waterlogged ('It can rain here as much as 300 mm in one night,' the Scenic Reserve ranger told me proudly) that I've camped in my tent on the floor of one of the draughty dank cabins, which is more comfortable than sleeping on one of the bare plastic mattresses. All I can hear is the loud rushing roar of the swollen Pelorus River and the sound of trucks' pneumatic brakes as the drivers throw their vehicles into the sharp corner outside my window before rattling over the single-lane steel girder bridge.

The only other people on site are an English couple from Cheltenham, sleeping on a mattress in a van they picked up for about £200 at the Sunday morning campervan market on the racetrack in Christchurch. They've both given up their jobs to travel for a year or so. The girl, who wears a trilby-style hat pulled low over her eyes like a 1930s gangster, leaving only her mouth to look at, is a dental assistant, whereas her chap said he'd jacked in his own business as an importer of racks – mostly American racks by all accounts. Racks for shops and shows. So far they've spent three months in Thailand and three months in Australia. They didn't think much of Oz. 'We just didn't find the people very friendly. They're much nicer here. And the scenery's a lot more varied too!' This from him, who I might add is wearing an interesting combination of clothing: long blue plastic mac, baggy white calf-length trousers (apparently fishermen's trews from Thailand), socks and sandals. He has at least apologised for the socks and sandals, explaining that as they had just done a big wash he was forced into wearing the remnants of his clothing. I said I forgave him, but only just.

Havelock, Marlborough, 14 May

Today I managed the grand total of twenty torrentially raining kilometres (including plenty of truck-suckings) before I decided to call it a day. Queen Charlotte Drive, the hilly and narrow bay-hugging road from Havelock to Picton, was rumoured to be so spectacularly scenic that I thought I'd give the weather a day to improve its ways.

As I entered the tiny town there was a garish sign saying: WEL-COME TO HAVELOCK 'THE GREEN MUSSEL CAPITAL OF THE WORLD'. Apparently these are green-lipped mussels (as opposed to red lips or purple lips?). All very lovely, I'm sure, but I think I'll stick to porridge myself. I feel I'm on safer ground there.

In the boomtown gold-rush days when gold was discovered down the road at Wakamarina ('forceful hitting of elaborate docking facility for pleasure craft') and thousands of miners flocked to the area to live under canvas at nearby Canvastown ('tent city'), Havelock had twenty-three hotels. Which might not sound very many until you consider that Havelock today has a population of

500. The main street, although pretty uninspiring, still has a touch of the pioneering look about it. Two people that Havelock likes to put on their high horses, and who had their early education here at the local school before going on to bigger things, were Dr William Pickering of the US space exploration programme and Lord Rutherford, the nuclear physicist who first split the atom. Not a bad score for such a sparsely populated place. Maybe there's something in those green-lipped mussels after all.

I'm doing more cabin-camping tonight. Despite a comfy-looking bunk, I am sleeping on the floor within the confines of my inner tent because that's where I'm happiest – plonked out on the hard flat ground. In the clean and spacious campground kitchen I found a magazine called *PROPELLER* '*The Trailer Boat Magazine*'. The main inside features were advertised on the cover with macho abridgements such as: *BIG RIGS*; *RAMCO'S BIG BOYS*; *35 HOURS WITH A FICHT*. Whatever a 'ficht' is. I delved inside to discover that this particular ficht was an 'EVIN RUDE FICHT RAM 225'. Well, that's good to know. I might have known a sheep would find its way in there somewhere.

Havelock is sited right at the head of Pelorus Sound and the wharf was busy with fishing vessels with names like *Loosen Up*, *Glitterwake, Silver Moon, Sin Bin* and *Yesss!* Overlooking the wharf was the big warehouse belonging to 'Sanford Havelock – Sustainable Seafood – Putting the MUSSEL into Marlborough'.

After a wander in the rain, I walked up The Slip past the Slip Inn and returned to my camping cabin, where Radio Pacific was once again interrupted by the horseracing and an excitably hoarse man yelling out the current positions of Come Away With Me, Touch My Pocket, Straight Edge, Give It A Whirl Girl and Is She Faking It? Not being a horse person I soon switched stations and heard a presenter on News Talk ZB ask whether New Zealand and Australia should have a common border and a single currency. The first caller to ring in was not impressed with this suggestion. 'I think that's a stink awful idea, mate!' he said. 'I'll tell you why. Do you know what Aussies think the capital of New Zealand is? About fifty bucks!'

Sea, sun and a silly load. Coromandel Peninsula, North Island

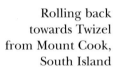

Rolling back towards Twizel from Mount Cook, South Island

More tripod dodging. Near Manapouri, South Island

Sunbathing seal.
Kaikoura
Peninsula, South
Island

Lily – my little
Maori tent mate.
Whakatane,
North Island

Drying out in the
Blue Boar Tavern.
Ruatoria, North
Island

Gary framed by the Kauri twins. Waipoua Forest, North Island

Flogging up another hill. Near Broadwood, North Island

Gary anchoring me down in the wild wind at Cape Reinga, at the top of North Island

Disappearing into the lush, dripping ferns of Waipoua Forest, North Island

Waiting for the ferry from Bayswater to Auckland city centre, North Island

Picnicking miles from anywhere – Gary forlornly searching the horizon for an all-day breakfast cafe. Aupouri Peninsula, North Island

Gary not happy with more rain, more hills, more mud. Near Cape Reinga, North Island

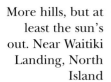

Wild weather – Gary blown clean off the road in storm-force wind and rain. Near Aranga, North Island

More hills, but at least the sun's out. Near Waitiki Landing, North Island

Another possum victim of the Josie Dew rolling road-train. Near Waitangi, North Island

Chilly camping. Twizel, South Island

Jagged edge – icicles at Haast Pass, South Island

Bluff – the Land's End of South Island

Typical New Zealand –
sheep, floods, fish and
steaming land: the
river in Masterton,
North Island, and the
steaming land in the
Champagne Pool,
Wai-o-Tapu, North
Island

A splash of driftwood. Hokianga Harbour, North Island

Gary cycling into the sunset. Waipoua Forest, North Island

Picton, Marlborough, 15 May

Saw the sun for the first time in days this morning. Why Queen Charlotte Drive is called Queen Charlotte Drive, heaven only knows, because it should be Queen Charlotte Cycle. The narrow winding road that hugs the hilly coast is made for bicycles. It dips, it dives and it springs surprises of utter loveliness around every corner.

Back in Picton I met an Australian couple who told me they were from Perth. 'That's Western Australia,' said the man, just in case he thought I thought he meant simply Perth, Australia. 'There's a difference. A big difference.'

The man was a big storyteller and told me of every shark attack that had occurred in his area in the past year. The only remains of one of the victims was the woman's bikini washed up on the beach. He also told me a story about an Aboriginal mate of his who went travelling to Alaska. Once there, he was out in the wilds practising some throws with his boomerang when the boomerang landed on the head of a bear. The bear took unkindly to this so gave chase to the Aborigine, who was a very good runner and just managed to outpace the bear all the way to a hut in the forest. He threw open the door, hurled himself inside and quickly slammed it shut again, but the bear was travelling at such speed that it shot straight through the door and out of the back wall, trampling another man in the hut to death in the process.

14

Following another rocky crossing across the Cook Strait aboard the Inter-island ferry, Wellington slowly merged from the gloom looking just as wet and windy as when I'd left. This time I managed to locate the friends of a friend of a friend that I'd had no luck locating when I'd last been here getting wet and wind-blown. Not far from their home in Miramar, I stopped at a corner dairy store to buy them a bottle of wine. This was where I first met Caroline. She had just nipped out to buy a bag of sugar. I had no idea at the time this was Caroline, but I looked at her a little oddly because it was freezing cold and wet outside and yet she was wandering around the dairy in bare feet dressed for summer in winter. Likewise, she had no idea I was who I was, but still looked at me a little oddly – probably because I was dressed for winter in winter. Then she saw my bike and that was that – she led me down the pavement to her home apparently oblivious to the fact that she was wading bare-foot through icy cold puddles.

Caroline used to be Tracy. But she hated the name Tracy so when she was six she changed her name to Caroline. She was married to Allan and they had four boisterous young children: Cameron, Morgan, Conner and Jamie. Allan and Caroline, who were both vets, met twenty years ago at vet school when they were dissecting an embalmed dog. 'So I always tell people we met over a dead dog,' said Allan. Another slightly unusual thing was that Caroline's dad, Richard, had been born with his heart on the right-hand side of his body instead of his left. He'd been told he wouldn't live past fifty, but he was now sixty-seven. Judging from my brief sighting of him in Twizel, where he ran a salmon farm with Caroline's mum, Margaret, he looked in good nick.

Before I left, it came up in conversation that Allan and Caroline had a friend whose surname was Leper, pronounced Leaper. The Leper married a 'de Post' and they double-barrelled their names together so that they were now known as an athletic-sounding Mr and Mrs Leper-de-Post.

Ohakune, Ruapehu, near Lake Taupo, 18 May

Now that Gary has a definite date for flying to New Zealand (June 6), I'm putting my legs into gear and high-tailing it back up to Auckland. Over the last couple of days I've ridden 250 windy and wet, chilly hilly kilometres. Because the two state highways, SH1 and SH2, are the only roads into and out of Wellington and because both are death highways (I had already experienced the unpleasant busyness of Death Highway 2 when cycling into Wellington via the Hutt Valley back in February), I decided to take a train to free me from the vehicle-rushing suburbs. This was easier said than done. Firstly, the guard was no help at all. There was a big step up between the platform and the guard's van – quite a struggle when you've got short legs and a severely weighty bike. All I needed was for the guard to balance the back of the bike while I climbed up into the van to haul it in. Instead, the rotund guard just stood with his hands on his portly hips and said, 'It's not our duty to help. I'm not risking putting my back out just to give you a hand.'

So, feeling much vexed, I shoved the whole lot in myself.

The train was supposed to depart at 8.40. Half an hour later we were still sitting in the station. A long-awaited announcement told us that the delay was due to the train 'waiting for an engine'. Always a useful addition to a train. 'And then, when the engine arrives,' continued the disembodied voice, 'we will make the connection before testing the brakes.' You'd have thought they would have run through all these elementary preliminaries back in a siding.

A lot of backward and forward shuntings later, we were finally off. But only for ten minutes before we ground to a sudden stop. Nothing happened for a while. Eventually an announcement informed us that we were currently having an 'operational stop'. Whatever that meant. Maybe they were running back down the track to retrieve a lost wheel. Eventually, we moved forward with a lurch. Only to stop again. With a lurch. We then managed about ten minutes of walking-pace travel, before stopping again. This time the announcement explained this was because 'we're waiting to cross a southbound train'. Hopefully not literally. A derailment would be all we needed. When the guard walked through, a woman in front of me complained at the late-running of the train. 'This train is always late,' he replied. 'And anyway, this is nothing. Last night the train took three hours to cover a distance that normally takes fifteen minutes.'

Just when I was beginning to lose the will to live, the train came to rest at Paraparaumu station. I don't think we were supposed to stop here, but I took the opportunity of a platform to hurl my bike off the train and exchange the slow-moving clutches of the carriages for the Kapiti Coast.

Having become so fidgety on the train, I was now eager to go and I hit SH1 with alarming enthusiasm. With blurring legs I tore through the likes of Waikanae ('forceful hitting of organ of sight'), Otaki ('how sticky!'), Manakau ('personnel despatched to steer bovine into action'), Levin, Foxton, Himatangi ('he's a flavoursome smell'), Sanson and Bulls. So far the road had been flat and open and windy. But heading north from Bulls to Hunterville the road took a few dives as the hills closed in. By the time I hit Vinegar Hill, things had started to twist and turn. Then came viaducts and steep river cliffs as I followed the far-below rushing Rangitikei River into Mangaweka – an odd wishy-washy nowhere sort of place with an oddly sited low-flying tearoom situated in a battered roadside DC3 plane. Mangaweka also offered an eighty-metre bridge-plunging bungee-jumping option for those of a deprived childhood. I thought about camping near the giant corrugated-iron boot in Taihape, the region's prime farming town, which prided itself as being 'The Gumboot Capital of the World' as well as 'The Halfway to Everywhere Stop', but the Abba ('Dancing Queen') Motor Camp down Old Abbattoir Road was closed – quite a relief really as it looked (and sounded) a pretty unappealing place.

More uphill panting took me through Hihitahi ('hello, hello, thank you, hello') until I emerged on a bleak tussock plain erupting at the edges with volcanic cones of snow-crusted mountains. At the approach to Waiouru, the New Zealand Army's main training base, a sign at the side of the road warned: 'FOR YOUR SAFETY STAY ON THE ROAD. LIVE FIRING AND EXPLOSIONS AT ANY TIME'. A shame this, as I was dying for a pee and had hoped I might be able to sneak a quick one in behind a tuffet of tussock. But with admirable mind over bladder, I managed to hold on until I arrived at the litter-strewn public conveniences in Waiouru.

Waiouru is a cheerless place consisting of a wide-open strip of takeaways, fast-food cafes and service stations sprouting incongruously out of the desolate windblown plateau. It's the sort of place most people pass through on the way to other places. You don't really want to stop unless you have to. Waiouru is also the place where you don't want to get stranded in winter. Plenty of people do, though, because it sits at the southern tip of the Desert Road – a remote and exposed road often closed because of ice and snow. The population of Waiouru hovers just over one-and-a-half thousand and if you live here you are likely to live either on base, or off base in army-owned houses. The climate is hard around here and the clusters of army houses are bleak. A garden in Waiouru looks to be nothing much more than a flax bush and a spindly knot of conifers shaped in a rough sort of topiary by the wind. Every house has a satellite dish. Obviously people don't want to spend any more time outside than they have to.

After stashing a handful of dollars into my wallet at the Westpac Bank, filling up with water at the Fastlane Coffee Lounge and sending a small package to Auckland-based Jacquie from Waiouru's shed-sized Post Shop, I cycled out of town past Subway, the Lion Red Oasis pub, the Hiway Robbery Cafe and the multiple outlets for Tip Top 'Real Dairy Icecream'. Still on SH1 on a course for Rotorua, I joined the Desert Road. As I rode up on to the exposed volcanic plateau, the bitter wind socked me in my face and turned my hands and feet to stone. The Desert Road crosses the Rangipo Desert, which is not a true desert but named as such due to its barren near-desert area and hostile appearance. Hour after hour I battled onwards, all the time watched over by the brooding conical form of volcanic Mount Ruapehu. At one point, huddling in the cold beside a clump of wind-tossed tussock while devouring a bagful of food, it suddenly occurred to me that it would be more fun to save Rotorua's volcanic mud baths and thermal pools to do with Gary. So I jumped back on my bike and headed back the way I'd come. Instead of heading north, I would now head south, then west, then south, before veering west around Mount Taranaki – New Zealand's Mount Fuji, occupying the bulge on North Island's western coast – before riding north up to Auckland.

Back in Waiouru I turned right to skirt the southern flanks of Mount Ruapehu and bowled along following a stepped downhill. At Tangiwai, about 8 km west of Waiouru, I passed the spot of New Zealand's worst rail disaster where 151 rail passengers were killed when the overnight express train between Wellington and Auckland plunged into the flooded Whangaehu River on Christmas Eve in 1953. The accident was caused by a sudden release of thousands of tonnes of water from the crater lake of Mount Ruapehu which surged down the Whangaehu River in a massive wave. The swift and turbulent deluge, known as a lahar, uplifted massive quantities of sand, silt, boulders and muddy debris. Sometime between 10.10 and 10.15 p.m. the lahar struck the concrete pylons of the Tangiwai railway bridge, sweeping away three-quarters of the decking and track. Minutes later a young Taihape postal clerk saw the light of the approaching locomotive Ka 949. In a desperate attempt to warn the driver, he ran towards the train waving a torch. The driver saw the torch and braked, but not soon enough and the train plummeted into the river. Of the 285 people on board, 131 bodies were recovered and twenty people were never accounted for; it was presumed they were washed 100 km down the river and out to sea.

Somewhere between Carrot Corner and Wanganui, 19 May

I was welcomed into Ohakune last night by a gaudy model of a giant carrot, as tall as a tree, sprouting from the ground in tribute to the town's primary product. Most visitors to Ohakune came here not to indulge their passions in the simple delights of a tapering orange root vegetable, but to go skiing or tramping, or horse-trekking or jet-boating or white-water rafting. This is because Ohakune (Maori for 'place to be careful') was known as the gateway to the Mount Ruapehu ski areas and Tongariro National Park. As if to validate this claim, a woman drove past in a car with a licence plate saying: SHE SKI. Never mind alpine lodgings or après-ski facilities – all I wanted was information on the state of the road to Wanganui, as rumour had it that it had borne the brunt of the February storms and had partially disappeared. The woman in the tourist office told me that the road was now open though reduced to lots of single-lane sections where the landslides still encroached upon it. She also said that, from Ohakune, the road to Wanganui was mostly all downhill.

All I can say to that is she can't have been a cyclist. As State Highway 4 followed the Mangawhero River, the road went up and down and up and down and up and down as it climbed away from and dropped away to the river. During the February floods this river, which cuts deep into the mudstone hills, caused havoc in the area by flooding farmland and washing away bridges and trees. The road was still full of hazard signs warning 'SLIPS!' where the rain had caused numerous mudslides, washing away whole strips and chunks of road that collapsed into the river. Teams of road gangs in day-glo orange coats buzzed about rebuilding the highway and trucking heaps of mud and rockfall out of the ravine. Down below, the riverbanks looked like the aftermath of a battle, with an entanglement of drowned and river-washed trees lying ensnared like a mesh of snarled corpses.

Along this 100 km-odd stretch of road there was just one tiny settlement, Kakatahi, which made for a virtually traffic-free ride. Just south of the very splashy Raukawa Falls, I spent the night camping down by the river at an in-the-middle-of-nowhere YMCA. The place was run by affable Rosaline, a terrifically sturdy woman with a gammy leg – a result of having wrenched it climbing on to her sit-on mower. She was preparing food in the industrial kitchen for an onslaught of young teenagers on parole scheduled to arrive by bus in the morning to pick sack-loads of walnuts for a company in Wanganui. Rosaline was a generous soul and gave me a big bag full of silverbeet, cauliflower, tomatoes and mushrooms for my tea. Back in my tent I heard on the news that three boys had been caught red-handed smashing up a school in Invercargill, causing $10,000 worth of damage. The boys, who were aged six, eight and ten, were referred to on the news as 'pint-sized vandals'. They should get them up here to pick walnuts.

Hawera, Taranaki, 22 May

Somewhere around Otomoa ('to cut grass mechanically') Road and Bennyfield Hill, I looked out across a spectacular choppy sea of emerald green hills. At Upokongaro ('United Possum Organisation of Central African State of Kangaroos') I merged with the mighty Whanganui River before coming to rest in the historic city of Wanganui itself. Stretching nearly 300 km, the Whanganui is the third longest (and the longest navigable) river in New Zealand, whereas Wanganui is one of New Zealand's oldest cities (founded in the relatively ancient times of 1841), but it's obviously not as important as the river because it lacks the extra 'h'.

All over New Zealand there are 'Fire Risk Warning Monitors' on big billboard devices at the roadside with an arrow pointing to a

colour-coded 'Low', 'Medium' or 'High', depending on the current wet or dry situation of the ground. But on the busy truck-laden road to Hawera, I passed a similar sort of roadside device claiming to be a 'Facial Eczema Monitor'. There was something in the corner of the board referring to 'Pet Care'. Quite what all that was about I don't want to know.

It was all big dairy and sheep country round here, the sleek steel Fonterra milk tankers being the most prominent trucks on the road. The rain poured from the grubby skies, the spray splashed in a filthy wet cloud from the passing thundering trucks. Patea was a depressingly deserted and run-down place with boarded-up shops and the odd bored-looking Maori wandering around. Loud music reverberated from shabby houses whose front gardens lay stacked full of old car parts. One gate had a picture of a pitbull terrier nailed to it with the warning words: 'DOG WILL BITE YOU'. Don't think I'll be going in there, then.

By the time I reached Hawera I was a mobile puddle. Water dripped and drained from every catchment area. I could even feel waves in my shoes. The woman in the tourist office said to me, 'I could never imagine travelling alone on a bike.' Shame that, because I can fully recommend it. Even in the rain.

New Plymouth, Taranaki, 26 May

In Hawera, due to all ground being flooded, I camped in a cabin at the motorcamp with the camp cat called Fluffette. The middle-aged skinhead in the next-door cabin was a big bloke covered top to toe in tattoos. He liked his fags and his drink and knocking on my door for a chat. 'I come down here every weekend,' he told me. 'The woman I'm going with at the moment – a hairdresser in town – lives just down the road, but her daughter don't much take to me. She's in the army, you know. I call her GI Jane. So when she comes home at weekends, I move up here to the cabin.'

Another time he stuck his head around the door and said, 'You smoke dope, mate?'

I said, 'No, sorry!'

He said, 'No worries. I just thought all backpackers smoke dope. Mate of mine grows a big patch of it. If you change your mind, give us a shout. I've got a bagful if you want it!'

From Hawera most traffic heads north on SH3 direct to New Plymouth. I veered off on the coast road that is known as Surf Highway 45. At first I thought this appellation referred to the splooshing surfing effect of all the water on the road (it was still raining a storm), but then it dawned on me that it was alluding not to the undulating aquaplaning but to the surfing Mecca spots that adorn these shores.

If you'd asked me where I might find the Bread Capital of the World, I would have said somewhere like Germany or any patisserie in France or the cobble-hilled, bicycle-pushing Hovis-filmed advert town of Shaftsbury, Dorset. But no, no and no. Just west of Hawera I rode past a large and tasteless plastic model of a loaf of bread on a pole heralding my arrival in the rather nondescript town of Manaia, the one and only 'Bread Capital of the World'. Well, blow me. Apparently Manaia, which served the local farming and petrochemical industries, had a local bakery that exported worldwide. A quite staggering fact, I think you'll agree.

Somewhere near Pihama ('mother's ham pie') the sun came out and for the first time I had a proper sight of the mountain that looks just like Mount Fuji, so much so that Tom Cruise had not long since left the area after filming *The Last Samurai.* ('*Ah so desu-ka?*') This 2,518-metre mountain, known to some as Mount Egmont and to others as Mount Taranaki, is the symmetrical centrepiece of this land-bulging province. Although the region in which Mount Taranaki sits is called Taranaki (the Maori name for the dormant volcano), the national park containing Mount Taranaki has retained the name of Egmont National Park. Egmont is the name Captain Cook gave the volcano, calling it after the Earl of Egmont, who had encouraged his long-range expedition. Just to confuse things further, Taranaki's cape is known as Cape Egmont, whereas the waters on either side of the cape are called the North and South Taranaki Bights.

The sun accentuated the colours of the area to the extreme – the fertile lushness of the green pastures, the coal-black volcanic sand of the beaches, the dazzling white snow on the mountain and the astonishing blue of the sky. In places, where lava had long solidified into heaps, the shape of the land turned to crowds of little green hills with rounded tops. Some of the hills bore curves and divots and wave-like ribs, but in other areas the ground had a pocked and tousled look. All of this hummocky land was clothed in an unreal green and dotted with cattle.

Although it was most pleasing to feel the warming rays of the sun on my back again, I knew it wouldn't last – I could see the dark smudge of clouds piling up on the Tasman's westerly horizon and feel the wind rising once more and smell the nearness of the rain. By the time I had arrived in New Plymouth and propped my bike on the seafront at the base of the severely wind-bending Wind Wand (a weirdly attractive 45-metre red flexi-stick designed by the kinetic artist Len Lye that can bow and sway in the fierce Tasman winds up to 20 metres from the vertical) it was pouring again, the cold and violent wind hurling the rain across the streets in sheets.

Te Kuiti, Waitomo, 28 May

All I can say about the last two days is: storms, gales, hills, saddles, mounts, tunnels, gorges and bush. Lots of bush. Stretching for unpopulated miles and miles. At the roadside the variegated greens of the bush begin, then give way to the black-green of distant hills. The region I'm in now is called Waitomo, meaning the place where *wai* (water) disappears into a *tomo* (hole in the ground, otherwise known as cave). There are hundreds of limestone caves all over the area whose watery caverns have been turned into a tourist-luring 'experience' for such delights as abseiling into them down water-spouting walls, floating among them on giant inner tubes or being guided through them in boats to see cave-dwelling glow-worms. Well, I can do without all that drenched and dripping rigmarole, thank you very much. After all this rain, I'm like a Waitomo myself – a place where rainwater disappears into the various caverns and crevices about my person.

Eventually I emerged into yet another 'capital of the world' – this one Te Kuiti (verb: 'to quit, to go, to leave'), 'The Shearing Capital of the World', marked by the prominently domineering statue of a sheep-shearing man. On a male theme, if not a sheep one, I was now in what's called King Country – named after the Maori king movement of the 1850s, which developed locally and sought to unite the tribes on a national basis. New Zealand may be currently lacking a Maori king, but this is more than made up for by a mouthful, namely Te Arikinui Dame Te Atairangikaahu, the

Maori queen whose official residence is at the Turangawaewae Marae, at the northern end of Ngaruawahia – the Maori capital of New Zealand.

Auckland, 30 May

As it happened, I passed the abode of Te Arikinui Dame Te Atairangikaahu in Ngaruawahia, but I couldn't see a lot as it was raining so heavily. Ngaruawahia, which is Maori for 'broken open food pits', sits at the confluence of the Waipa ('electrically operated blade with rubber edge wiping a windscreen clear of rain or snow') and Waikato ('querulous calling of domestic feline') Rivers. The Waikato is the longest river in New Zealand, flowing 425 km from the icy slopes of Mount Ruapehu on the volcanic plateau, passing through forest and steamy thermal areas and thundering down waterfalls before making a more placid journey through farmland on its way west to the Tasman Sea. What with these two fat swollen banked rivers, together with all the horizontal rain and dripping clouds of truck-sperlunking road-splashed spray making it feel akin to cycling into the flow of a fireman's hose, my abiding memory of Ngaruawahia is an exceptionally wet one.

In true New Zealand style, the weather remained atrocious as I careered past Lake Waikare ('questionable possession of his car' – otherwise known in Maori as 'rippling water'), Te Kauwhata ('to water a cow'), Pokeno ('no prodding allowed'), Bombay, Ramarama ('ra-ra-ing mother'), Drury and Papakura ('papa can cure her').

The last leg was so abominably wet and traffic-laden that to spare myself from a premature death I boarded a bus driven by a man called Lindsay. Suddenly I was among a world of rules. Having been too wet outside to eat anything in my normal roadside grazing manner, I was banking on hungrily scoffing a pannier-load of fodder once seated on the bus. But Lindsay was having none of it. 'I allow no eating or drinking on my bus,' he said, 'because I'm sick of clearing up other people's chunder off the seats and carpet.' Well, it's amazing how much you can eat surreptitiously behind a hand, even when sitting up front behind the rule-making driver as he keeps an eye on you in his mirror.

Apart from his no-eating regulation, Lindsay was a good and informative soul who told me that the clumps of New Zealand flax that sometimes manage to grow in trees are known as 'widow makers', due to their propensity to fall from a great height on to a man's head and kill him. As we whooshed through Papatoetoe ('father of two-digit foot'), Lindsay informed me that we were about to pass over the narrowest strip of New Zealand – all of a few strides wide. The street across this one-and-a-half kilometre strip is called Portage Road because the Maori discovered it was far easier to carry their canoes over this slender neck of land from Otahuhu Creek to Manukau Harbour than it was to paddle right up and over the top of North Island among the big seas off Cape Reinga.

During the bus journey, the wipers working furiously to clear the buckets of rain from the windscreen, it occurred to me that I had been in this Land of the Long White Cloud and Never-Ending-Rain for almost half a year now. And drawing on my thought processes I accumulated a few ruminations on various aspects of New Zealand from a cyclist's point of view. Here they are:

WEATHER:
Couldn't be wetter if it tried, but then I have landed here in the wettest, windiest, coldest, most floodiest and horriblest summer on record.
TIP: Bring clipless welly boots, a floating tent and a set of sixteen small anchors in place of tent pegs complete with buoys to facilitate location in morning.

WIND:
Strong and gale force from every direction but always against you.
TIP: Hoist the mizzen and tack hard on wide roads to ease your journey (method not recommended in close proximity to 50-tonne logging trucks).

ADDED EXTRA: Fold down wing mirrors to reduce wind resistance, close mouth and tape back ears to help with aerodynamic properties.

ROAD SURFACE:
METALLED ROADS: Chippings vary from fist to saucer-size resulting in an energy-sapping tyre-munching ride. Otherwise fin-*tis*-tic.
UNMETALLED ROADS: Vary from lung-choking dust to hub-sinking mud and from loch-sized water-filled potholes to slinky smooth if you manage to slalom among the copious gravel and bouncing boulders.

VOLUME OF VEHICULAR TRAFFIC:
Far from a cyclist's paradise in this department. For a country reputedly full of sheep there's an awful lot of cars and volumes vary from constant flow to sporadic flurries based on ferry timetables to rugged remoteness of road.

ATTITUDE AND SKILL (OR NOT) OF DRIVERS:
Diabolical! Worst ever experienced! The majority seem convinced that the only place for a cyclist is in the ditch and if you're not in it, they will soon put you there. Oncoming vehicles take perverse pleasure in overtaking directly into your path. In essence, Kiwis drive too fast, too close, too aggressively and too inconsiderately. Give me the kamikaze bus drivers in India any day.

GENERAL STANDARD OF CAMPGROUNDS:
Top notch. Most have kitchens with fridges/freezers/ovens/hobs/microwaves/gas barbecues and instant boiling water 'Zip' machines, which saves a lot on ye olde camp fuel.

WILD CAMPING:
Find a bit of bush, look this way, look that way, making sure no one else is looking or lurking, then dive on in.

EVOCATIVE SOUNDS OF BUSH CAMPING:
Squabbling possums hissing, morepork owls moreporking, unidentifiable creatures squawking and flapping and scurrying, heavy rain, heavy wind, howling rain, howling wind, crash of large falling branches and trunks, gush of rivers rising, distant screech and squeal of boy-racers racing (yes, they get everywhere).

PEOPLE:
In a generalising way of course: frank, matey and to use one of their oft-used expressions 'good as gold'. (That's before they get behind the wheel).
DOWNFALL: They think that anyone who rides a bike around their wildly mountainous land 'bloody nuts mate!' (How wrong could they be?)
QUIRK No. 1: A fetish for sporting short welly boots (often white) which they remove before entering country stores/petrol stations/pubs etc.
QUIRK No. 2: If they're not welly-booted they're bare-footed – even in the middle of winter in the middle of the street in the middle of the rain. Must be a back-to-nature mother-earth sort of thing.

GENERAL UNPLEASANTRIES AND ANNOYANCES:
Possums; boy racers; logging trucks; driving standards; un-rollable toilet paper dispensers in public conveniences; sandflies.

GENERAL COUNTRYSIDE QUIRK:
For a land reputedly full of sheep there's an awful lot of cows.

Once back in Auckland I dived through the rain on to the ferry to Devonport. Riding north out of town the blazing pohutukawa trees of last Christmas were now standing dull and lifeless after their December spree. And then I was back at Jacquie's where I discovered that, since my last visit, she was lacking a lodger. Milly the cat was now deceased, having been run over by a car. When alive, Milly had been almost as partial to a harvest moon as she had been to leaping out of the first-floor kitchen window on to the adjacent balcony before jumping back in again. So keeping to a similar line of attack in memory of her much-missed cat, Jacquie waited for the great orb of a harvest moon to hang suspended in the sky. When at last it appeared, she leant over the balcony to sprinkle the considerable collection of Milly's ashes ('much more than I thought they'd be for a cat,' said Jacquie) to the moon. Unfortunately, Jacquie had not only failed to take into account the direction of the wind but also to close the kitchen window, resulting in clouds of Milly's remains blowing back in through the window to land all over the kitchen. The parts of Milly that didn't make it back in through the window ended up covering the windows and prize plants of Mrs Basham, the elderly woman who lived downstairs. Mrs Basham never said anything. And nor did Jacquie, despite the fact that half of Mrs Basham's house and garden resembled the aftermath of Pompeii.

Auckland, 5 June

I've spent the past week based at Jacquie's while scuttling around the environs of Auckland on my wheels purely for investigative purposes. I've also used the opportunity of some dry floor space to sort through my kit and burrow to the bottom of my musty panniers, the contents of which, after nigh-on six months of solid on-the-road usage, resemble the layers in an archaeological dig – the various strata of squinched and creased possessions each relaying a story through the history of time.

Tomorrow morning at 05.00 hours Gary is scheduled to drop out of the sky with a boxed bike. A journey that took me two months of watery slow motion will have taken him a mere cloud-racing, DVT-induced twenty-four hours. I'm getting some good strong builder's tea in for him to make him feel at home in case he's already suffering from workshop withdrawal symptoms. Talking of strong tea, Jacquie told me that her grandmother, who was Scottish and disliked wasting money, would spend hours cutting each teabag in half before sewing each half up with a couple of sturdy stitches.

Auckland, 6 June

I nearly cycled off with the wrong man today. Jacquie and I got to the airport at some unsociable hour of the morning and sat in the arrival lounge waiting for Gary to appear. As we were sitting watching crowds of bleary-eyed passengers shuffling round the corner of customs dragging their wheelie cases and pushing trolleys piled high with perilously stacked mountains of luggage, Jacquie asked me if I was nervous. I was a bit, though in a nervously excited way. I also told her I felt a little perturbed because as I hadn't seen Gary for nearly eight months I might not recognise him. He might slip through the net and walk out of the airport without me even realising it was him. Jacquie asked for some landmark features of what he looked like.

'Short hair, big shoulders and wheeling a long cardboard bike box,' I said.

No sooner had I said this than a man with short hair, big shoulders and wheeling a long cardboard bike box swung round the corner into view.

'That must be him!' said Jacquie excitedly.

He swivelled, scanned the crowds and, spotting us, waved and grinned before moving at speed in our direction.

Jacquie said, 'He's coming, Jose! Run and greet him!'

But I just remained rooted to my seat, almost cowering back into it, while staring at this bike-box-carrying person scooting towards me.

Jacquie looked at me and said with a degree of urgency, 'What are you doing, Jose? It is him, isn't it?'

'Errr, I think so,' I said, suddenly feeling very hot. 'But I'm not sure!'

He was practically on top of me now and yet I still couldn't respond. All I did was remain rigidly in one position with a nervously shocked smile fixed upon my face as a rush of blood flooded my head. He kept grinning, looking straight at me, and then, at the last second, he advanced one pace beyond where I was sitting to be greeted by an elderly woman who was positioned directly behind me. I looked at Jacquie and we both exploded into laughter.

It took me a good few moments to recover before remembering I still hadn't found Gary. And then I saw him, travelling at speed for a side door with his bicycle box-mounted wide-vehicle trolley. The next thing I knew I had landed in his arms in an ungainly heap of guffaws, telling him how I had nearly gone off with the wrong person. Things then turned even funnier when, referring to my bed-head hair, which is never good even at the best of times, Gary's first words to me were, 'I see the rooks are nesting early, Jose!'

15

Parakai, Auckland North, 15 June

To escape the traffic throngs of Auckland in one easy swoop, Gary and I took the suburban train out of the city. It seems not many people enter or escape Auckland by train because no one we asked, all of them locals, had any idea where we would find the main railway station despite the fact that it sits right on Queen Street, the commercial heart and main shopping drag of Auckland. Once inside Britomart, as the station is called (sounds more like a giant hypermarket) it was about as far removed from London's mainline railway stations as you could imagine. For a start, the place was deserted. It was like Waterloo or Paddington after a bomb scare or anthrax attack. But unlike Waterloo or Paddington, the station was spotless. It was all glass and silver and shiny mirrors everywhere. Made us feel like lifting the bikes instead of wheeling them lest we left an unsightly tyre track in our wake. And what's more it was cheap – $12 (about £4) for an hour's train ride for two people and two bikes. As the train rumbled through the suburbs past such buildings as King Dick's Liquormart and another splayed with the words 'INDUSTRIAL STRENGTH FOOD', the only other person to enter our carriage was the train guard, a friendly Indian from Bombay – the Mumbai Bombay, not the Bombay south of Auckland. I asked him how he liked New Zealand. 'I am liking it very much indeed,' he said. 'I am finding it a very empty place. I have come from living in a city of twenty million people to living in a country with a population of under four million!'

He told Gary and me he had emigrated here with his family over a year ago. 'It was very easy for us to come and live here,' he said. 'But we arrived here just in time because three months later the New Zealand authorities clamped down on immigrants and made it very much more difficult to apply for residency.' The only trouble he found was that, as a chemical engineer, he was over-qualified. So he had to take a job on the trains instead.

At Waitakere we left our empty train for another empty plat-form. In fact it was a mini platform, like a toy town platform only a few paces long, containing a locked shed. That was all. The only other person within sight was located about a mile down the road. He was a road mender, a big-handed Maori. With no useful sign-posts to be seen, I asked him to point me in the right direction for Kumeu and Parakai. For a moment I lost him because he went off at a tangent about various weights of road-crushing equipment. He then said, 'Bloody year it's been for weather, bro. Never seen this amount of road damage since I've been on the roads, eh?'

I said I couldn't agree with him more, before steering him back to the matter of directions. He then went on for some considerable time describing a complicated route to lead me on to State Highway 1 – just the road that I had dragged Gary all the way out here to avoid. I had a little banter with him and told him I didn't want to go the long way round on Death Highway 1; I wanted to go the quieter back route through Woodhill.

'What you want to go through Woodhill for, bro?' he asked.

'Because the road goes through it – on the direct route to Parakai,' I said.

He rubbed his chin with his big hand in deep thought and said, 'Woodhill? Hmmm. Well I guess yous want to take this road what we're standing on here now.'

So we did. And that's how we came to join a busy road loaded with overly close-passing tankers and logging lorries and Kenworth aggregate trucks to arrive in Kumeu, home of The Hot Breadshop. Unusually for a hot bread shop, The Hot Breadshop sold no hot bread but it did have hot pies – egg and bacon and mince and cheese, a hefty stack of which Gary hungrily devoured within minutes of our arrival. Along with The Hot Breadshop that sold only hot pies, the only other notable thing about Kumeu was the number of people hobbling about on crutches with a broken leg encased in plaster. What could have caused such an endemic fracturing of the limbs? Maybe they had all fallen over each other in a frantic stampede to reach the The Hot Breadshop when, during a lapse in concentration, it had errantly baked a batch of hot bread instead of hot pies?

We now appear to be camping in a swamp opposite Black Pete's Bar and Grill, which advertises 'Beer, Bait and Free Ice' for sale, apart from the ice, which is of course free. The swamp is in fact an official camping spot of the Parakai Aquatic Park, but although we are not camping directly in the aquatic department itself, you'd hardly know the difference due to the excessive amount of water underfoot. Everyone else on the site is sensible enough not to be sleeping in a tent, but that's because every other person is a permanent resident in a permanent caravan.

Having said that, a retired couple pulled up into the site in their vast bus-like motorhome, adorned with the words 'JUST UZZ'. I discovered that the Just Uzz twosome were country music fans and were here for a country music event occurring this weekend in nearby Helensville. They suspected it would be a washout as the forecast was, as usual, spectacularly wet.

This evening, Gary was just in the process of picking a big beetle with a body the size of a penknife out of his packet of Tim Tams (two-layered chocolate biscuits with a lightly gooey interior of chewy caramel) when one of the permanent residents, a man with a large angular body and very wet moccasins, asked uzz, I mean us, if he could buy our bikes for a couple hundred bucks. Gary was a little too keen for my liking (I think the wet has already got to him), but I held fast. I like my wheels and I was not going to sell them to a man in moccasins even if he did originally hail from Tilbury (on the Thames Estuary – the London Thames that is, not the Coromandel one), which meant we were able to share a little conversation about the delights of the Fobbing Landfill

Site that I happened to pass on these very same wheels back in the autumn of 2001.

Helensville, 19 June

We're making good progress – all of 3.5 km in four days. Well, it has been a bit wet. The first night in the tent it rained so hard we were almost set afloat into the chop of the Tasman. It was still raining the following day so, as we were wet already, we endeavoured to get a little wetter, though warmer, by wallowing in the virtually empty (save for the odd local Maori) hot thermal mineral pools of the neighbouring aquatic park. Night number two within tent was wet again, albeit with some improvement because the rain stopped for all of ten minutes – time enough to stick my weather-monitoring head out of the door to glimpse a dark sky with a small patch of clear sky studded with rain-washed stars.

On the third day we rose again to find no improvement in the weather but a need for a new location. So we packed a wet tent into a wet pannier and exerted ourselves the two miles until we reached Helensville.

Helensville is situated at the bottom of Kaipara (Maori for 'eat fern root') Harbour, New Zealand's largest harbour with a shoreline of over 3200 km (there are lots of indentations). The town used to be a bustling place. It was founded on timber that was conveyed on ships across Kaipara Harbour or floated to the town on huge rafts before being loaded on to wagons. Now most of Helensville seems to be run down and closed up. Antique shops and shops selling 'collectibles' are what appear to keep Helensville going, though who knows how as even most of these, like the Lock, Stock and Barrel Antiques and Memory Lane Furnishings, were boarded up. Gary and I sat in a cafe for a good chunk of the day watching the heavy logging rigs and Kenworth aggregate trucks stonking down the uninspirational main street in the pouring rain.

Finally, when the rain looked like it had no intention of stopping, we made a move up the road to Malolo House, a nineteenth-century kauri villa, which had rooms, dorm beds and camp spots. We were going to camp, but when the Dutch owner, who hailed from Hoek van Holland, told us the weather was set to get worse with damaging gale-force winds, we took one of the old, creaky wooden-floored rooms instead. Mr Hoek van Holland lived in the other half of the house with his children and Dutch wife and he told us he had been a contract cleaner all his working life. 'It was always a very busy and fast life,' he said. 'In Holland I had a BMW and would drive very fast everywhere. When I came to New Zealand I kept up the fast lifestyle. For me it was impossible to drive without speeding. But when I was caught the third time and lost my licence for three months, I thought maybe it was time to slow down. So we bought Malolo House just before Christmas and at last I am living at a sensible pace!'

Mr Hoek van Holland was right about the weather. The heavy rain turned to even heavier rain with a large helping of wild winds on the side. Gary and I were busy with tent-drying and sleeping-bag airing when a very weather-battered backpacker (a car-free one at that – rare species!) tumbled through the door. This was Ivor, a long-distance hiker who was walking up the coast to Cape Reinga.

Ivor was originally from Tauranga. A baker by trade, he had given up the profession many years ago because instead of starting baking at 4 a.m., like all bakers had for years, the times were changed to start baking at 10 p.m., which Ivor found too tiring because he was not a night person. So he started travelling and had not long since got back from Korea, where he spent two years working as a teacher. The current incarnation of Ivor sounds like a bit of an action man, travelling as he was with not much more than a bush knife, a billycan and a tarp shelter – though he was now thinking of relenting and buying a tent. The only food he carried was a 500-gram bag of muesli and maybe a packet or two of two-minute noodles, both of which he ate dry. He was having a rare rest here because, to take a shortcut across a mangrove swamp (in an Indiana Jones fashion), he had removed his boots and in the process cut his feet badly on oyster shells. He seemed quite excited to find some fellow travellers heading for Cape Reinga in all this winter rain and, presuming we were of a hardy nature, asked us how far we had travelled today.

'See that tree over there?' said Gary, pointing out of the window and getting Ivor to follow the line of his fingers. 'Well, we've come all the way from just beyond that point.'

Ivor thought we were joking.

'No, really, we have,' I said, trying to stop myself from laughing. 'Exhausting it was too!'

Ivor looked decidedly concerned and gave us a wide berth for the rest of the day. But before I packed myself off to bed, Ivor took me aside and gave me a word of warning.

'Beware this travelling as a couple thing,' he said. 'In my experience – and everyone I've known who's given it a go – it inevitably ends in disaster.'

Makarau Bridge, 19 June

It was still raining when we woke up this morning, but then the sun came out. Time to hit the road with gusto. And we did. At least for the first twenty kilometres. Progress then came to a rapid halt not far past Kaukapakapa (Maori for 'to swim with too much flapping') when, at Makarau Bridge – a rather splendid iron bowstring truss bridge, at that – we met Carol Forsyth, who invited us to spend the night in her big red barn of a home down by the river. Carol, who seemed to be about the only resident of Makarau Bridge, was a coastguard 'day skipper tutor'. After marrying at sixteen and travelling and working around New Zealand while living in a van for nine years with her two young children, Carol had spent most of her working life living on or around boats. Her jobs included being anything from master on a yacht in the 2003 America's Cup to skipper on the very same passenger ferry service that I'd caught to the Coromandel on New Year's Eve. Carol now lived with her teenage son Benjy and fat cat Widdles in their red barn, a home with a large high-roofed room centred around a big log-burning stove with the kitchen and bathroom and bedrooms (all with handleless doors) squeezed off to the sides.

Down the muddy track and in one of Carol's working outer barns lived her friend Fran. Fran's barn was a dusty cobwebbed jumble of a junkyard workshop-cum-studio. Sitting in pride of place was a 1914 clinker-built boat called *Butterfly* that she had found down in the nearby creek sinking into the mud. Fran was restoring the whole of the wooden boat herself and was currently in the process of a spot of caulking. She led us up the wonky ladder and into the cockpit and low-slung cabin so that she could talk wood with Gary. Gary, being a chippy and whose life revolves around ancient joints and the whole history of wood, was more than happy with this. Pouncing skittishly all over the boat was the more-kitten-than-cat ship's cat, Pappy. 'It's short for Papillon,' said Fran. 'French for butterfly.'

Fran, like Carol, had had a life of boats – more recently working as a skipper on one of the yachts used for ferrying some of the 450-odd film and supply crew around an undisclosed Pacific island location for the TV series 'Survival'. Along with being an experienced sailor, Fran was also an artist and writer and was known by both her maiden name, Whitworth, and married name, Bird. Her husband Cliff had been killed – electrocuted – when working on the electrics of their boat over thirty years ago.

Wellsford, 21 June

In a normal upright state of events, today would have been the longest day of the year, but being in an inverted position as we currently were, we had to make do with the shortest day instead. Still, despite Gary reminding me that we could be basking in the balmy heat of an English summer day (a bit of an oxymoron if you ask me), today has not been a day to be sneezed at.

It started out on a dry footing, at least for the first hour. While Gary mended one of Carol's broken bikes, suffering from an obstinate fixed freewheel and found lurking among cobwebs in yet another outer barn, Carol took me on a tour of her fig trees and orange trees and veg patch, a veritable jungle of silverbeet or, as we northern hemisphere dwellers call it, Swiss chard. As the rain pounded down, I made a triple batch of flapjack biscuits to leave in our wake for Carol and Fran. When the sun suddenly and unexpectedly burst out, Gary and I took this as a sign of our summer solstice and, dawdling no more, left Carol making fig jam and cranberry bread while we took off up the road for Wellsford.

We were now in the district of Rodney. To cycle to Northland from Auckland there was a choice of two roads: traffic-pounding Death Highway 1 or SH16, the quietly winding out-of-the-way road that Gary and I followed. Because the bulk of the traffic travelled on SH1, leading to multiple crashes and delays and jams, Transit New Zealand was trying to encourage motorists to branch out from the crowds and take to SH16 instead. Courtesy of Transit, the *New Zealand Herald* had recently run an article in an attempt to woo the stampeding hordes off SHI on to the more sedate SH16. In a letter to the *Herald* headed 'SH16 NO SOLUTION', Crispin Caldicott from the Kaipara Coast Highway begged to disagree with this suggestion. He wrote:

> Your article 'Just far enough from the crowds' is not entirely accurate. SH16 does meander through some very beautiful countryside. It does offer great views, and stopping to admire them at the absent lay-bys would be the only way to avoid a stressful ride. For many reasons it is not a good road, or a sensible alternative to SH1.
>
> There are no passing lanes, very few long straights, a high degree of curvature and some pretty hairy hairpin bends and hills just south of Wellsford. The 47 km from Kaukapakapa to Wellsford are without motoring facilities of any kind – there is at least a warning sign at the former heading north.
>
> Transit consistently advertises the road as an alternative route to the North, failing to point out that it is considerably longer and much slower. Shifting the problem away from SH1 has failed

to solve it – SH16 does not have the capacity for fast, heavy traffic.

And a good thing too. It was perfect for cycling. If a little hilly.

After a 5 km climb, we arrived at the top of Cleaseby Hill. The view from up here was tremendous, encompassing the mottled pasturelands of the valleys rolling downwards to the pewter-like reflections of the distant sea. To the east tatters of cloud hung like rags on the shadows of Conical Peak. All about, vast messy clouds were banking around the heavens.

It was at this scenic high spot where we stopped for some food in a dip by the road out of the wind. After eating we were having a frolicsome moment on the ground when the only car that had passed in a long time pulled up beside us. Out piled two elderly men. One was twig thin and bird-boned. The other had an almost spherical body, the flesh of his face sagging in hound-dog folds. Both men looked rather concerned. That is, until I jumped up and bid them a chirpy hello. They then looked quite relieved because, as one of them explained, they had seen two bikes on their sides in the verge with two bodies beside them and immediately presumed we'd had a bit of a spill. All quite touching really. After a bit of a chortle, they went on their way, assured that all was well.

Down the hill in Wellsford we were about to camp in a small green patch behind the Sun Valley Motor Lodge when the Sun Valley suddenly turned into a flooded valley, thanks to a violent thunderstorm that struck out of the blue with all-consuming fury. One minute a tui and a bellbird had been perched in a nearby tree singing their competitively fluted tunes with their usual indefatigable beauty, and the next the tree was thrashing around wildly in the chaotic wind as a tumultuous rain poured from the skies, hammering on the tinny rooftops and rushing down the gutters deafening all other sound.

Paparoa, 23 June

With Wellsford under water and all tuis and bellbirds blown into
oblivion, we gave the camping a miss and took a room at the motel
instead. The motel was owned by a friendly house-proud couple
called Bill and Sue, but I think they were a bit concerned about
two scruff-bag cyclists occupying one of their rooms, especially
when we stayed an extra day due to adverse weather conditions.
Sue was itching to get into our room under the guise of changing
our towels, but really because she wanted to see the filthy tip that
she presumed we had turned the room into. We told her to save on
the washing as we'd be fine using the same towels twice, which only
made her all the more agitated and determined to sneak a look
into the assumed bombsite of our room.

Actually, Sue had no real reason to be concerned. I veer towards
a tidy nature as I like to pile and file or, as Gary puts it, tidy things up
so effectively that no one can find anything. Gary, on the other
hand, prefers to upturn things and thrash through them in an
alarming manner before leaving every flung-about possession in a
splayed heap like a mini landfill. This time, however, because we
wanted to demonstrate to Sue our fastidiously pernickety leanings,
we went completely overboard by stacking all our panniers in neat
rows, making the bed to perfection, folding the towels, cleaning out
the shower and polishing the taps. We even gave the toilet paper that
carefully folded and pointy edge that you find cleaners doing to
toilet paper in hotels, presumably for aerodynamic reasons. For the
first time in history, Gary folded his clothes. In fact he didn't just
fold them, he ironed them out as best he could with his big builder's
hands before stacking them to perfection on the spare bed as if he
worked in the clothes-folding section of Benetton. Gary even
scolded me whenever he spotted my pile of scrupulously folded
clothes a millimetre out of line with the parallel edge of the bed or
saw an edge of plastic bag poking from the corner of a pannier.

All through our exaggerated tidying campaign, Gary acted in an
amusingly straight-faced manner which, combined with his absurd
shop-folding hand movements, evoked an almost continuous

cackle of hilarity from me. My cackles were further increased whenever we saw the shadowy form of Sue passing outside our large net-curtain frontage. Quite what she thought was going on within, I hate to imagine, but the thought of what she was thinking only made it all the funnier.

Tidying practices finalised, we at last ventured out into the flooded streets. At one point a hailstorm hit with such force that to avoid severe denting to our skulls we jumped into the doorway of the Phat and Phunky store to shelter from the savagery of the elements. Further up the street we paid a visit to Hammer Hardware for Gary to buy a jubilee clip, as he had noticed a crack in the frame of his rack braze-on attaching to the seat stay.

Wellsford, like Helensville, is a dull and humdrum place. It has one main street, its two rows of uninteresting shops separated by SH1, which scythe a vehicle-rushing path down the middle. Signs in the town tried their best to lure us down the road to something called Sheep World, where presumably you could have an 'experience' living in a world of sheep. Thankfully we never got further than the Four Square supermarket, because another hailing downpour forced us to take cover. Sheltering in the foyer of Four Square came as a lucky stroke of luck because, as it happened, it was by far the most interesting place in Wellsford – far more interesting even than the local museum (a room filled with everything that anyone had ever acquired and no longer wanted). The interest attained from the Four Square was down to its noticeboard advertising offerings along the lines of:

'PINECONES – $5 a bag'

'FIREWOOD FOR SALE – dry, split, blue gum.
$70 m^3 delivered'

'PIG
Sow raised for breeding 18mths old. Long White / Landrace –
nice temperament.
$295.00'

'I'M LOOKING FOR MY OWNER IN A GOOD HOME
I AM A YOUNG CALICO
I HAVE NO COLLAR
I'M VERY AFFECTIONATE
MY PAWS ARE UNIQUE, I HAVE AN EXTRA TOE ON EACH'

'TOMARATA PRE-LAMBING CALVING DOO
"The Academy Awards"
with the band "Sticky Fingers"'

'SALE
Clearance of Pre-loved clothing for adults and children'

As SH16 ran out at Wellsford, we had to head north for 30 km on Death Highway 1 – a nightmarish scene of thick-fast traffic and cyclist-hating logging trucks. Nor did the weather help matters: strong headwinds and heavy rain. At Brynderwyn, where we could turn off westwards on to a quieter road, we stopped to warm up and dry out at the Swinging Cow Cafe and were served by a woman wearing a cow cap that said, 'Love one an-udda'. A man bustling about behind scenes wore a cow hat that declared, 'There ain't no bull here but luvvabulls!!!' Oh dear, what had we let ourselves in for? Behind the counter hung cow-shaped blackboards serving

'MOO-SHAKES'. The tables were littered with bovine-flavoured jokes: What kind of cowfee do cows like? De-calfinated!! Why do cows wear bells? Because their horns don't work!! Why did the cow cross the road? To get to the udder side!!

We continued down the road to Maungaturoto, which according to the roadside sign was 'A real New Zealand town!' – though I'm not sure why as it looked pretty indistinguishable from all other New Zealand towns. Maybe it was the bright blue painted pillbox-like public conveniences that earned it such a title. Or maybe it was the hairdresser's called Urban Fringe that sat across the road from this concrete bunker. Whatever reason, it wasn't worth lingering around to find out as it was getting rainier and colder and windier by the minute.

By the time we arrived in Paparoa the weather had deteriorated even further so we dripped our sodden way through the doors of The Old Post Office hostel (an old kauri building circa 1903) where a worried-looking woman showed us to a small blue room with an electric blanket fire-hazard (circa 1952) on the bed. Down the hall blazed a pot-belly stove (with the door left open) to warm our cockles. Hazardous heating appliances aside, the most note-worthy thing about the part of the house we were in was the amount of dead possums used about the premises as wall and floor furnishings – most of them in the form of a sheet of leather adorned with a grimacing set of teeth at one end.

Maybe the worried-looking woman had been partaking in the Pahi Possum Patrol. I'd been reading about this particular possum patrol in the *Paparoa Press*, 'The Village in the Valley' local community magazine, which was paying its thanks and

> . . . congratulations to those people who've acted with a wee bit of dosh, and baited and trapped possums. Some have been surprised at how many possums they've been feeding, but not for long! That many hands make for light work is absolutely true. If everyone did their bit, we'd have possums, rats, ferrets, stoats, and weasels licked with relative ease.

The article went on to say that there were now 70 million possums running havoc all over New Zealand (seventeen-and-a-half per person!) consuming 21,000 tons of vegetation nightly – much of this being native trees. The paper said:

> Female possums are now carrying young that will appear in spring as joeys. If we can deal with these now, we'll have more than halved next year's population.

Further down the page, the reader was asked:

> Did you realise it takes about 20 Northland possums to supply 1 kg of fur? That 1 kg is worth $80+. The best fur is hand plucked from a warm possum and enough at a time to make the trip worthwhile.

We were then informed that Pahi Possum Patrol was assisting a local trap designer in his efforts to produce a multi-live trap capable of holding up to fifteen possums all caught with one lure they didn't get to eat.

> We hope to report outstanding success with these over winter. It is hoped they can make controlling possums a valuable activity even for amateurs. Remember – You can't get anywhere unless you 'spread ze legs'!

Matakohe, 24 June

Things got off to a bad start this morning. First we were awoken by more rain. Then, as we were preparing ourselves for another soaking, the worried-looking woman about the house accused me of stealing one of her lacy doilies off the top of the chest of drawers in our room (the previous night I had stored it in a drawer of the chest to prevent it getting ruined by our wet clobber and this morning had forgotten to remove it). Anyway, quite what she thought I might want with an old doily, I don't know, because doilies aren't a vital part of long-distant travel inner tent decoration. There again I could sport it like a skull cap, worn in fetching manner draped over my head beneath my helmet with the dangly lacy bits trailing over my eyes like an errant fringe.

Thirty seconds after leaving Mrs Happy, we stopped. A small Four Square store beckoned us to grace its shores. So, despite having not long finished breakfast, we were eating again. This time: two bags of liquorice, a packet of raisins and a bunch of bananas. Once refuelled to tackle the wet and to overcome the shock of being mistaken as a purloiner of doilies, we set sail once more, only to stop again a mere 6 km up the road. Trouble was, we got no further. It wasn't rain or food that stopped us in our tracks this time (though it was still raining and we did somehow demolish another bagful of food without any noticeable difficulty) but a large museum devoted to kauri, those vast and ancient trees comparable in age and size to California's giant sequoias.

New Zealand's economy was once heavily dependent on the exploitation of kauri timber and kauri gum. In fact, it wasn't that long ago that the whole of the north was covered in kauri forest. Then, along came Captain Cook who, on seeing his first kauri forest in 1769, wrote: 'The banks of the river were completely clothed with the finest timber my eyes have ever seen.' Uh, oh! Not for much longer. Human greed was all too soon to destroy something that had stood untouched for millennia. Acres upon acres of these magnificent trees, many of which had been on earth for over 2,000 years, were seen as lucrative money-makers. Cook's report inspired the Royal Navy to send ships to New Zealand to harvest these fantastically straight trees for spars. Then came the bushmen, gum-diggers and farmers, who felled kauri for their timber, dug up the gum to make resin and cleared the forests to form pasture.

The enthusiasm of those early settlers for harvesting (or decimating) this seemingly limitless resource, together with the privations they endured, was all part of the woody package that came with a wander around the Kauri Museum – a veritable temple to all things kauri, including a century-old steam-powered mill with life-sized mannequins, apparently modelled on the descendants of the men who worked the mill, busily slicing giant logs into rough-sawn boards.

A mind-boggling proportion of the museum was devoted to lumps of kauri gum (the amber-coloured fossilised resin of the kauri tree) and the uses of its resin, one of those being as an essential ingredient in the manufacture of Victorian false teeth. As the immigrants rapidly depleted the country's native kauri forests (by the early twentieth century less than 10,000 hectares remained), the new industry of kauri gum began to emerge. Resin, exuded by the trees, became a valuable commodity in the production of varnish and linoleum. It was mostly the Yugoslav immigrants who carried out the job of locating the lumps of resin by poking long rods into the ground near dead trees.

The largest kauri on record, though the trunk height is not known, grew at the head of Tararu Creek on the Thames coast, Coromandel, in the 1870s and had a diameter of 8.54 metres (28 feet) and a girth of 26.83 metres (88 feet). Further up this way, on the Kauri Coast, the largest kauri ever to be officially measured grew on Tutamoe Mountain near Dargarville. It had a diameter of 6.4 metres (21 feet), a girth of 20.12 metres (66 feet) and a trunk height of 30.48 metres (100 feet). S. Percy Smith, New Zealand's Surveyor-General, documented his reaction when first setting eyes on this tree:

> I was constructing the triangulation north of Auckland in 1870–74, and on one occasion was in advance of my men, they carrying the instruments and myself using my long knife to cut a track up one of the south-east spurs of Tu-ta-moe Mountain, when I saw (out of the corner of my eye, as it were) in a slight depression, what I took to be a cliff! But as I advanced a few paces I saw that I could look round it, and then it dawned on me it was a kauri tree of enormous size.

One of the most amusing moments at the museum occurred when Gary and I were walking back past the ticket desk. A very large and loud American tourist had just arrived to buy a ticket and the woman at reception asked him where he was from.

'The motorcamp down the road,' he said.

'I mean what country are you from?' asked the woman.

'Why d'yer wanna know that for, lady?' he asked.

'Because we're doing a survey,' replied the woman politely.

'What d'yer do with the survey?'

'We're not sure yet. We're just accumulating data.'

'So why d'yer wanna know where I'm from?'

'Knowing where our visitors are from is of great interest to us.'

'Well, I sure think it would be a good idea to work out what you're gonna do with the data before you trouble your visitors for the information.'

This uneasy exchange went on for a few more moments. I thought the woman, who was beginning to look more and more harried, was about to call for security. Instead she took a deep breath before attempting one more time to ask which country her difficult customer was from.

'Jeez! I'm from the USA, ma'am. So, are you gonna sell me a ticket or arrest me?'

Outside in the museum grounds stood Matakohe's simple 'pioneer school' – a one-room wooden building built in 1889, full of old wooden desks and a blackboard on the wall at the front. The room was barred off, but in the entrance hung a framed list of 'RULES FOR TEACHERS – 1915', which sounded more like punishment before you'd even started:

1. You will not marry during the term of your contract.
2. You are NOT to keep company with men.
3. You MUST be home between the hours of 8 p.m. and 6 a.m. unless attending a school function.
4. You MAY NOT loiter downtown in icecream stores.
5. You MAY NOT travel beyond the city limits without the permission of the chairman of the board.
6. You MAY NOT ride in a carriage or automobile with any man unless he is your father or brother.
7. You MAY NOT smoke cigarettes.

8. You may not dress in bright colours.
9. You may UNDER NO CIRCUMSTANCES dye your hair.
10. You must wear AT LEAST two petticoats.
11. Your dresses must NOT be any shorter than two inches above the ankle.
12. To keep the schoolroom clean you must:
    - Sweep the floor at least once daily
    - Scrub the floor with hot soapy water, at least once a week
    - Clean the blackboard at least once a day
    - Start the fire at 7 a.m. so that the room will be warm by 8 a.m.

Talking of schools and length of dresses, I spotted a small piece in the *New Zealand Herald* headlined: 'SKIRTING DISASTER'. It was all about a school back home, Kesgrave High, near Ipswich, which had banned girls from wearing skirts and ordered them to switch to uniforms with long trousers. Two years ago the school had asked parents to ensure that their girls' skirts were just above the knee. But it seems that since that time the hemlines had crept up to 'inappropriate' levels. 'We simply do not want our girls going outside with a "come-hither look",' said the governor, Margaret Young. The school had 1600 pupils, a large number of whom cycled in every day. This was apparently upsetting Madge because she said that the short skirts looked 'dreadful' on girls who cycled.

All this reminded me of the hoo-ha that occurred back in my own school days. The direct route to school was a return cycle of twenty miles. Because I was keen on cycling, I would often go the indirect route to boost my daily mileage to nearly half a century – as I believe they call it in the trade. Trouble was, I was the only pupil who cycled to school and the school didn't take kindly to this. They thought it was unladylike behaviour, especially as I refused to wear the school uniform skirt while cycling. But then I like to think I had a point: short skirts are not the most practical kit to be sporting on a bike, particularly on icy winter mornings when plummeting down 1:4 hills – a procedure that would turn my legs purple with cold from ankle to upper thigh. So I wore my elder brother's ripped jeans instead. And because I wasn't arriving at school in school uniform I was punished. So I began to cycle almost all the way to school in jeans, and then at the last moment would leap over a wooden five-bar gate into a nearby field and change into my skirt behind a hedge. All went well for a while until, apparently, one of the male teachers spotted me doing this (what, I'd like to ask, was he doing peeping at me anyway?) so I was punished again. Didn't stop me from cycling, though.

Dargaville, 29 June

Oh no! What's this? Not more capitals! This one is Dargaville, 'Kumara Capital of the World'. Dargaville was once a thriving kauri timber port, reached after a difficult journey across the treacherous Kaipara Bar and 64 km up the winding and strongly tidal Wairoa River. Today the kumara (a sweet potato) is grown extensively in the area. The Maori have always had a soft spot for kumara, being a staple Polynesian food. It was brought to New Zealand by the migratory canoes of the Maori from their Polynesian home, Hawaiki. In bygone days, they used to eat it raw but, according to Maori legend, when Rongo-maui (who seems to have been an early day type of TV chef) returned from the heavens and informed all his viewers (so to speak) about the joys of cooking, he instructed that kumara should be baked in underground ovens, otherwise 'men would have lived like birds, insects, animals and other tribes of people who eat their food raw'.

Kumara weren't only cooked underground. They were also baked in the embers of the fire, steeped in seawater or dried in the sun, or stone boiled in a *huahua* – whereby food was cooked by dropping hot stones into containers holding the food and water. Cooked kumara were served in flax (phormium) baskets with garnishings on top of dried shark, boiled fish or any savoury morsels that could be rustled up. The whole kumara plant, roots and all, was boiled in a gourd and the liquid was applied to pimples and skin eruptions, or drunk to assist feverish conditions.

*

I'm almost feeling a need to get my hands on a gourd myself and feeding the boiled kumara liquid to Gary, who is on his sick bed suffering from feverish conditions. I think it may be an allergy to cycling. It's come as a bit of a bitter blow to me to discover he's not as keen as me on cycling almost continually uphill through almost continuous rain. Heaven knows why. I find it quite a splendid pastime, myself. Especially when you haven't got anything better to be doing with yourself.

That's why tonight is going to be our fifth night in Dargarville: to try to get Gary into some sort of functioning order again. I must admit that Gary being ill is really quite amusing. You know what men are – a simple cold becomes man flu, and man flu becomes a terminal death-bed scenario. I've been acting as Florence Nightingdew to my patient, mopping his brow with a cool cloth while he mumbles away deliriously.

Last night I said with urgent tone, 'Do you think you'll survive until morning?'

'Only if the good Lord permits my passage through the night!' groaned Gary, with such dramatic effect that I couldn't stop laughing for the next half an hour. In fact, Lords permitting passages through the night have now become a holiday stock phrase along with 'Good as', 'Sweet as' and 'Yiis! Fin-*tis*-tic!'

For the last few nights the sanatorium (soon morgue) has been an old insulated railway goods wagon that a century ago was used for transporting meat, fruit and dairy products. The owner of the grand-sounding Dargarville Holiday Park (for which read 'car park in the middle of town in midst of mass building construction') has a thing for old goods wagons and, by cramming inside them a couple of bunk beds and a micro toilet and shower, has converted them into liveable cabins. Saying that, we've been doing most of our living (or in Gary's case, semi-living) on the wooden veranda that juts out in front of the wagon. Our vista is quite marvellous: along with a busy side street lined with warehouses and auto-shops, we look out on to the rears of two beaten-up flat-bed trucks belonging to the Maori road-building team dwelling in the wagon opposite.

Dargaville has long been known as a cow-town and is now trying hard to shake off that image. But I think it could have a battle on its hands; it's a mostly remarkably unremarkable service town for the region's farmers. Dargarville's saving grace is the wide Wairoa ('when you can take the bridge') River. Even the local radio station is called Big River FM (radio catchphrase: 'From the banks of the River to the mouth of the Big Stuff').

My patient and I have spent many hours sitting on a bench by the riverbank watching small private planes heading inland up river only to crash into a nearby hillside. At least, that's what it looks like they are all doing from where we are sitting. Our exaggerated intakes of breaths and urgent rising to feet, coupled with a desperate smack of hand to the forehead, whenever we spot another potential air disaster has drawn quite a crowd of onlookers. We manage to fool them for a while before they wander away looking rather baffled. It's all most amusing.

Here's a selection of Dargarville's main street shops: Just Jewellery; Molly's Fashions with Peter Rabbit Children's Wear; Lynleys Lingerie and Linen; Mags n' More; Dargaville Sports Hunting and Fishing – which, I might add, has 'HUNTING SEASON' painted in large letters across the front window. Beneath this, written in bright eye-catching paint, are this hunting season's offers: ESCORT AUTOS $799; 5 SHOT PUMP GUNS $499; DECOYS $79.95; AMMO $99. At first I thought they were advertising old Ford Escorts for sale and was about to suggest to Gary that maybe he could buy it – would save all this messing around on bikes in the rain business – when I realised the Escort Auto was actually a ferocious killing machine. Which on reflection, I suppose is not that much different than a car. Anyway, it was in Mags 'n' More that Gary picked up a magazine called *Outdoor*. On first glimpse, I presumed it was a sort of travel–tramping–camping mag – the 'mag' I refer to here being of course the magazine of a periodic paperback publication containing topical articles etc. nature, and not the metal case holding several cartridges used in some automatic firearms. But then I saw that under the title it said, 'NUMBER 1 FOR BIG GAME HUNTING', and tried to woo potential buyers by advertising across the cover: 'WIN YOURSELF A REMINGTON MODEL SEVEN SHORT ACTION 7MM ULTRA MAG'. Inside was a double-page spread devoted to children hooked on hunting. Beneath the title 'KILWELL KIDS PHOTO MIX' (I'm not sure whether this is a take on kids killing well or whether there is an actual place called Kilwell) were rows of photos of children, one as young as four, triumphantly holding aloft a rifle in one hand and the severed head of a boar or pig or goat or deer in the other. They looked like mini Rambos, dressed in combat camouflage and grinning with a murderous look of evil triumph in their eyes. All quite scary. Don't they have Sindy Dolls around these parts?

In the shoot-to-kill *Outdoor* magazine there was also plenty about 'Bow Hunting'. Looked quite savage. Think I'm going to invest in a flak jacket before I next venture into the bush for a pee behind a ponga fern. And I'll keep my cycling helmet on for good measure. All in the name of life preservation. Anyway, I certainly feel for any four-legged creatures up here in this neck of the woods. They don't stand a chance. Not when the Kiwi hunter's motto is: 'If it's brown, it's down.' Just this morning I saw a ute (the Kiwi name for

a 'utility vehicle' or pick-up) with a bumper sticker that said, 'DON'T BE A BOAR: GO SHOOT A PIG'.

The benefit of all this rain has been a surplus of rainbows – whole ones, fat ones, double-decker ones. And if you want a rainbow, you've got to put up with the rain, as I believe Dolly Parton once put it. When it's been raining too hard to sit beside the river watching planes crash and causing general crowd chaos, we've planted ourselves in the Blah, Blah, Blah Cafe and Bar where my sickly patient has worked hard at taking his medication – copious quantities of grandé mocha coffee and vast slabs of chocolate and passion-fruit cheesecake. It was over one such Blah, Blah, Blah session that Gary told me his granddad used to weigh crisp packets and if they were underweight he sent them off with a letter of complaint to the manufacturers, who in return sent him a boxful back. The things you learn when you sit around convalescing.

Kaihu, 30 June

Every morning at 7 a.m. on the noddle, we've been awoken by the shattering alarm of an air raid siren. This was not the Third World War breaking out but the Dargaville fire brigade. Our goods wagon motorcamp owner man said that for years the fire brigade had tested their alarms at 7 a.m. without fail. But when the firemen were issued with pagers they put a stop to the practice. The silent mornings didn't last long, though. There was a public outcry by local residents complaining that they used the siren as an alarm to leap out of bed and that when it stopped they were subsequently late for work. So the fire brigade restarted the daily wailings and everyone was happy again.

I forgot to tell you that when cycling to Dargaville a few days ago, we passed a high fenced-off area with a sign stuck on the front saying 'GOLDEN MILE OSTRICH FARM'. Funny ostriches, if you ask me, because this variety came with coats of fluffy white wool and four legs. There's been no sign of any ostreep this morning, but in the little cafe at Kaihu I did spot an advert in the window saying:

INDIAN OR TAMWORTH BOER WANTED FOR MATING
FOR RENT OR WILL BUY

I thought that sort of thing was supposed to be illegal these days. But then I suppose we are out in the sticks where you can probably get away with anything once tucked out of sight behind a thicket of mamaku ferns.

Have I mentioned the rain in New Zealand yet? Well, this morning it swept up from the sea, covering the whole land in its methodical advance. I don't mind torrential rain because once I've got acclimatised to its ridiculous ferocity it can be quite stupidly fun. But not only was this rain torrential, it was also numbingly cold. And although this quiet (save for the odd logging, aggregate and cattle trucks) road had its hilly moments, it wasn't hilly enough to get any internal core temperatures hot enough to warm up the frozen extremities. Sometimes the rain enhances the countryside far more than the sun, and up here the greenness of the land and the dripping woods and filigrees of mist suspended over the hills was startlingly beautiful. Being winter, many of the trees are bare now, clawing grey-fingered at cold wet winds.

During our aqueous ride we came across Kaihu Farm Hostel, stuck out in the middle of nowhere. It advertised itself as 'perfect for cyclists'. The hostel, maybe, but not the hill that led down to it, which was as steep as a mineshaft. I'm not looking forward to the ride out in the morning.

So here we are now, in the hostel, trying to dry out. Appropriately there's an anonymous poem stuck to the wall in the kitchen that says:

It rained and rained
The average fall was well maintained

And when the tracks were simply bogs
It started raining cats and dogs
After a drought of half an hour
We had a most refreshing shower
And then the most curious thing of all
A gentle rain began to fall
Next day also was fairly dry
Save from a deluge from the sky
Which wetted the party to the skin
And after that the rain set in.

Omapere, 30 June

I was nearly mown down by an excitable herd of stampeding cattle today. They came en masse, hurtling down the road towards me with cow-dogs and farmers on quads and trail bikes in hot pursuit. I think they were making a break for freedom.

The weather has been wild and wet for most of the day. On exposed ridges and hills the punching wind slammed into us with such force that it was impossible to cycle without being thrown off the road or under the wheels of a logging truck. Even pushing the bike along the road at a forty-five degree angle took immense effort because of the thumping wind gusts smashing into us from the side. At one point I was blown clean over like a pack of cards, my heavy body-squashing bike landing squarely on top of me.

Despite the weather, Waipoua (Maori for 'water that comes from night rain') Kauri Forest was wonderful. Dense dripping bush as green and impenetrable as a jungle enveloped the quiet and narrow twisting hilly road. On several occasions we stopped to walk into the kauri forest and stand insignificantly beneath the likes of the mighty Tane Mahuta and Te Matua Ngahere, or what the Maori call the Lord of the Forest and the Father of the Forest. These vast, ancient, serene entities – Tane Mahuta is the country's largest living kauri with a height of 51 metres (168 feet) and a girth of 14 metres (46 feet), its first branch is 12 metres (39 feet) off the ground – have been on earth almost as long as Christianity and were mature well before the first humans arrived in New Zealand.

Among the kauri forests lives the kauri snail, a type of large carnivorous snail that can make short work of worms – sucking them in like a strand of spaghetti. Kauri snails are found only in New Zealand (but with relatives in Tasmania and Victoria) and their shell is a dark green flattened spiral around 8–10 cm in diameter. These snails, which can live for up to forty years and have the ability to climb kauri trees and travel hundreds of metres while foraging for worms at night, have phenomenal radulae – rasp-like structures of tiny teeth used for scraping food particles off a surface and drawing them into the mouth. Each radula comprises between 150 and 200 rows of teeth, with up to 700 teeth per row. The teeth at the front are worn down or dislodged at a rate of three to five rows per day. The whole radula moves around, bringing fresh teeth into play while replacements are formed at the back. This, in effect, makes kauri snails like the slow-moving chainsaws of the forest.

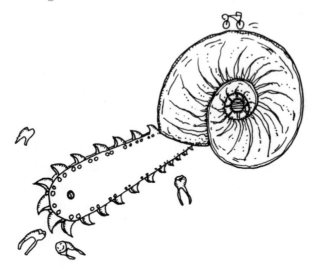

Other residents partial to the kauri forests, and which (like so many of New Zealand's ancient fauna) display gigantism, include native earthworms that can exceed one metre in length. And then there are the wetas, New Zealand's most primitive ancient creatures, having changed little in the last 190 million years. The wingless giant weta is the heaviest insect in the world, weighing almost as much as a thrush. Despite its size, the giant weta is harmless (it's related to grasshoppers) and unable to bite. But I bet that's down to it being of New Zealand stock. Were the weta to be found in Australia it would undoubtedly be a hazardous killing machine, capable of sawing off your head with torturous ease.

Between Motukaraka and Kohukohu, 2 July

After two nights spent beside the mountainous golden sand dunes at the head of Hokianga Harbour, we cycled on through the thrashing wind and rain following the twisting harbour and mangrove swamps. At the head of Rawene Peninsula perched the tiny town of Rawene, whose timber buildings cantilevered over the waters of Hokianga Harbour in fetching style. For such a small and out-of-the-way place, Rawene had a strangely large hospital plonked on top of the hill. Back in the 1820s, this spot was a site for a proposed settlement, but when the English settlers arrived it rained so relentlessly they thought 'sod this for a lark' and, refusing to stay, sailed on to Sydney instead.

While Gary wandered off to the local chippy to get what turned out to be dory and chips, I had a look around and came across a white wooden building with a plaque on the wall that said, 'Dog Tax War 1898'. I soon discovered this building was the old police station where the Mahurehure Hapu of the Ngapuhi (the local tribe) refused to pay a tax on dogs – a refusal that led to the last armed conflict in New Zealand.

All this part of Hokianga Harbour is literally a backwater, with precious little employment now that timber milling and farming have declined. In other words, it's a perfect cycling route with virtually traffic-free roads and a jaunty little ferry to take across the choppy harbour from Rawene to the Narrows just south of Kohukohu.

*

Tonight Gary and I are sleeping in a wooden cabin surrounded by sheep and groves of orange and grapefruit and tall wind-waving trumpets of yellow canna lilies at a backpacker's eco lodge called The Tree House.

The only other people staying are an ill English couple. They've spent the past five months backpacking around various South Pacific islands and suspect they've picked up some incurable disease. They said they'd tried 'every drug under the sun' to try to cure themselves, but nothing is working. 'We've got no energy,' said the girl, 'so we're just here to chill.' I told them about the hospital-in-the-middle-of-nowhere handily situated across the harbour, which might be able to sort them out. They were initially keen to pay it a visit until they discovered it would cost them all of $14 to take them and their car across. I said they could leave the car behind and walk and it would then only cost them $2 each. They said they couldn't be bothered with that, so we left them to die.

The Tree House is owned by Phil and Pauline. Phil (who built the place himself) said that just after they had opened, an American cyclist who had spent the night at the lodge sneaked away without paying. Phil gave chase and found him waiting for the ferry over to Rawene. 'He said he forgot to pay and handed me a $100 bill, presuming I wouldn't have the change on me, hoping that would put me off. But I simply returned to the lodge to get change, making sure I took a very long time so that he'd miss his ferry. Which he did! I gave him a bit of a lecture, telling him how I had built the place myself and that they were cheap rates anyway. Then, when I got back home, I got on the "phone tree" and made a couple of calls to the next couple of hostels on his route warning them about an American cyclist who likes to get away with a free night. They then made a couple of calls warning hostels further down the line. And that way, we spread the word!'

Herekino, 3 July

About 1200 years ago, there were around 12 million kiwis (the birds, not the fruit or the people) in New Zealand. Today there are only 7,000. But last night we heard the hoarse whistling cry of one and this morning we found a kiwi feather outside our door. We're taking this as a good omen. Even if it is still raining.

There wasn't a lot happening when we stopped up the road in Kohukohu. The only signs of life came from the small store where the owner was playing loud country music (Dwight Yoakum – 'Guiii-tars and Cadillacs') to no one but himself. Gary bought the country music-liking owner out of chocolate and then we stepped outside to see the only other form of life around: a hirsute hippy in pointy cowboy boots pulling up helmet-less at the store on a long trike motorbike. Every other building in Kohukohu was closed – every other building being the Waterline Cafe and the Palace Flophouse and Grill.

These days there's not a lot to Kohukohu. It's a far cry from the 1830s when the area was the heart of New Zealand's timber indus-try, making Kohukohu a busy port and the main means of transporting all the straight and knot-free kauri that had been felled for ship spars. Being such a thriving milling town (the double mill employed 5,000 men capable of milling 6 million feet annually) Kohukohu was a bustling place full of wooden buildings. Then fire struck. The hotel was the first to go when it became engulfed in flames in 1900 and had to be pulled into the tide to prevent the blaze from spreading. Twenty years later, the general store caught fire; the flames arched across the road and destroyed the library, the reading room and the Courthouse. Thirty years after this, another hotel and a supply store, a bakery, tearoom and dressmaker's shop were burnt to the ground. Then in 1967, Andrewes Store caught fire and was destroyed along with the Bank of New South Wales, the tobacconist, a men's hairdresser, the police station, tearooms and the offices of a lawyer, a dentist and an electrician. Some of the buildings might have been saved if the tide had been in at the time. As it was, the fire hoses were not long enough to reach the water. All that remained were the post office, the library and the butcher's shop.

Despite the torrential downpours, it was a lovely ride over rolling hills to Herekino, passing through bush and undulating farmland and heady-smelling groves of eucalyptus and cedar. The only vehicles on the road were battered utes with dogs chained to their rears. Kingfishers were everywhere, either perched on poles or flitting around like blue-green starbursts. There was no shortage of herons either, standing stock-still admiring their reflections in unmoving water or ensconced in magnificently ponderous-winged pterodactyl flight. Every field seemed to have a couple of Paradise ducks releasing their mixture of high-pitched calls and deeply discordant warning cries whenever they spotted us breezing by.

Tonight we're staying at the Tui Inn, a bit of a back-to-basics hunting shack with no electricity, a long-drop toilet and a handful of soiled mattresses dumped on the floor. The kitchen has candles, a singing kettle and a grimacing boar's head above the fireplace. Over the door is strapped an eight-foot, two-man salmon-belly crosscut saw. The inn belongs to Grant, a real backwoods country boy who seems to live for hunting. Nailed to the top plank of his long sheds are a score or more of boars' skulls, while hanging from a hook outside his house is a fly-buzzing cow's carcass. A neighbour brought the cow over because it was diseased, so Grant cut its throat and strung it up to drain. 'Can't have good meat going to waste, you know, bro,' he said. Grant is married to Tangi, a Maori, and runs hunting adventures for those in need of a kill. The visitor's book has comments from satisfied customers singing Grant's praises and esteeming the virtues of possum shooting and boar killing. One American wrote: 'It sure felt good to stick that knife in the pig.'

Kaitaia, 4 July

Was awoken this morning by the sound of Grant hacking into the hanging cow carcass with an axe. Grant's yard was covered in severed bones, sending his heap of dogs into crazed excitement. When Gary and I appeared, Grant said, 'Awright, bro?'

Yes, lovely, thanks.

More rain, mingled with welcome bursts of steamy sun. Climbing up one hill that skirted Herekino Forest we passed beneath two pairs of trainers, tied together at the laces, dangling on the power lines above our heads. We took this as another good sign. A good sign of what, I'm not quite sure. Maybe of the art of power-line shoe-hanging. And then the rain started. Again. Still in the middle of nowhere, I was chased down the road by a yappy mutt in an Elizabethan ruff. Quite where it had sprung from, I don't know. Nor do I know why it felt the need to sport a bonnet in the shape of a satellite dish. I suspect it was on the run from a vicious needle-jabbing vet.

There were cars all along this stretch of road. Not live ones, but corroding corpses, abandoned in fields and rivers. Gary and I stopped to admire a small rusting cuboid wall of oxidising metal, comprising twenty-two cars tightly compressed into an impressively compact space. If the world's got to have cars, this is how I like to see them: crushed into blocks, impotent to do any damage. Better still, they could be melted down and built into bicycles.

It is a big Maori area around here; they live in mostly ramshackle and shabby abodes with old armchairs and tattered sofas pulled out on the veranda and yards full of car wrecks and rooting pigs. Despite all the rain and occasional cold, we were in subtropical climes up here and the cluttery homes and worn three-piece suites on the deck were all very South Pacific island. One veranda even had a ropey piano propped against a wall, and there was always someone plonked in one of the armchairs, usually male and sturdily built, watching the world go by. One cheery young woman, hanging up washing, saw us swoosh by and, waving, called, 'Whes yous goin'?'

Gary called back, 'North!'

'Yous ridin' north?' she replied with an excitable shriek, 'Waaaaaaaaa!'

*

My camping days seem to have fallen by the wayside. Our top priority for accommodation in Kaitaia was to find a cheap motel with Sky TV so we could watch the Tour de France. Oh, and an electric blanket would be nice, too, as the nights are getting rather chilly, you know. Fortunately, Kiwis like their electric blankets. (See what a bad influence Gary is having on me? Two months ago I thought nothing of sleeping out in minus 7°C. Now when I take a room, I check the bed for wired heating devices and the television for satellite capabilities.)

Since arriving in Kaitaia, the rain has been torrential. But for some reason there's a pink van driving around with a pig painted on the side brandishing the sunburn advice: 'ONLY PIGS LOOK GOOD PINK! SLIP – SLOP – SLAP –WRAP.' I suspect they're a bit mixed up round here.

Kaitaia (promisingly, Maori for 'food in abundance' – must be due to the giant Pak 'N' Save just around the corner from the motel) is the main town of the far north of Northland. It was founded by Croatian settlers who came here in search of kauri gum. A number of local signs are still written in English, Maori and Serbo-Croatian, reflecting the influx of Dalmatian settlers.

Nearly every face up here is a Maori face – some of them with impressive full-face tattoos. The town has swags of men hanging around on street corners, smoking and drinking. Some of them are plainly off-their-heads drunk. The owner of our motel, a fat and ham-faced Pakeha, said that the dole is the biggest employer up here. 'A lot of these Maoris are the second or third generation in their family to be out of work. They've got no need to work. Their house gets passed down from generation to generation and they can claim the dole for their daily dollars. Most of them have a boat, or else they work the boats and get paid under the counter.'

Walking around town we saw cafes and clubs with signs on their doors saying: 'No gang insignia. No patches. No beanies, wellies, muddy boots, torn clothing'. Which just about ruled out every inhabitant of Kaitaia.

This whole area, known as the Far North, has no counterpart in New Zealand. For a start the subtropical climate places it apart from the rest of the country. Known as the 'cradle of New Zealand history', the whole district has cultural importance for the native Maori inhabitants and historical importance for Europeans. Early whalers, sealers, missionaries, explorers and settlers made big impacts up here, but despite its early start off the blocks, European development continued at a much slower pace here than in many other parts of New Zealand. Compared with other areas of the country, the Far North's social and economic development has been quite different, owing to a long period of neglect. From the beginning there was little interest in the interior because the few roads were often impassable and so transport was by coastal vessels calling at river and estuary ports. Small settlements grew up in semi-isolation and independence.

When the Church Missionary Society established a Maori mission station in Kaitaia in 1833, they purchased around 260 hectares of land from the Maori. But instead of giving the Maori money, they handed them articles of trade: 80 blankets, 70 axes, 30 iron pots, 40 plain irons, 30 pairs of scissors, 10 shark hooks, 2,000 fish hooks and 50 pounds of tobacco. Sounds more like the products of a car boot sale than a commercial transaction for a hefty lump of land.

Kaitaia, Northland, 7 July

We've been here three days now and the rain has been relentless. It did stop today for a few brief moments, prompting us to mount up and take off on a side trip to Ahipara – a scattered village at the southernmost section of Ninety Mile Beach. This vast stretch of beach, receding into the far distance as a haze of misty sea-spray, is a little too optimistically named; it is in fact more like 90 kilometres (56 miles). Still, it is an amazingly long beach, referred to by the Dutch explorer Abel Tasman as a 'desert coast'. The sand below the high water mark is almost concrete hard, making the beach popular as an alternative road to the north for 4WDs and specially adapted tour buses.

I was keen to cycle up the beach before joining the dirt road for the final leg up to Cape Reinga before cycling back down the middle of the peninsula on the road to Kaitaia. Gary, though, thought it would be more sensible and far less hard work to do the whole thing by bus. I looked at him, thinking he was joking. But no, he was perfectly serious, which came as a bit of a shock. 'We don't have to cycle everywhere, Jose,' he said. This came as even more of a shock because I've got it programmed into my system that we do. I couldn't travel to the top of New Zealand by tourist bus! That would be far too unexcitingly easy. Think of all those nooks and crannies only seen from a bike that would pass us by. What's more, we would miss out on feeling all this heavy winter rain splooshing off our skin. There again, maybe that's not such a bad thing.

Gary and I left the motorhomes parked up on the beach (motorhomes with names like RAMBLIN' ROSE; AWAYAGEN; IMAROMA) and cycled back to Kaitaia, where we discussed further the final assault on the north. Gary was quite happy to give Cape Reinga a complete miss, unlike me, who was as keen to cycle to the very north of North Island as I was to cycle to the very south of South Island. But I was forgetting that Gary, who'd been working hard, building buildings in all weathers virtually every day for almost twenty years, had come out here for a holiday, not an endurance test. Whereas cycling for me is a way of life, cycling for Gary is a fun activity to do from time to time, as long as there are no hills, no wind and the sun's shining. A bit of a tall order for New Zealand, then.

So we came to a compromise: we would take the bus up to the top and cycle back. But when we walked round to the two bus companies, Sand Safaris and Harrison's Cape Runner, and were told by some unhelpful people that they wouldn't take our bikes, we had to think again. A very friendly Bet in the tourist office came to our help. She thought her mate Lyall, a local farmer, could help us out. So by our slipping him a few dollars into his back pocket, that's what's going to happen. Lyall is scheduled to pick us up tomorrow morning at 9.15 in his dark green Mitsubishi ute.

Waitaki Landing, 8 July

True to Bet's word, Lyall appeared and we threw our heap of bikes and panniers into the back of his pick-up and took off up Ninety Mile Beach. Lyall was a good sort, a cattle farmer with 540 of the beasts, which he kept down on a farm near Ahipara. Many years ago he did the big Kiwi OE (Occidental Earthworm) thing but got no further than London, where he stayed for months working in pubs in Potters Bar and Stevenage.

'The pub owner told me not to serve "travellers",' said Lyall. 'I wasn't quite sure what he meant by this because I felt travellers were people like me, and if I turned up in a pub I'd feel pretty hard done by if the barman refused to serve me. So I served them. I remember the landlord coming up and saying to me, "I told you, mate. Don't serve travellers. They're gippos."'

We kept driving up the wide and empty expanse of spray-lashed sand, me itching to be out there riding along it, but doing an admirable job at keeping my mouth shut. Every now and then we would pass a small group of Maori bent over digging in the sand. Whenever they spotted us they would suddenly straighten up, trying to look all innocent. Lyall told us they were illegally digging for toheroa, a shellfish delicacy prized since ancient Maori times.

'They eat them raw, steamed open or cooked up in frittas,' said Lyall.

Along with the shellfish, there were also a lot of shags along Ninety Mile Beach. To me shags are wonderful diving birds, but Lyall had a mate, a fisherman, who, as Lyall put it, 'hates the bastards.' Lyall explained why.

'He accuses them of eating all the smaller fish so he used to drive up here in his ute and hang out the window with his semi-automatic and shoot as many as he could. He hated them so much he'd empty the whole mag into a shag. After a while, he was sure the shags began to recognise his vehicle because they would fly off when ever they saw him coming!'

Lyall, a tough-looking bloke, told us that he had a sister who lived on a sheep station in Queensland. Although he liked his sister well enough, he'd never been to visit her. In fact, he'd never even been to Australia. Said he didn't fancy it.

'Why not?' I asked.

'It's the snakes,' he said. 'One of my mates used to live in Australia and when he came back to New Zealand he told me that 75 per cent of Aussies have got a python living in their attic. Then there're all those snakes and spiders that lurk in the toilet. I can do without living in a country where you have to check under the toilet seat every time you want to take a shit!'

Along with foreign snakes, Lyall also had a deep aversion to possums, or 'squash 'ems' as they are more fondly known once splayed out on the road.

'Man, I hate the bastards!' he said, addressing them with similar hatred as his mate to the shags. 'If I see one in front of me, I will do everything possible to flatten the bugger.'

His wife used to cringe when he slaughtered them this way, but she had hardened up considerably, so much so that when she was at the wheel she took immense pleasure in aiming at the possum herself. According to Lyall, the trick when driving was to 'aim for the possum's head, mate, and listen for the double boomph of the front and back wheel hitting'. He explained that this method resulted in a clean kill requiring no hosing of the ute's bodywork. I must admit that, due to the slower pace of life on a bicycle, the efficiency of this method could be seen to be very effective, judging by the large number of road kill possums we passed in the road suffering from 'Dunlop Disease'.

Come to think of it, when riding in New Zealand, it often feels as if cyclists have little more than the status of a possum. Motorists appear to hate us two-wheeled travellers as much as they do their pesky Australian import-of-a-rodent. Gary and I all too frequently found ourselves the target of this manic possum-like killing charge, the direction only being altered at 10 to 15 metres from the point of impact by a wild swerve accompanied by frenetic honking and shouting as the driver-cum-hunter vented his anger at not being able to pull off the kill. This abuse was often used in conjunction with the passenger hurling a cocktail of hand signals, spit or empty 'stubbies' (small glass beer bottles) at the cowering cyclist.

Quick but nonetheless highly scientific tests carried out during idle moments (e.g. roadside toilet stops) concluded that, yes, from a distance of several miles, a heavily panniered bike could bear a faint resemblance to a possum straying on to the sacred 'I've-paid-my-taxes' stretch of tarmac of a motorist's domain. And thus, complying with the Kiwi hunter's mantra of 'If it's brown, it's down', the accelerator would be mashed flat to the floor in a frenzied attempt to eliminate this unlawful intruder.

Such hazards fare lowly in the fear stakes when compared with the simultaneous passing of opposing 50-tonne logging trucks. The saving grace has been our handlebar-mounted mirrors – a must for the cyclist in New Zealand, for the trick is, on spotting a fast approaching logging truck from the rear, to bale out – get off the road as far as possible even where this means into a ditch, up a bank, through a hedge, into the bush or over a bridge. These thundering multi-wheeled monoliths stop for no one.

It's not that there's not enough room for the logging trucks to pass. It's the sucking and wrenching vacuum that exists between their front and rear trailers which threatens to drag you under their wheels. The woman in the Dargaville tourist office told us that recently this logging truck vacuum had resulted in an eight-year-old schoolgirl being literally sucked out of a bus stop to her death.

But I digress from possums and Lyall, who was still in full flow about his hatred of these vegetation-destroying blighters.

'One night,' he said, 'a possum had climbed a tree outside our bedroom window and was making a bloody awful racket, hissing away like they do. So I went outside and climbed up a ladder and knocked the bastard out of the tree with a stick. It then ran across the yard with me hot on its heels, but because it was walled in it realised it was cornered, so it ran directly for me because a possum will climb the tallest thing around, no matter that it might be human! Luckily my dog caught the possum before it got to me, but one of my mates, he had a possum run straight up him and land on his head.'

After seeing no one for mile upon mile, and catching sight of the odd half-submerged vehicle (abandoned by drivers who had mis-judged the tides and become bogged down in soft sand – 'They tend to be the Asians,' said Lyall), we passed a small figure standing in the waves: a Maori man fishing for mullet with a net. Lyall pointed out how green the waves looked around where the man was standing. 'That's plankton,' he said, 'which the Maori take as a good sign as a spot to dig for toheroa, as the toheroa like a good bit of plankton.'

Lyall dropped us off in the middle of the sand opposite a mountainous ridge of sand dunes. These dunes are where the tour buses stop for their passengers to go sand tobogganing.

'When I was a boy,' said Lyall, 'there was none of this tour bus business. But from time to time I used to come up here with a few mates and we'd toboggan down the dunes on nikau palm leaves.'

Big handshakes all round and then Lyall climbed back into his ute and started back towards Kaitaia. But twenty foot away he stepped on the brakes and thrust his head out of the window.

'I forgot to tell you,' he called, 'to mind the mosquitoes round here. They're as big as sparrows!'

Gary and I set off cycling inland up the Te Paki Stream across the watery sand into a spanking wind. We then joined a sandy dirt road that took us south to Waitiki Landing, the last stop before the land runs out at Cape Reinga, comprising a petrol station, small store, cafe (serving 'Mrs Mac's Famous Beef Pies') and place to camp with cabins all rolled into one. So this is where we are now, sitting in the cafe out of the wind and rain. The only people around are the couple who work here and a small group of Maori propped up at the bar, smoking and drinking. I'm drinking pot loads of tea and Gary is eating an ostrich burger and chips. Says it tastes like chicken. As does anything odd. Like snake.

Waitiki Landing, Northland, 9 July

We're now on the Aupouri Peninsula, a narrow, 100 km-long slither of forest and dunes and hills. This is the Maori's *Te Hika o te*

Ika ('the tail of the fish'), recalling that legend of Maui hauling up the 'fish' of the North Island from the sea while sitting in the canoe of the South Island.

From Waitiki, the dirt road to the Cape is only 21 km, but thanks to the weather (wild, wet and exceptionally windy) and state of the road (pot-holed, rocky, corrugated and, in parts, wheel-sinkingly muddy), it took us a good three hours to cycle and occasionally push. There was only one point where the road grew smooth for a few hundred dirt-packed yards, but then it settled back to the same old scabby, stippled surface. Matters weren't helped by the odd fat-tyred 4WD and high-bottomed Unimog (ex-army truck) tour buses like the Dune Rider or Sand Safaris that did nothing towards reducing their speed when they passed, leaving us to nurse wounds where the big stones kicked up by their wheels bounded off our bodies like large lumps of shrapnel. But despite the drivers, weather, hills and road, the seascape of scenery was as dramatic as it was wild and beautiful.

The advantage of spending so long cycling this stretch of rough road was that by the time we arrived at the Cape the last of the bus passengers were climbing into their bus to be bussed away. We fought with the lusty wind on the track down to the fat, squat white lighthouse. The wind was such that we had to cling to the lighthouse to avoid being blown over the nearby sharp drop of a cliff. Had we been blown over the cliff we'd have ended up in the sea – a confused and lumpy sea that stretched on for ever and ever. Somewhere to the west lay Australia. Big as Australia is, the ocean is bigger and it would be easy to be washed clean past it. Somewhere to the east and far above lay the tail end of South America. But mostly it was just the vast Pacific. We didn't want to fall into the Pacific, or any other sea for that matter, and so after braving the obligatory photographs we took of each other with bikes in our Michelin Man-like wind-inflated waterproofs, we took ourselves off into the hilariously scary wind to a position of less likely cliff-falling drowning.

The sea reflected the viciousness of the weather. This is the point where the snarling waves of the Tasman meet the manically swirling currents of the Pacific in a furious gnashing of surf. A Maori in the ostrich burger cafe told me that this is the only place in the world where you can see two oceans meeting. (What do the other oceans do, I wonder? Cross to the other side of the street?) In really stormy conditions, this colliding point of seas can produce waves up to 10 metres high. Today, looking out towards a buckled horizon and a boiling frenzy of leaping waves, these two oceans were not so much meeting as knocking each other senseless.

Although Cape Reinga sits at the northern tip of New Zealand, it is not the northernmost point of the country. That honour goes to the Surville Cliffs on North Cape, 30 km to the east, which beats Cape Reinga by a few latitudinal degrees. But the Cape is the northerly most accessible point on the peninsula and holds great significance to the Maori. Reinga means 'place of leaping' because the Mauri hold that, after death, their souls journey to this point to climb down the roots of an ancient pohutakawa tree that still clings to the cliffs, before leaping into the sea for their final departure to the spirit world in their traditional homeland of Polynesia.

Apart from wild seas, the Cape has seen some interesting comings and goings. First on the scene was the early Maori explorer, Kupe, who canoed this way more than a thousand years ago. Some four centuries later along came the Great Maori Fleet. In 1642 Abel Tasman sailed by and named the land Niuew Zeeland, after the Netherlands province of Zeeland. But he didn't linger long in New Zealand after his only landing attempt (in South Island's Golden Bay) resulted in the murder of three of his crew.

One of the strangest episodes of European exploration in New Zealand waters occurred in late 1769, when Captain Cook and Captain Jean Françoise-Marie de Surville were sailing around here off the northern coast. Unknown to either of them, their vessels *Endeavour* and *St Jean Baptiste* must have been as close to each other as 70 miles. In the age-old tradition of help freely being given to those in peril on the sea, Captain Cook would most likely have assisted Captain de Surville had he known of the predicament faced by the French captain. After all, Britain and France were not at war at the time, and Captain Cook held the secret of how to prevent and cure scurvy, which at that time was killing de Surville's crew at the rate of one per day.

Pukenui, 10 July

The ride back from the top was even slower and harder than the one going – but only because the wind had swung around to smack us in the face and the rain had made the bone-rattling road far soggier and bumpier. When we finally hit the stretch of sealed road outside Waitaki Landing, it felt so astonishingly smooth that it prompted Gary to proclaim, 'I *love* roads and tarmac!' He said it in a tone of such exaggerated heartfelt silliness that I fell into a bout of hysterics and had to bring my steed to heel as it made my legs go weak.

Today the wind was still feisty and still in our faces but the sun was out, making the rigours of yesterday feel a world away. Apart from being a lovely ride following the only road (Death Highway 1 – which is pleasantly un-deathlike at the moment as it seems precious few people want to come all the way up here in the dead of winter) down the middle of the peninsula offering occasional views of the Pacific and the Tasman and inlets and outlets and harbours, the only things of note are the bamboo hedges, a field full of cows and turkeys, me being chased by an ostrich (possible doomed burger material?) when I climbed over a fence for a pee, and all the kingfishers dipping and diving alongside us like wagtails before landing on gateposts and telephone wires. We also passed a house whose owner was using an old microwave as a postbox. Further down the road, I spotted a *Sunday Star Times* headline board with the words: 'HE BASHED ME BUT I STILL LOVE HIM'. Better buy that, then.

Awanui, 13 July

Keeping to the tradition of getting nowhere fast, we are getting nowhere fast. I was banking on getting a good few hilly miles under our belts, but Gary spotted a motel on the junction of Death Highway 1 and SH10 and, seeing as it had Sky TV (hence *Le Tour*) and an electric blanket, in we went. The motel was owned by Patrick and Jannette, a friendly Dutch couple with a high standard of cleanliness (the toilet had a Miss World-like 'Sanitised For Your Convenience' sash draped across the lid). They had been in New Zealand for two years. Jannette told us why they had given up on Holland. 'Life there was just too hectic,' she said. 'It was impossible to relax. One of the many things that used to get on our nerves was how, whenever we were asked out to dinner and we didn't want to go, we felt we had to make an excuse. But here we can just say, no, we can't come that day. And people leave it at that. They don't question why we can't come, or feel put out. They simply ask you again another time.'

There's not a lot to Awanui – a couple of stores and something called The Nappy Shack. It's located on the banks of the Awanui River and was originally established as a port for Kaitaia. Scows plied the twisting waterway to Awanui to load kauri logs and, in later years, kauri gum. A huge mass of giant peat-preserved kauri logs, recovered from swamps where they had been submerged for between 30,000 and 50,000 years, were stacked up in a sawmill just up the road from the motel. The sawmill was all part of the tourist-luring Ancient Kauri Kingdom – a workshop and shop where you could wander among slabs of wood made into odd-shaped furniture at quite shocking prices. A salesman told me that one highly uncomfortable-looking kauri three-piece suite which had a 'sold' label attached to it had been bought for $60,000 by a German couple. 'And that doesn't include the freight cost for shipping it to Germany,' he said.

During our extended stay in Awanui we went on the odd hunter-gather cycle mission into Kaitaia to replenish food supplies. Kaitaia may have looked on the surface as if things were going on in the usual uneventful way, but there was more to the town than met the eye. While we were there, a man was accused of burglary. More interestingly, he was found by police to be wearing two bras, a petticoat and a pair of bright red knickers.

Kerikeri, 17 July

A sudden flurry of activity. We've been washed down the coast in more extreme weather: sheets of torrential rain and wind so strong that when looking into it for a second you could feel your eyes depress. In the process of keeping all hands on deck, we sploshed through such places as Kaingaroa ('kangaroo in rowing boat'), Mangonui ('tropical fruit of the night', famous for its fish and chips – or as they say in these parts, 'fush and chups'), Pupuke ('unwell undeveloped butterfly') and Otoroa ('Tarka by boat'). In a camping store in Kerikeri, just along from shops with names like Manzone, Unichem Pharmacy, The Sound Lounge and Bin Inn Foods, I bought Gary a birthday present – a Primus PTL 2245

Alpine EasyLight for battery-saving inner tent activity. The shop owner was an elderly man called Mr Simpson, a Pommie who had come out here in 'sixty-four. 'I hold no love for the homeland,' he said. 'I threw away my passport in the seventies. Britain had nothing for me then, and has nothing for me now. I owe it no favours.' He used to be a shipwright in the Merchant Navy. 'When the Falklands War came along, my mates said, "They'll want you back in the navy again!" But I said I'd refuse to go. The only interest I have in the place is the football. Wolves. I've supported them all my life.'

Paihia, 18 July

Apart from the logging trucks, the most frequently sighted vehicle on the roads up here have been big bulbous water tankers delivering, funnily enough, water. Most farms and houses out in the sticks have no mains water. Instead they all have hefty tanks sitting on blocks outside the home, topped up from time to time by these tankers. You'd think in a land of so much rain all they'd have to do is take the top off the tanks and let nature fill it up for free. But I suppose it's not quite as simple as that.

We're now in Paihia, pronounced 'pie here' though it actually means 'here's a good place' – not for pies, apparently (though Gary begs to disagree), but for being the site of New Zealand's first church, made of reeds. It's since been rebuilt in more sturdy stone. Never mind churches or pies, this place seems particularly keen on its sea and its fish. Here's a taster of some of the names of the eateries: Tides, Only Seafood, Saltwater Cafe, The Wheelhouse, The Beachcomber, The Ferryman's Restaurant, The Lighthouse Tavern, Cafe Over The Bay and The Blue Marlin Diner. And whereas you might expect to find some sort of nightclub in a touristy town of this size, Paihia does have a club but it's a Bay of Islands Swordfish Club.

The reason Paihia sounds so nautical is due to its position: plopped in the heart of the Bay of Islands – a beautifully watery region embracing an irregular 800 km coastline and some 150 green-topped islands of varying size, clustered in clear blue waters, that stretch out like stepping stones to the horizon. For such a scenic setting, it's a shame the 'township' can't reflect it in comeliness as it's little more than an unremarkable stretch of motels and touristy shops sitting at odds with the quiet allure of the island-studded waterscape.

Following several lengthy sessions spent bobbing about on the pouncing chop and slap of the ocean wave in bobbable kayaks (wildlife encounter: small blue penguin unexpectedly surfacing off portside prow), and after a high-speed, wave-skimming excursion in the touristy Mack Attack speed boat to surf through a hole in a rock called the Hole in the Rock, we thought we'd better give ourselves a bit of Treaty of Waitangi treatment. So up the road we cycled to Waitangi, one of the earliest sites of permanent European settlement in New Zealand and said to be the single most symbolic place in the country for Maori and Pakeha alike, as it was right here on the wide green sweeping lawns running down to the bay in front of a white clapboard colonial house (known as Treaty House) that the Treaty of Waitangi, the founding document for modern New Zealand, was signed. On 6 February 1840, with Governor William Hobson signing on behalf of Queen Victoria (who was a little tied up with something more pressing on her plate), Maori chiefs and a bunch of well-to-do folk from England inked a pact ostensibly to end Maori–Pakeha conflict, to guarantee the Maori land rights, to give them and the colonists Crown protection and to admit New Zealand to the British Empire before the 'bloody French' (who were already making inroads on the Banks Peninsula) could get their hands on the country. This treaty, which was apparently to 'signify a partnership between races', has been found, without too much trouble, not to signify any such partnership. The barge-poling British expected to rule New Zealand alone and did so.

Since the signing at Waitangi, the treaty has remained as the hub and central nerve of New Zealand's race relations. Many

Maori argue that their rights, guaranteed by the treaty, have scarcely ever been maintained and that they struggle for recognition every day. There's a lot going on in the news at the moment about the so-called 'privileges' of the Maori. Some Pakeha are very unhappy about it, which reminds me of the nurse I met in South Island who complained to me how her daughter was having to pay to go through nursing college (and battling along on the subsequent debts) while her partially Maori friend at the college had all the fees paid for her. Just the other day I read a letter in the paper written by Sydney Keepa, a Maori from the North Shore:

> As a Maori I would like to give my definition of being a 'privileged Maori'.
>
> I wonder, is it a privilege to have 10 per cent of my people unemployed; is it privilege that our lifespan (male) is nine years less than Pakeha; is it privilege that Maori make up almost 50 per cent of prison inmates; is it privilege that 40 per cent of Maori do not own their own homes; is it privilege that most Maori end up in low-skilled, low-paid jobs; is it privilege that Pakeha came to our land and stole 95 per cent of it; is it privilege that 163 years ago Maori entered into an agreement with the Pakeha giving Pakeha rights and then those same people trampled on Maori rights; is it privilege that when politicians want to lift their ratings they use Maori to do it; is it privilege that 45 per cent of the population agree that this is what being privileged is all about?
>
> Maori don't want to be privileged. All Maori have been saying is that we have rights – and the agreement that was signed 163 years ago guarantees that.

Auckland, 23 July

The water around one of the small islands rising out of the bay just off Paihia was mesmerising to watch, especially in a choppy swell when the waves rode in bumper to bumper each side of the island, then forgot which way to go. I was leaning against my bike watching these waves when a man called Tony, who owned a backpackers' hostel up the road, said, 'How're you finding riding up all these hills we've got round here?'

'Some are a bit of a struggle,' I said. 'But they're mostly fine as I quite enjoy cycling uphill.'

Gary, who was standing close by, gave me a worried look before mumbling something to Tony about me being not well in my head.

Tony told me how last summer he had been driving along in his pick-up when he passed a girl with a bike crying at the side of the road. Tony stopped and, thinking she had taken a spill, asked if she was okay. 'Turned out she hadn't come off the bike. She was crying because she was at her wits end – she just couldn't take cycling up any more hills. So I gave her a lift back to the hostel and she continued around New Zealand by bus.'

Before Tony headed back to his hostel he said that he thought that the girl should have chosen the South Island for cycling. 'They say the South Island has hills to look at, the North Island has hills to drive over.' I'm not so sure about this. More like the South Island has mountains to cycle over, the North Island has saddles and hills like mountains to cycle over. After all, 60 per cent of New Zealand is higher than 300 metres (1000 feet) and 70 per cent of it is either leg-quiveringly hilly or steep.

Gary and I were the only passengers climbing aboard the bouncing little passenger ferry that whisked us, plus bikes, across the bay to Russell, New Zealand's first capital and most historic village. With a population of 800 it's a tiny place, but very lovely in a dainty sort of way with its colonial villas tucked along a waterfront lined with pohutakawa trees. The village is a far cry from its early days as a port of call for rowdy whalers in the early 1800s. Then called Kororareka, it was dubbed the Hell Hole of the Pacific for its brawling seamen, runaway convicts, grog shops and orgiastic brothels. When Charles Darwin came this way in 1835 he wrote that the majority of the British there were the 'refuse of society'. A year later another early traveller observed that it was 'notorious at present for containing, I should think, a greater number of rogues than any other spot of equal size in the universe'. Missionaries, who are easily shocked at the best of times, were no more impressed by the amount of debauchery. One commented on finding it 'a dreadful place – the very seat of Satan'.

Kororareka is Maori for 'sweet blue penguin' and the place originally started out as a fortified Maori settlement. It got its name after a Maori chief, wounded in battle, asked for some penguin broth to be brought to him. After drinking the broth he said, '*Ka reka te korora*' – 'How sweet is the penguin.' By the 1840s the settlement was deemed far too bawdy to be worthy of capital status and so, after the signing of the Waitangi Treaty, the capital was moved south to Auckland, leaving Kororareka to be renamed Russell in an attempt to expunge its notorious swashbuckling past.

Russell may have the oldest surviving church in the country (built in 1836), complete with cannonball scars (from HMS *Hazard*) and musket ball holes (made by Hone Heke and his warriors when they ransacked Russell in 1844), but it also has the ubiquitous Four Square. I was shopping for picnicking material in this particular Four Square when I overhead on the local radio station how some professor in Maryland had just discovered a fifth chewing muscle that ran from the eye socket to the lower jaw. The excitable presenter seemed quite taken with this bit of news. 'Wow!' he said. 'Just when you thought there were no more cheek muscles there's *another one!*'

The sun has shown itself in the past few days but it has always been pretty short-lived. Rain is at the forefront of all weather agendas, with yet more floods (latest paper headlines: 'TWO DIE AND THOUSANDS ARE EVACUATED AS FIRST FLOODS AND THEN QUAKES HIT THE BAY OF PLENTY'). The thing with rain is that it either makes you stay put in a place until it moves on to be problematical for people elsewhere (which in New Zealand is generally for a long time), or else it makes you scurry the miles away in an attempt to outpace it. Since leaving Paihia we have tried to outpace it, but then the minute we get ahead (or behind) one rainstorm, another one soon comes along to make all efforts worthless.

Death Highway 1 hasn't helped matters; it's busy, it's fast and, judging from the number of white crosses at the side of the road, it's full of death. 'SLOW DOWN. HIGH CRASH RATE' said one sign. 'DANGER. DRIVE SLOW. THIS ROAD TAKES LOVED ONES' warned another. Most motorists, of course, pay no attention to such advice. They tailgate, they overtake on blind hills and blind corners, they slice off our elbows, they drive like demons. There comes a point in life when you think that dying for the sake of an idiot encased in a tonne or more of metal and buffeted by springy airbags is not a good option when a possible life-preserving one lies just around the corner. So, for the last fast burst into Auckland, we slid our bikes into the undercarriage of a bus and let our driver Les, with fetching slicked-back hair, transport us back to the city. Every time a passenger joined the bus Les would murmur, 'Sit back . . . relax . . . and enjoy the journey.' And we did.

16

Sometimes you do something which you don't realise you're doing until you discover after you've done it just what you've done. In my father's case, it's usually my mum who discovers that he's put the butter in the jam cupboard and the jam in the fridge instead of vice versa. And after climbing Rangitoto volcano on Rangitoto Island off Auckland, it was only a few days later when I had an X-ray that I was told I had broken a small bone in the top of my foot – though I didn't notice breaking it at the time.

Foot is fine now, at least for cycling. And just as well as I've got some sizeable mileage to be putting under my wheels. This is because travel plans have taken a surprising turn. As Gary only has a month left before he flies home to get building again, we have two choices: either continue getting very wet and not very far by bike in North Island; or hire a camper van so that Gary can see South Island. So, as I feel Gary can't fly all the way to this other side of the world and not see South Island in some shape or form, we've gone for the van option. Gary is going to be the man in the van with his bike on board, whereas, apart from the roads that I have already cycled, I'm going to chase him on my bike.

It's amazing how frisky my bike feels without its usual excess of unwieldy clobber (I'm riding with just handlebar bag and front panniers). Gary and I have been going like the clappers (and Gary has naturally been clappering along a lot faster than me) through a green and rolling rain-lashed area of mostly M's: Mangatawhiri, Maramarua Mill, Mangatarata, Mangateparu (*manga* is Maori for a stream), Morrinsville and Matamata. Matamata had a sign on the outskirts saying: 'WELCOME TO HOBBITON'. Something, I presume, to do with all the feverish *Lord of the Rings* hype.

Other roadside signs I spotted told me such diverse things as: 'BUCKLE IN BIG KIDS TOO – IT'S THE WAY'; 'ADOPT DON'T ABORT'; 'WATERCRESS (NOT HYDROPONIC) FARM'; 'SAW DOCTOR SHARPENING SERVICES'; 'PLOUGH THROUGH SNOW NOT TRAFFIC'; 'DROWSY? PULL OVER OR SLEEP PERMANENTLY'; 'TIRED DRIVERS END UP IN NIGHTMARES'.

Matamata might be trying to lure visitors with its Hobbiton connections, but, according to the town's tourist leaflet, what the place is really noted for is its importance as a bloodstock region. As a long-time devourer of various countries' promotional material, I can't say the enticement of a top bloodstock region is one I've come across too often. Certainly it's an unusual angle of approach for seducing the holidaying masses.

There's no getting away from the fact, though, that there are cows aplenty around here. When Gary and I dropped by on Rob Edwards, an old friend from my village who'd been living in New Zealand for years working as a cattle farmer, he told us that in just a small area around Matamata there are over a million head of cattle. Rob used to have 450 cattle himself, until he gave up farming to go into the building trade, although ultimately he wants to be a funeral director. He never intended coming out here to live. When he left home in the eighties his plan was to have a year out. He got as far as Australia where, at a motorsport event (Rob loves motorbikes – he had a Honda 1100 Blackbird in his garage) he met Karen, an Australian nurse. They married and now have two young children, Georgia and Maddie. Rob is a good sort, funny and friendly. It's no wonder he has a lot of friends, many of them Maori. Just last night he spent the evening with his Maori mates. 'Everyone gets on well round here,' he said. 'It's only politicians and extremists and hardliners who make it sound like we don't.'

*

We're now in Rotorua, which has to be one of the few places in the world that can be smelt before it is seen. Nicknamed 'Sulphur City' due to the pervasive rotten-egg whiff of hydrogen sulphide that hangs over the town that the locals call a city, Rotorua sits on an active fault line known as the Taupo Volcanic Zone. It is a narrow belt of vociferous activity characterised by volcanoes and earth-quakes, and although it is only 20–40 km wide, it spans a distance of 240 km from White Island off the coast of the Bay of Plenty to Lake Taupo and the volcanoes of the Tongariro National Park in the Central Plateau of North Island. Rotorua is full of oddities: steam rising from cracks in the tarmac, craters of boiling mud and hot springs, gaseous bores and ground fissures, explosive geysers (outside this region, geysers occur only in southwest Iceland and in Yellowstone National Park in the United States) and multicoloured terraces of sulphur and silica deposits. After George Bernard Shaw visited Rotorua in 1934 he wrote, 'I was pleased to get so close to Hades and be able to return.'

Situated on a thermal belt, Rotorua puts its steam heat to good use, piping it from beneath the town's thin crust to heat homes, hotels and mineral hot spas. In some parts house-building is risky because digging the foundations leads to the release of unwanted thermal activity – some residents have woken in the night to find their front garden transformed into a hot bath.

Rotorua is full of Maori history and mythology. For centuries the Te Arawa tribes lived beside the boiling hot pools, believing in *utu* (revenge) and killing their enemies with jade war clubs and sweet potato digging sticks. The town still has the greatest concentration of Maori residents of any in New Zealand. What with being such a hub of Maori culture and all the weird geothermal splutterings, Rotorua is, not surprisingly, a tourist hot spot – one of its streets (Fenton) has the longest stretch of motels in the whole of New Zealand.

Luckily, being winter, the area is relatively quiet. Most tourists seem to be of the Japanese variety ('*Ah so, desu-ka?*') who arrive on tightly scheduled bus tours to be disgorged into the popular Polynesian Spa public pools built around the town's most famous hot springs, with water ranging in temperature from 34°C to a skin-scorching 43°C. A nineteenth-century Catholic priest claimed that the waters cured his rheumatism. I'm sure they did, but I'm also sure they are likely to have ruined other parts of his anatomy. 'The patients emerging from this bath,' wrote a bather from the same time, 'look like boiled lobsters.'

They still do. Gary and I had a wander within, but we didn't participate in a boiling of tender regions as it was just too crowded. So we went for a cycle instead, but not before noticing a sign at the baths saying: 'ASIANS. PLEASE REFRAIN FROM SPITTING IN THE POOLS'.

Twenty fast-pedalling kilometres later we were at Hell's Gate, a highly active thermal area, where we had the spa pool to ourselves. We followed our dunking with a wander around the steamy and gurgling reserve, peering into waking mudpools that bubbled and klopped like boiling porridge. Beside a mudpool called The Inferno, varying between 100°C and 115°C, a sign said: 'WARNING – PERSONS WHO THROW LITTER OR STONES INTO THE THERMAL POOLS MAY BE ASKED TO RETRIEVE THEM'. It was worth hanging around to watch for anyone who might fall prey to such treatment, although it wasn't just litter-throwing tourists: more than a handful of visitors to the area, unprompted, liked to walk where it was not a good idea to walk and had ended up falling into bubbling mudpools or dropping into steaming vents with all the nasty results that a boiling alive entails.

Talking of death, after riding 50 km around Lake Rotorua and getting rained on hard out of clear blue skies, and then nearly knocked on the head by the end of a full and fat rainbow, we paid a visit to Whakarewarewa, known as Whaka and pronounced (in that way that Ws turn to Fs) Fa-ka. Whaka is a thermal reserve and much tourist-trampled Maori village (currently quiet) that sits suspended 35 metres over the surface of an underground thermal lake. We came away from this geyser-gushing place having discovered that, traditionally, the Maoris here had three ways of burying the dead. They either hung the bodies in trees from fibres of New

Zealand flax and used mussel shells to scrape the skin before burying the bones in caves and holes. Or they trod and stamped the
bodies into the hot mud until the bodies dissolved. Or they placed
them in tombs over the steam to cook slowly, over an extended
period of time, like a good Lancashire hotpot.

Kaikoura, South Island, 11 August

It's been a busy week chasing Gary over hilly volcanic ridge and windy
desert dale. From Rotorua we headed south to Taupo via Waiotapu
(Maori for 'sacred waters') – a freakish, fantastic landscape of deep
sulphur-crusted pits, jade-coloured ponds, silica terraces and a steaming lake edged with red algae and bubbling with minute beads of
carbon dioxide. Oh, and a large American tourist screaming abuse at
his son to keep away from the boiling cauldrons of mud.

And so to the largest lake in Australasia, Lake Taupo. This huge
body of water, 40 km long by 30 km wide, is so big that it's tidal. It
fills a massive crater formed originally some 25,000 years ago but
also the scene more than 1800 years ago of a cataclysmic volcanic
eruption, one of the most violent in history – six times as violent as
Krakatoa's in 1883. Enormous volumes of ash and pumice were
blasted up to a height of 50 km, producing spectacular sunsets that
were recorded by contemporary Chinese and Roman scribes.

Taupo is now known as the 'Trout Fishing Capital of the World'.
Even by New Zealand standards, the fish are monsters, with rainbow trout hitting the scales up to a weighty 9 kg. Somewhere
around here is Huka Lodge where the Queen Mother used to stay,
apparently fishing out of her bedroom window. Maybe it was a desperate measure. Maybe she wanted to buy some nice trout at her
lodge to send home to the Queen, but then came upon one of
New Zealand's quirky laws which states that it is illegal to sell trout
in this country. If you want a slab of trout you have to catch it.

I left Gary in the local museum looking at things like long sharp
stones shaped like a hand axe that the Maori used to thrust with a

twisting action into the upper nasal cavities of their enemies (must have made their eyes smart), while I took off at a canter on my wheels around the lake and on to the Desert Road. It was freezing up here, sleeting horribly, the roads treacherous with ice and wheel-eating potholes. The only traffic was the odd army jeep and the big articulated trucks that go stonking up and down the country, with the now all too familiar writing on the side: Streight Freight; Owens Global Logistics; Freightlines; Opzeeland Transport; SR Selwyns Freight; Linfox Integrated Logistics; TNL Freighting. Everything looked as remote as the last time I was up here – wind-tossed tussock grass, brown scrubby trees, dish-rag skies, wintry volcanoes and those miles of marching pylons, their high-tension wires cantilevering across the broad flat sweep of land.

More museums in Waiouru, this one the Army Museum, which made a change from all the kauri gum, logging and gold-mining ones that we have frequented over the rest of the country. Any mention of armies, wars or weapons and Gary is in his element, but, much to my surprise, I too found the Army Museum to be an engrossing place, albeit in parts very sad. Although New Zealand has never had a foreign war of its own, it has sent thousands of its young men to die in other people's. In the Gallipoli campaign alone, 7,473 out of the 8,450 New Zealand soldiers who disembarked were either killed or wounded.

Museum visits over, it was on down the same way I had come up, past more drivers roadside signs: 'STOP REVIVE SURVIVE'; 'TIRED DRIVERS MAKE MISTAKES – TAKE A BREAK'; '"PEACH TEATS" – CALVES LOVE 'EM!'; 'THINK BEFORE YOU DIG – THINK PIPELINES'; 'FLATHILLS FOR FOOD'; 'HUNTERVILLE – HUNTAWAY CAPITAL OF THE WORLD'. At one point I even had a truck of carrots overtake me with a sign on the rear tailgate saying: 'WARNING: CARROTS ON THE MOVE'. What, to a little holiday bach by the sea, perhaps?

And then along came the junction at Bulls, with its copious assortment of Bull-adorned stores: BULLOCKS; YE OLDE BULL; COMMEST-A-BULL; SOCI-A-BULL; COMPUTE-A-BULL. All I can say to that is bull the other one.

For the last flapping flat sweep to Wellington, I was back in the cockpit of the van, marvelling at how easy motoring is compared with the wind-blasted, jelly-leg-making rigours of cycling. When it started raining hard (again), instead of stopping at the side of the road to heave my jacket on hurriedly while being drenched by spray from a stream of trucks and then being blown for a Burton in the spanking wind, all we had to do was wind up the windows and flick on the wipers. As easy as that. Gary says: 'Trucking is the way to go, Jose!' But I'm not so sure. Although it's a bit of a novelty travelling at ease at speed in an armchair, the trouble is everything happens too fast and there's no sense of endorphin-popping satisfaction that comes from the element-lashed struggle. Also, driving doesn't feel like travelling. It feels like a hermetically phoney sham.

And so here I am back in Kaikoura for the third time. Am beginning to feel quite like a local, which is perhaps why I'm walking around with my hands tucked up into my sleeves. Seems to be what every third resident is doing. But then it is cold, a snarling wind hurling itself against the town off the ridge of snow-heavy mountains.

Balclutha, South Otago, 15 August

This new style of bike touring (chasing after vans) is quite fun for a change. Whereas I normally make a meal out of my mileage, I'm now moving down the map as fast as a witch. The good thing about New Zealand is that because there's a dearth of roads and people, it's not hard to spot Gary. Out in the bushy sticks, he's either waiting for me in a lay-by reading the paper, or in a town I'll inevitably find him ensconced in a museum or in a cafe scoffing down an all-day breakfast. Some days, he eats three breakfasts a day. One day he even ate four. I say: 'What about your waistline, Gary?' He says: 'Never mind that, Jose. I'm on holiday!'

This is true. So I let him be. I, after all, am at work. At least, that's what I try to tell him. Gary thinks I have a funny idea of work.

*

The last few days I hit the 4,500 mile mark (7,240 km) on my bike computer while bowling south across the Canterbury Plains to Timaru, where the hills start again until somewhere around Makikihi ('Kiki Dee's mother') where they decide to peter out to become flat until Oamaru (site of penny-farthing races, yellow-eyed penguins, little blue penguins and a motel with a placard outside saying 'SPEND A NIGHT: NOT A FORTUNE'). It was in Oamaru that I heard an advert on Port Radio, the local station, berating people for littering the land. 'Don't be a tosser,' said the no-messing voice, 'use a bin.' You couldn't get away with an advert like that on British radio – there'd be too many complaints from Tunbridge Wells.

After Oamaru: more hills. And a surplus of swedes for sale at the side of the road. Not normal swedes these, but ones as big as Viking helmets. Then came the peculiarly large Moeraki Boulders (Devil's Marbles) – huge spherical boulders scattered along the beach. They were formed some 60 million years ago and two of them have been found to contain dinosaur bones. Maori legend has it, in the way that Maori legend does, that these boulders (about fifty altogether, with circumferences of up to four metres) were gourds that fell out of the voyaging ancestral canoe when it was wrecked nearby.

I met up with Gary in the cafe on the cliff overlooking the boul-ders. The car park looked like a gathering for a 4WD convention – big, shiny, bike-bashing tinted-windowed gimmicky beasts – and for some reason the loud-voiced owners were all wandering around in rolled polo-neck jumpers. Maybe it was a tosser-bonding thing. Some of these polo-necked owners were causing much fuss in the cafe: apparently the coffee wasn't hot enough and one woman was complaining like a braying donkey to the woman behind the counter, accusing her of microwaving the milk, which she said tasted 'bloody disgusting'. Gary was quite happy with his. As for my tea – lovely.

The weather, which had been cold and often wet, turned to snow as the humping great hills of Dunedin approached. The front page of *The Press* was full of pictures of snow and closed roads and head-lines reading: 'TORNADO KILLS TWO'; 'LIGHTNING STRIKES FARMER'; 'NEW STORM ON WAY'; 'WEATHER DANGER NOT OVER'. We were told: 'Hundreds of people have been stranded by closed roads and cancelled flights as extreme weather grips the nation.' Forecasters were warning of a southerly snow storm brewing to rival the October 2000 blast that caused extensive damage around this area. Oh well, it's all part of the package of travelling around New Zealand in winter. Trouble is, it's not far off the mark of what I had thrown at me in summer.

Dunedin is the old Gaelic name for Edinburgh, underlining the Scottish origins of the city since the first Presbyterian settlers arrived in the mid-nineteenth century. People round here speak with a Southland burr, which some say sounds like a Scottish accent, but is more Kiwi with a mouthful of Rs.

Clinging to the walls of the natural amphitheatre at the western end of Otago Harbour, Dunedin is a seriously hilly city. One of its streets, Baldwin Street, is officially the world's steepest street at 38 degrees. I fancied bursting a lung by trying to cycle up it, but owing to current weather conditions of ice and hard-packed snow, it was impossible to walk up it, let alone cycle.

On through Waihola ('questionable Spanish greeting') and Milton with its store advertising 'FROSTY BOY ICECREAM – OFTEN LICKED NEVER BEATEN'. Just outside Lovells Flat I passed Old Sod Cottage, making me briefly wonder who the old sod may have been. We're now the only people in the small, snow-covered motorcamp in Balclutha (Gaelic for 'town on the Clyde') owned by an old boy watching TV in a small cabin. I don't think he is very well. He's surrounded by more bottles of drugs than a pharmacy and, oddly, more hose fittings than a plumber's merchant.

You could tell we were in the thick of sheep country around here. Apart from all the sheep, that is. Everywhere there was a profusion of stock trucks and lay-bys. These lay-bys were definitely not for picnics. They were, according to the signs, STOCK TRUCK EFFLUENT DISPOSAL areas for the trucks to jettison their loads of effluent into a tank rather than spill it all over the roads. Then there were the stores with names like 'Dave Bateman Shearing and Manure Supplies'. And the *Otago Daily Times* went into great detail reporting the latest stock sale. Not stocks and shares or Hang Seng Indexes, but far more riveting things saying how 'top lambs made up to $111 and prime ewes up to $66 on a small yarding at the Waiareka stock sale'. Apparently there was 'a large yarding of store cattle' too (what a relief!), which 'sold strongly throughout the sale'. Just in case you're wondering, 'Top 1-shear ewes' were going for $61–$66 compared with 'Top lighter ewes' (presumably this type come with convertible roofs to reduce the weight), which were being snapped up for between $41 and $45. Then there were the 'Prime steers' and the 'Store cattle' and the 'Bobby calves' and the 'Simmental cross bulls'. I'd never heard of Simmental bulls before. I wonder if they bear any relation to simnel cakes and make their appearance on the table only at Easter?

While we're on the subject of the *Otago Daily Times*, towards the back of the paper they had a game called WORDPLAY, which introduced itself by saying, 'More offerings in our regular word feature in which readers take a word from the dictionary, add, subtract or change one letter, then supply a definition.'

Here's what M. Urquhart from Owaka came up with: **Lumpered**: sauce gone wrong; **Blank statement**: no money left; **Implessive**: admired by orientals; **Clampion**: a person who immobilises vehicles; **Inmaterial**: a stubborn stain.

Debbie Williams from Mornington had offerings along the lines of: **Subduet**: tame the singers by force; **Agundance**; plenty of weaponry; **Pardone**: chef's excuse for under-cooked food.

Well, I suppose you've got to amuse yourself down in these parts somehow. There's only so much fun you can have with livestock.

Riverton, Southland, 18 August

Snow still lined the road as I cycled out of Balclutha past WONGY'S COD AND TATIES, SOFT ICES, THICK SHAKES. Thick streamers of smoke leant from the morning chimneys. I was following the Catlins Coast, one of the more forgotten corners of the country. The area is constantly strafed by roaring south-easterlies while the unforgiving relentlessness of the sea has moulded the coastline into plunging cliffs, windswept headlands with skeletal bushes and contorted remains of trees, deserted white sand beaches, rough boulder-strewn bays and gaping caves. The area is a lot quieter now than it was in the nineteenth century when all those extractive industries competed to lay siege on New Zealand. First the sealers arrived, then the whalers, then the first settlers intent on farming. Next, along came the timber millers, the loggers attacking the dense stands of native beech forests to serve the voracious needs of the Dunedin market. The gold-diggers weren't far away either. But before any Europeans had appeared on the scene, the Catlins once teemed with Maori hunters, as the region was one of the last refuges for the flightless moa.

As I rode through this fantastic stretch of hilly country, along a road that was half sealed and half slushy tyre-skidding potholed dirt, the weather that threw itself at me was a monkey's breakfast of sun, snow, rain, hail and sleet. But all the time the air was sharp and aggressively fresh and pure, and felt like new.

After riding past no signs of habitation save for the odd sheep station all morning, I arrived in Owaka ('forceful hitting of female species), the largest place in the Catlins. Which isn't to say that Owaka is big. There was a pub, a petrol station, a Four Square, a motel, a 'Blowhole' backpackers, a takeaway, a tearoom, a restaurant called Lumberjacks, a cyber cafe (of all outback things) and a museum the size of a broom cupboard (closed, but it could have been 'open by arrangement' – arrangement of what, I wonder: dusty ornaments?). There was also a sign offering Bottom Bus tours. Tours of bottoms in a bus. Now that's unusual.

In the summer people come to the Catlins to swim with the Hector's dolphins that frolic in the waters close to shore. In fact all along this coast the area is so thick with wildlife it's like a natural zoo. There are fur seals and Hooker's sea lions (sounds saucy), whales and elephant seals, blue and yellow-eyed penguins, shags and sooty shearwaters (obviously avian chimney sweeps), blue ducks and yellow heads.

At Curio Bay, Gary and I wandered among one of the world's most extensive and least disturbed examples of a 160-million-year-old Jurassic fossil forest, embedded in the rocks. The forest became petrified after being buried by a volcanic eruption (I'm not surprised, I'd have been pretty scared too). Over time the wood had been replaced by silica, leaving the remaining structure of the trees. It's quite a thing to jump across the rock pools from trunk to trunk knowing how incomprehensively old these trees are. The prehistoric cyads, tree ferns and ancestors of the matai and kauri resemble fossils found in South America, confirming that New Zealand was once part of the great southern supercontinent of Gondwanaland.

The last burst into Invercargill, the most southerly city in the world, was as flat as a tray and almost Roman road-like with long stretches of straight. Every wind-blasted tree down here was a sculpture. Like Dunedin, Invercargill was originally a Scottish settlement – many of its wide, wind-funnelling grid-type streets are named after rivers in the Highlands. To the Maori, the area was known as Murikiku, 'the tail end of the land'. To the tourist bureau people, who possess a worrying penchant for branding anything they can get their hands on in a measure of desperation, Invercargill's motto is 'The Friendly City' – a cry for help if ever I heard one. During my cycles around New Zealand a lot of Kiwis not from Invercargill had warned me about the city. They said it was a rough place full of hoons and drunk drivers (whose conduct prompted one newspaper to describe it as 'bantam behaviour' – 'intoxicated young men, chests out, strutting from bar to bar, eager to take on anyone who annoys them'). I'd also been told more than once that Invercargill was the 'Gum Boot Capital of the World' (I thought Taihape was, but I'll let them fight that one out) and that it never stopped raining. Well, they were wrong on this last one. I've been in and out of Invercargill several times now (in from the Catlins, out to Bluff and back from Bluff) and the weather has been cold and perfect with clear blue skies and, currently, no wind. In fact this unusual lack of wind even made headlines in the *Southland Times* saying how the maximum gust yesterday reached a mere 15 km/h, and that at 6 p.m. the wind was clocking in at only 6 km/h. This made for riveting reading, especially when you're used to a continuous battering.

Perching at the tip of a peninsula in the shadow of a massive aluminium smelter massed with fishing fleets (oysters are the town's claim to fame), the bleak outpost and straggly port of Bluff is known as the Land's End of New Zealand even though the South Island's southernmost point is actually Slope Point in the Catlins. (As south as this south point may be, it is a still a long way north of the most southerly part of New Zealand – Campbell Island – lying 590 km south of Stewart Island, which is but a penguin flop from Antarctica.) But because SH1 runs between Bluff here in the south and Cape Reinga on the north of North Island, the two points are taken as being the End to End of Enzed. The actual highway terminates opposite Land's End NZ B&B and The Drunken Sailor Cafe and Bar at the Stirling Point signpost, indicating distances to the likes of the South Pole (4,810 km – not far!), Sydney (2,000 km), the Equator (5,133 km) and London (18,958 km – blinking miles away!). Kiwis call this point the End of the Earth, even though on a clear day, like today, you could see another bit of Earth in the shape of a large island 35 km away over the notoriously rough Foveaux Strait. Had I not been with Gary on a hasty schedule to get back to Auckland to see him off on his flight home, I would have taken the boat from Bluff to what the Maori call 'The Anchorstone of Maui's Canoe' (the weight that held the other islands together), otherwise known as Stewart Island, a virtually unexplored area of nearly 2,000 square kilometres.

Maybe another day.

The flax-lined dead-end road to Bluff was flat and exposed. There were deer farms and yellow-bright bushes of gorse, and more swedes (75c each or 3 for $2) for sale. Any trees around here were scrub-like and wind-warped, having grown at a drunken angle leaning to lee, blasted by the endless southerlies. Talking of drunks, you could tell what the local beer was around here, not so much from the pubs and billboards, but from the amount of bottles of Speights ('Pride of the South') hurled on to the verge and into the ditches. The local paper, like many New Zealand papers, listed the worryingly large number of names of those convicted for drink driving over the past week:

AINSWORTH, Brett, 43, engineer, 900mcg, fined $2500, disq 12 mths. AMUIA, Tavita, 22, car groomer, 829mcg, 100 hrs community work, disq 8 mths. BEYNON, Michael, 34, roofer, 465mcg, disq 6 mths, vehicle confiscated. HAAR, Patrick, 42, bricklayer, 95 mcg, supervision 9 mths, disq 12 mths. HARTLEY, Mildred, 65, retired, refused blood, 150 hrs community work, disq indefinitely, vehicle confiscated. LAL, Bevan, 28, vinyl layer, 176 mcg, imprisonment 6 mths, disq 12 mths. THOMPSON, Raymond, 48, labourer, refused blood, imprisonment 10 weeks, disq 24 mths. VANDERCOLK, Matthew, 20, stable hand, 483mcg, fined $400, disq 6 mths . . .

And on and on and on.

For the fourth time I was in and out of Invercargill, past Withy Woos Farmyard Zoos, the Ballance agri-nutrients factory, the South Pacific Meats Ltd meat processing plant, Clifton Wool Scour, Brick 'n' Cobble Maori Construction, the Robin Hood Milk Bar and Headhunters Hair Design. Still on the broad coastal plain it was a flat fast ride to Riverton, where I found Gary parked on a hill at the sparse and mostly residential caravan park (dubious bogs; chaotic shambles of a kitchen; strange old man in cock-eyed blue bobble hat who kept following me everywhere). Settled in the 1830s by sealers and whalers, Riverton ('The Paua Shell Capital of the World') is one of the oldest European settlements in New Zealand and the road is lined with many of the original wooden cottages still in good nick. Riverton is keen on preserving the past. Two years ago the New Zealand Historic Places Trust offered a whaler's cottage for sale for the sum of just NZ$1 (30p), so long as the purchaser promised to preserve it according to the trust's specifications.

On one of our many encounters, the old boy in the skew-whiff blue bobble hat kept saying to me, 'Never had so much rain as this year . . . never had so much rain. Just never had so much rain . . .' Then he said that he thought it wasn't right that Gary was driving when I was cycling and that I should ride 10 km, then Gary ride 10 km, then I ride 10 km again. I told him that I was keener on cycling than Gary and Gary was keener than me to sit in cafes eating all-day breakfasts so it worked out quite well. But the old boy still didn't think it was right. He gave me an iridescent paua shell (big mussel-shaped shells found on local beaches), which he had been using as an ashtray and receptacle for his chewed chewing gum. 'To remember New Zealand by,' he said. Then he suddenly said, 'Must go, mate. Got to get to the store for some fried kidneys. Full of iron you know.'

Later, in the chaotic kitchen, I was leafing through a pile of ancient Australian *Women's Weekly* magazines, one issue of which advised me in the 'Home Hints' section not to discard 'a rubber hot-water bottle that's sprung a leak', because 'filled with scraps of soft material, it makes an excellent kneeling pad which can be easily washed'. This from a certain R. Moran, Helensvale, Qld. What a marvellous tip! Could preserve my knees for years to come if tip utilised for inner-tent-kneeling activities. I was interrupted from picking up any more indispensable 'Home Hints' by the reappearance of my bobble-hatted friend. He pointed to a small domestic appliance on the counter top, shaped like a mini microwave but burnt black from its never having been cleaned. It was called 'A Lean Mean Grilling Machine'.

'Cooks a steak in ten minutes flat,' said my bobble man. 'Beau-da-full!'

I asked him how long he had been living on this site.

'Two months,' he said.

'And how long do you think you'll stay?'

'When the left hand tells the right hand what to do,' he said.

He told me he used to live in Bluff. 'The windiest town in the country,' he said, clapping both hands on to his bobble hat as if to signify holding it down in a strong wind. 'The main street there runs west to east so is bang on full frontal to the winds. In Riverton, you know, the main street runs north to south, so you can plot a course from the two towns!'

Later, when I went to wash up, the old boy was still there, staring at his 'Lean Mean Grilling Machine'. He looked at me as if he had never seen me before and asked me what I was doing. So I told him. He then said he thought I should cycle 10 km, then Gary should ride 10 km, and then I should ride 10 km again. I told him that he had already told me that, but I don't think he realised. 'I'm sixty-six . . .' he said before ambling back out into the cold night and back to his dilapidated caravan.

Tuatapere, Southland, 19 August

Just when you thought I must have exhausted all capitals of the world, I arrived in another one: this time 'The Sausage Capital of the World'. Gary, who likes his sausages (generally accompanied with fried egg, hash browns and beans in abundance), was pleased about this, though I can't say there'd been that much evidence of any sausages so far apart from a small shabby blue shop next door to the Four Square (which incidentally had a caged parrot outside that barked like a dog). The shop was called 'LL BUTCHERY'. Written across the front were the words: 'Quality Small Goods "A" Grade Meat SAUSAGE CAPITAL'.

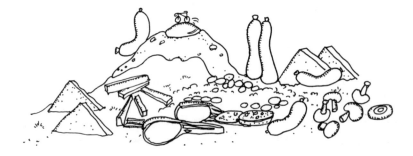

Never mind sausages – the town had plentiful supplies of saws and axes. At least it did in the little local museum. Once known as the 'The Hole in the Forest', Tuatapere went back to its early days as a sawmilling centre for the bushmen cutting their way down through the extensive lowland forests of native trees that once covered the area. Along with old black and white photographs showing the local loggers embroiled in the town's annual sawing and tree-axing competitions, the museum was full of various axes and cross-cut saws from those industrious forest-ruining wood-chopping days. There were axe handle slashers, mattock hoes and grubbers, timber twitches (used on rail tractors) and log hooks for hauling massive logs on the Waiau River. The museum was just a side room reached through the tourist office. No one else seemed very interested in the place. The tourist woman had to get up and unlock the door and turn on the light before sliding the door shut again and closing us in. It was not a museum of carefully lit display cabinets. They didn't have enough money for that. Instead, displays were simply placed randomly on shelves and tables. Anyone could quite easily have walked off with anything if they felt that way inclined.

Perched on a shelf over by the building's electricity meter was an old bottle. A few token explanatory words told me that this bottle was a 'Tea Bottle, Favoured by early Bushmen'. A little anonymous ditty followed:

> Let those who never drink strong tea
> Stick to their way of thinking
> But let them never interfere
> With other people's drinking.

The tourist office museum woman told us that a local man had found a 12-foot moa skeleton in a cave not far away so brought it in to show the museum. This museum then sent it off to a large museum for intricate study. And that museum still had the moa because it said it wouldn't send it back here until this tiny non-money-making museum got a $100,000 humidity controlled display cabinet. 'As if we can afford something like that!' said the tourist office woman. 'So we will never see that moa back here again.'

It's a shame the Maoris had to eat all their moas. I've seen a few skeletons of them during my time in these Antipodean parts, but I think clapping eyes on a live moa would have been quite a sight to be seen. A large sight too. The largest moa was the *Dinornis gigantis*, which attained the lofty height of three metres when standing to attention. All moas seem to have had a digestive system based on the foundations of Chesil Beach. As birds don't have teeth for chewing, moas encouraged plant digestion by swallowing up to five kilograms of pebbles (usually quartz – they had high standards those moas – because of its hardness) as gizzard stones to grind down the tough cellulose and fibres.

Tuatapere (which means 'ceremony before singing and amusement') may once have been a hive of milling, but it is now a rather slumberous farming centre. The only urgency about the place came care of the local radio station. At home, the adverts on local radio tend to centre around the opening of the latest optician or two-for-one deal down at the Cock and Bull, but around here they were about the best chemicals to use to prevent aborted lambs or, as one low rustic voice said, to 'come and test drive the latest Massey Ferguson!' Ooh, yes please.

Kingston, Southern Lakes District, 21 August

The road from Tuatapere to Te Anau was a joy of virtual emptiness, making up for the bone-chilling nor'westerly that cut like a knife. The gorse was yellow and wafting rich on the wind. There were larks and harriers and oystercatchers and paradise shelducks and tyre-squashed pukeko and possums and mailboxes of a mannequin's woman's torso and a man's lower half padded out with a cricket box. And near Clifden Suspension Bridge there were roadside signs saying things like 'SYD SLEE PINE CONES $3 A BAG'; 'HORSE POO 50c'; 'HUNTERS – BE SAFE BE SEEN'. Recently a hunter had been shot by another hunter who mistook him for a boar.

As I was riding I had layers of mountains on my eastern elbow rearing their heads into the pure air, where colours were honed by the sunshine to an almost surreal radiance. The near low ones were grassed, the mid-distance mid-height wooded, the far-off wall of jagged peaks rock and snow. This is the southern snub of the Southern Alps, the ridged ruffle of land that the earth's crust of this lively country had scalloped and buckled to half the height of Everest. Away to the west and south lies the World Heritage site of Fjordland National Park, the largest in New Zealand, covering 1.2 million hectares along the remote south-western coastline of the South Island. It contains fourteen fjords, from the famous Mitre Peak-reflecting Milford Sound south along the coast to Preservation Inlet, some stretching as far as 40 km inland as they trace the paths of the ancient glaciers that created them. Most of Fjordland is swathed in impenetrable bush. Wet bush. It rains a lot out there. The area is as inaccessibly isolated as it has always been. If Captain Cook were to return today to the same Fjordland inlet that he dropped anchor in over 230 years ago, he would recognise it still, for nothing has changed.

On past Belt Mountain, Diggers Hill, The Knob, Chimney Peaks and over Jericho Hill until I found Gary beside a big boulder on which a plaque said: 'THIS ROCK MARKS THE APPROXIMATE WATER LEVEL OF THE RAISED LAKE AS ORIGINALLY PRO-POSED'. We were standing fairly high up overlooking the broad plain of the Waiau River. Just over the way lay Lake Manapouri ('lake of the sorrowful heart'), which at 444 metres is New Zealand's second deepest lake and site of the country's largest power station, generating one-tenth of the nation's electricity. In the 1970s it was proposed to increase the level of the lake by 12 metres to provide more water storage for the hydroelectric station, but the prospect of irreparable damage to what is the most beautiful of New Zealand's lakes I've seen so far outraged New Zealanders and led to the Save Manapouri campaign becoming

the country's greatest environmental battle. Nationwide protests
and a petition with over a quarter of a million signatures eventually
led to the government scrapping the project. Some of the other
information where Gary and I were standing included the words of
Henry David Thoreau: 'In wildness is the preservation of the
world.'

By the time we were camping in Te Anau ('The Walking Capital
of the World') the sky had caved in and a brutish storm detonated
all around. The area had had a lashing of storms of late, so much
so that the one-way road to Milford Sound had been closed for
eight days due to avalanches. So that hit the idea of cycling up to
this overly photographed hot-spot on the head.

This morning a stinging, sleety rain fell diagonally on me as I
rode towards Kingston past overflowing rivers and floods, sheep,
deer farms, turnips, tussock and toetoe grass blowing merry hell in
the wind. Higher up, the mountains were covered in fresh dump-
ings of snow, but down here the untidy heaped hills were a
fantastic scrubby colour of purples and browns and ochres. At
Mossburn, where a sign said, 'Welcome to Mossburn: "The Deer
Capital – Northern Southland Naturally"', I turned off for Five
Rivers where I joined SH6, the main state highway that stretches
the length of the South Island (over 1,400 km) via the great West
Coast.

The trouble with these big highways is the big traffic. Suddenly
I had been catapulted back into the land of cyclist-sucking
double-trailer trucks and fast 4WDs – most of these ones full of
snow-seeking hoo-hahs with snowboards and skis piled high on
the roofs. I was now cycling over Jollies Hill Pass directly into the
full blast of the sleeting nor'westerly and could hardly move. My
face stung from the needles of icy rain and, no matter how hard
I tried to ride, my body grew progressively more numb. Despite
the slush-spraying roads and the ferocious buffeting winds, the
drivers' behaviour was appalling. All travelled too fast, too close.
Then three 4WDs, following an oncoming truck, overtook the
truck in a convoy, all gunning towards me at well over 100 km/h.
They missed me by inches, but none of the drivers in their heated

music-thumping sealed tanks looked as if they cared. Just north of Jollies Pass, the driver of an aggregate truck travelling in the opposite direction deliberately swerved into my lane and, with hand on horn, drove directly towards me before pulling away at the last second. Up in his cab, the driver thought this was the biggest joke; opening his mouth wide, he pulled a face of ugly guffaws.

At Garston ('New Zealand's Most Inland Village'), I sheltered for a moment beside the public toilets and an information board about the large amount of Chinese gold-mining that went on around here. Across the road at the Garston Hotel, where a lot of motorists stopped for a drink at the bar, a woman emerged with a bucket of water to sluice away a large pile of vomit from outside the door. By the time I got going again the wind was even stronger and my hands and feet were painful lumps of bloodless inefficiency.

On one long stretch of undulating road, two more vehicles overtook directly into my path. Moments later came the shock of a great cracking smack into my head. At first I thought a passing motorist had hurled a rock at my helmet. But then in my mirror I glimpsed a huge shape falling out of the sky towards me. I glanced over my shoulder and saw the massive shadowy shape of a bird as big as a buzzard dive-bombing towards me. Thwack! A direct hit. No matter how fast I tried to cycle, the bird, an Australian harrier, kept attacking my head. It's bad enough having an aggressive bird the size of a small seal crash into your head when you're walking out in the open far from anywhere or anyone (Iceland's great skuas spring to mind), but when you're trying to control a heavily laden bike in sleeting gale-force winds on a lunatic-speeding highway with the cross-sucking pull of passing vehicles, not knowing which angle the bird is going to come from next, it's an utter nightmare – enough to send you into a panicky nervous wreck. I turned into a nervous panicky wreck and, despite the near impossibility of cycling fast into the thrashing wind, I cycled fast, my legs whirring, my lungs bursting, using up every reserve of strength I could muster.

By the time I rolled into Kingston and spotted the camper

parked just down the road from an all-day breakfast cafe, I was in no great state. Hyperventilating vigorously, I stumbled through the sliding door of the van and collapsed on a seat, shaking with cold. Gary, cocooning me in his arms to try and get a bit of warmth generated, didn't know what had happened to me. And I couldn't explain. I was totally incapable of any coherent speech, which I suppose is nothing new.

Arrowtown, Southern Lakes District, 23 August

Kingston, with its grand population of 100, consisted of a small smattering of houses, a pub and a cafe-cum-store. There was also a motorcamp, which on the evening we arrived was a semi-frozen slush of mud. Apart from a couple of workmen living in a wreck of a caravan, no one else was staying. I told Gloria McEntyre, the motorcamp owner, about the episode with the dive-bombing harrier. She told me that during the early summer, when a lot of cyclists come this way, it was usually the aggressive magpies they had a problem with – so much so that some cyclists painted a pair of large eyes on the back of their helmets to deter further attack. 'Harriers have been known to attack people,' she said, 'but usually only when they are protecting a nest or sheep carcass.'

Every night since Gary and I have been sleeping in the camper I've had the sliding windows on my side open wide above my head. No matter that it's winter with below-freezing temperatures – I like a good dose of fresh air. So far I've woken up with leaves on me, rain on me and, during our Kingston stay, a small snowdrift on my head. This time, not for the first time, the windows froze over, making it impossible to slide them shut. Gary wasn't impressed.

Kingston had been hit by a heavy snowstorm over night and by morning everything was white and deadened by the grip of hard snow. Gary wasn't overly happy about me attempting to cycle to Queenstown, but being stubbornly difficult, I insisted I'd be fine. As it was, the gritters and snowploughs were soon busily at work clearing the road that hugged the shore of Z-shaped Lake Wakatipu.

Lake Wakatipu (or, to give it its full name, Wakatipuawaimaori – meaning a succinct 'the freshwater trough where the giant goblin lies') is New Zealand's third largest lake after Taupo and Te Anau. It fills a glacier-carved valley, surrounded by steeply rising mountains, and has an oddly behaving water level that rises and falls about 125 millimetres every five minutes. The scientific explanation is that this phenomenon is caused either by wind or by variations in atmospheric pressure. The Maori have other ideas and put it down to the giant demon that kidnapped a beautiful girl and took her back to his cave in the mountains. But while he snoozed the girl was rescued by her lover, who set fire to the giant. The giant's body burned a hole deep into the ground until the only thing left was his heart, which survived after the flames were doused by a torrential downpour. Rainwater filled the valley in the shape of the giant, but his heart is still beating, causing the water to rise and fall.

I followed the lake as occasional blizzards swept off the jaggedly towering Remarkables and Hector Mountains and out across the water to the mountains on the other side – Lambing Saddle, Mount Dick, Symmetry Peaks and the Centre Spur. The weather had put off a lot of people and so the traffic was light to non-existent. As I climbed up the icy road of the Devil's Staircase, I had the place to myself.

More capitals, this one Queenstown – 'The Adventure Capital of the World' – a busy place overflowing with bug-eyed adrenalin junkies spending a couple of hundred dollars to be strapped to someone or something and hurled off a high place. While cycling around New Zealand I kept meeting other tourists who were amazed I could spend so long here and not do any of the extreme things that so many people came here to do. Things like bungee-jumping, sky-diving, jet-boating, heli-skiing, parapenting, parabungeeing, river-sledging, scree-luging, cave-rafting, canyon-crunching, white water-drowning, paracrashing and scuba-dying.

I can't say any of these things took my fancy. The chancy uncertainty of cycling (mostly) alone seemed to be quite exciting enough. And you didn't have to queue up to do it, wear identikit tour-group costumes or fork out large sums of dosh for the pleasure. The simple pastime of surviving overly close encounters with 50-tonne logging trucks, dive-bombings by aggressive head-whacking Australian harriers or plummeting down the multiple hairpins of a mountain pass with ballast-laden panniers and bike-slamming crosswinds at 40 mph – or just cycling and camping in a land of unpredictably severe weather – flooded my veins with such a surge of adrenalin that I felt no need to throw myself off a totteringly high bridge or building attached to nothing more than a large elastic band wrapped around my ankles (and paying an arm and a leg for the privilege) while hoping that the supervisor or jumpmaster, or whatever they're called, was concentrating when they attached the correct life-saving clip to the appropriate toggle.

Up the road from Queenstown rushes the Shotover River, which gained a reputation as the 'richest river in the world' because of stories such as that involving a pair of nineteenth-century prospectors who set out to rescue their dog from a rock crevice and discovered over 11 kg of gold in a single day. The river still yields gold but these days most people flock here to be strapped into the Shotover Jet for a water-skimming ride between the sheer faces of the canyon walls. At Arthur's Point, Gary and I watched as one load of mouth-gaping jet-boaters climbed back up the hill after their ride, giving each other a lot of jet-boat-bonding backslaps and high-fives in the process, while shouting things like, 'Kicking!', 'Awesome!', 'Man alive!', 'Sweet!', 'Fin-*tis*-tic!' and 'Ultimate experience!' That was quite enough of that, thank you very much, so we took ourselves off to Arrowtown.

Wanaka, Otago, 24 August

News last night was about how an American woman ate fifty-seven lobsters in one go. I hear she is still alive, though she deserves not to be.

Since waking up yesterday morning in Arrowtown (surprisingly attractive old gold-mining town of weather-timbered shop fronts and white stone churches shaded by ancient sycamores) the weather has been unexpectedly glorious – icy cold but blue. Perfect, in fact, for cycling the Cardrona road over the Crown Range. At 1080 metres, the Cardrona road is the highest highway in New Zealand. Apart from the number of motorists driving SUVs with skis and snowboards on the roof without taking the black-ice state of the road into consideration, this ride rates as the most fantastically enjoyable and scenic ascent and descent of switchbacks I've had yet in this severely mountainous land. I flew down the Cardrona side of the mountain into a clean, ice-capped wind, at one stage passing a high deer fence

draped with hundreds of bras, among other items of intimate under-
wear. Just a Kiwi thing, I believe.

Before I knew it, I was back in Wanaka. Only difference since I
was last here at Easter: the poplars were no longer golden, there
were no tents in Lakeland Holiday Park, all the outdoor stores had
swapped their stock from bikes and tents to skis and snowboards
and polar tech wear. Oh, and my ankle worked.

Harihari, South Westland, 28 August

If cycling over the Crown Range was top-notch for snow and views
and plummeting hairpin cornering and the inexplicable appearance of multiple fence-strewn bras, Haast Pass had to be top for
dense rainforest-like bush and . . . well, rain. Because it's the rain
that makes the rainforest-like bush so dripping and leafy and lush.
And it's the rain that sends the water surging with powerful force
over the outlandish-sized riverbed boulders at the Gates of Haast
(site of an iron bridge that spans the river) and cascading over the
Fantail and Thunder Creek waterfalls. And it's the rain that helps
to form the drips into overhanging icicles like lethal daggers the
size of organ pipes.

But it wasn't the rain that rained down on me. For once it was
moving up the country just a step ahead. All I'd had since leaving
Wanaka was sun from a raw winter sky. Lake Hawea (beautiful
milky-blue lake overlooked by Mount Grandview) slid past on my
right, as did the equally alluring Lake Wanaka on my left. Then
came Makarora ('Paul McCartney bellowing'), where the hills rose
all around like the walls of a fortress, with the tiny hamlet (containing a cafe) sitting in a cleft, sheltered by the land.

Gary and I camped across the road from the cafe with a cyclist
from South Korea. Pusan Man, we called him. He was cycling in a
woolly hat and a heavy camouflage army jacket. When I rode up
behind him he looked like a moving bush. Strapped to the back of
his bike were two spare tyres and a hot-water bottle. Attached to his
handlebars was a mini MP3 player that he plugged himself into

when he rode, so that he moved along the road with no ears and imitating a bush. I thought: heaven help him. But heaven would help, because he was a Christian. I only found this out when he mentioned he wasn't that keen on cycling ('velly hard work travel method'), so I asked him why he did it, and he said he only cycled because it brought him closer to God.

Haast Pass is the southernmost road crossing of the Southern Alps. It's named after Sir Johann Franz Julius von Haast. Who the devil's he? I asked myself when I first heard his name. I also asked Gary, but because the question involved no references to undersquinted abutments or flyball governors he just gave me a look like a sheep in the rain. A little research later, I discovered that von Haast was an Austrian geologist who, obviously not in the name of modesty, named the pass after himself even though it was the gold prospector, Charles Cameron, who had been the first European to cross the pass. The Maori (who in the naming of grand passes of course didn't qualify in the eyes of the new settlers) had known about this route for centuries, using it to cross the Main Divide on food-gathering expeditions and in search of greenstone. These Europeans only discovered the route in the 1860s. When the great Haast gold rush of 1867 came along, considered to be a 'duffer' to hundreds of miners who found no gold, the Otago Provincial Government, excited by the prospect of a new goldfield, decided to have a track cut over Haast Pass. But when little gold was found the project was shelved and only revived at the prospect of a port at the settlement of Jackson Bay. By 1876 there was a rough walking track, which was improved sufficiently for a herd of cattle to be driven over in 1877. It wasn't until 1929 that an attempt was made to begin a road between Hawea and Haast, but nothing much happened until 1956. The road was eventually finished in 1960, with a link through to Fox Glacier in 1965. The whole lot was finally topped in tarmac in 1995. Quite a long-winded fiasco, all in all.

One part of the descent of Haast Pass is so steep that you feel as if you're going to be bucked clean over your bars. There was even an 'õh-fuk-a-ta-ne – my-brakes-have-failed!' runaway ramp to try to lessen the impact of an out-of-control crash. I continued plunging downwards alongside the swollen Haast River and on past Roaring Billy Falls, Roaring Swine Creek, Orman Falls, Imp Grotto, Dancing Creek, Dizzy Creek, Dismal Creek (things are going downhill fast, and not just in gradient), Glitterburn and Snapshot. About 10 km from where the broad Haast River meets the sea and SH6 swings north across the bridge, I passed a sign that said: 'ONLY 60 KM TO PARINGA LODGE'. Only 60! Not that I wanted to stay at Paringa Lodge, mind you, it's just that a sign like that can only be written for motorists. You wouldn't say to a cyclist who had just heaved themselves 80-odd kilometres over a mountain divide: 'ONLY 60 KM TO GO!' Well, I suppose you could, but I'd only hit you.

The scenery seemed to be getting better and better. From Haast the road runs up the coast, squeezed between the sea and the mountains. I bowled along over Coppermine Creek and Waita ('there's a fly in my soup') River, past Bald Hill and Seal Point. For a short while, the winds that normally torment this coast pushed me along as fast as if I was being chased by a pack of snarling rabid hounds before deciding they preferred to smack me in the face. Some of the trees around here, trying to make a stand against the weather, were so one-sidedly warped by the winds howling in off the stormy expanse of Tasman that they look as if they'd had a bad hair day: bald on the back with manes blown into a scraggy thicket on their east face.

Onwards and upwards through a forest of spindly, sky-scraping kahikatea, New Zealand's tallest tree. The West Coast was everything I had always imagined the rest of New Zealand to be: beautifully wild and sparsely populated with empty roads, unruly rivers, primeval forests, formidable mountains and waves crashing like avalanches on to a ruggedly deserted shore. Rudyard Kipling referred to the region as 'last, loneliest, loveliest, exquisite, apart'.

But although the sun had been shining down unbrokenly on me, the West Coast doesn't have a reputation for good weather. Rain tends to fall in buckets amounting to some 5 metres (nearly 17 feet! – or well over three times taller than me) a year, which at least accounts for all the luscious rainforests and dazzling greens. Many Kiwis refer to the area not so much as the West Coast as the Wet Coast. When Abel Tasman sailed this way in 1642, he was so unimpressed with the weather and what he could see of the impenetrable forests and inhospitable rampart of mountains that he hastily scarpered north. Captain Cook called it 'an inhospitable shore'. The next to pass comment on the unfavourable conditions was the Frenchman Jules de Blossville, who noted in his logbook in 1823 that the coast was 'one long solitude, with forbidding sky and frequent tempest'. His countryman Dumont D'Urville shortly afterwards summed it up in one word: 'Frightful'. So off-putting was the West Coast that European exploration inland didn't begin in earnest until the middle of the nineteenth century. After spending 550 days in the wilderness, and reduced to a diet of fern root, penguin, rat and finally his own dog, Thomas Brunner described the region as 'the very worst country I have seen in New Zealand. For what reason the natives choose to live here I cannot imagine.' But the natives – the Maori – took well to the area, they ventured across the mountains in small parties, prizing the West Coast for its quantities of fine greenstone.

It's no wonder the West Coast is so empty of people – or Coasters, as they are known. The population stands at around 38,000 (a mere 1 per cent of the country's 4 million people), slightly less than when it peaked at 40,000 during the gold rush days of the 1860s when men lit their cigars with £5 notes.

Since those hardworking, hard-drinking, hard-fighting days, there's still an air of Wild West to the place. A notice in the window of Fox Glacier general store was advertising not prams or kittens for sale, or ironing or baby-sitting services like you get in the post office window at home, but a rifle for sale ('BSA 270 Wooden stock, blued barrel, very accurate, excellent flat shooting calibre with great hitting power, ideal for West Coast thar, deer, chammy'). And in today's paper, I've just read about a man who's been charged after a West Coast armed offenders' squad call-out found him with unlawful possession of swords, blow pipes, a bayonet, knuckledusters, batons and 'other homemade weapons'.

Fox Glacier, like its neighbour the Franz Josef Glacier, is all about icy brilliance and eerie magnitude – those vast white tongues of old winter snow compressed to ice and descending down a valley about 100,000 times slower than a river while locked in a series of retreats and advances. Though these ones seem to be doing a lot more retreating than advancing. A sign at Fox Glacier said: 'IN 1750 THE GLACIER WAS HERE'. Sounds all a bit like the usual 'I WOZ 'ERE' graffiti you find carved into rocks and trees and bus shelters to me. I never knew glaciers could be such louts. Anyway, the tip of the 1750s glacier was a lot further towards the sea than it is today. Now it's shrunk back by a good five minutes' cycle ride.

So what makes a glacier like an army, with all this advancing and retreating? Well, if I've got this right, if the ice melts from the lower glacier faster than ice accumulates in the upper glacier, the glacier will retreat. But if ice melts from the lower glacier slower than ice accumulates in the upper glacier, the glacier will advance. So when the icy armies of Franz Josef are advancing, they are responding to heavy snowfalls (with fortunately precious little collateral damage) that occurred at the upper glacier about five years ago. Seems this response rate is much faster than the world average for valley glaciers, which is 10–15 years. Franz Josef likes to puts its skates on and is known as a 'dynamic glacier' (what, as opposed to a slothful couch-potato one?) and can advance or retreat at rates of over a metre a day.

Well, I stared at the wall of dirty ice of the Franz Josef for a considerable amount of time and didn't see it move an inch. Maybe I should ask for my money back. Not that I had spent any money, mind, as in New Zealand you can walk up to these large lumps of ice for free.

There are some big old hills . . . sorry, saddles around here for cycling up and over. And if that's not enough, there's a mount, in the form of Mount Hercules – a surprisingly enjoyable mount for cycling over if ever there was one. That is, apart from the hoons and boy racers out for a spin from Franz Josef.

Earlier, I'd found Gary polishing off an all-day breakfast and a Mrs Mac's steak and cheese pie at the cafe in Whataroa (not 'what a top oarsman!' but 'tall foodstore platform', even though I couldn't see any tall ones around – just ground-level ones like the one Gary emerged from looking like he'd eaten a fried egg too many). Whataroa was like something out of a spaghetti western, consisting of one straight windblown street (devoid of human life) lined with a scattered assortment of slightly shanty shiplap abodes. The only thing missing was a few big tumbleweed globes bowling across the road. A mini van parked on the pavement doubled up as the local school bus (there was a yellow sign with the silhouette of skipping schoolchildren that got propped up in the window when it was needed) and the tour bus for Rainforest Nature Tours (Whataroa is the home of New Zealand's only white heron breeding colony). The only thing I saw moving (apart from Gary) was the odd Westland milk tanker that came rumbling down the street.

Gary and I camped behind a pub in Harihari (an almost identical version of Whataroa) and the wind was blowing a spanking gale. When we arrived here, there was a goat in the field behind us. But when I last looked it was nowhere to be seen. Maybe it had been blown away.

Hokitika, Westland, 29 August

I met up with Gary in Pukekura ('remedy for sickness'). This metropolis (pop. 2) on the edge of the podocarp rainforest consisted of the Bushman's Centre containing the Bushman's Museum and, across the road, a pub, unsettlingly called the Puke Pub. The Bushman's Centre had a model of a giant sandfly hanging off the outside wall. Not that you needed a reminder that you were back in sandfly territory – the little buggers were everywhere, greedily piercing their blood-sucking proboscis into any exposed skin. Inside the cafe, which contained stools and benches lined with possum fur,

Gary ate an all-day breakfast followed by a Pete's Possum Pie. The wrapper of the pie not only had a list of ingredients including 'prime N. Z. possum meat', but gave a short history lesson about how 'possums were introduced into New Zealand in the 1800s to establish a fur trading industry'. The khaki-green wrapper containing a picture of a possum went on to tell you how possums 'have now become a major pest, destroying huge amounts of our native forest. When you sample our pie you are helping save New Zealand forests.' So full marks to Gary here for doing his part towards the preservation of native Kiwi foliage. It was no good being a vegetarian in a place like this, where the population (Justine – originally a Lancashire lass – and Pete, of Pete's Possum Pie fame) did not have much favourable comment to pass upon shrubbery-munching persons, and where you could buy stickers for sale declaring that: 'VEGETARIAN is an old Indian word for Piss Poor Hunter'.

Mrs Possum Pete told us that some people are so disgusted by the place that as soon as they walk through the door they walk back out again, appalled. 'And the health and safety people are always trying to close us down,' she added.

The miserable sods. I think there should be more of these sort of places, myself. Puts all those squash 'ems I keep passing in the road to good use.

Some eateries around here were all for BYO (Bring Your Own Bottle), but The Pukekura Road Kill Restaurant had a slight variation on the theme as it was down to you to bring your own road kill. Their motto was: 'You kill them. We grill them.'

As for the Puke Pub Possum Menu, well, there was quite a choice. There was the Road Kill of the Day. Or you could have the Guess that Mess Daily Special ('Possum straight from the highway to you'), Wheel-Tread Possum toasted sandwich ('All sorts of foreign filling'), Headlight Delight Pie ('Fresh from the roadside'), Sandfly Steaks ('Human Revenge') or Shovel Flipped Roadside Pizza. There again, if time wasn't on your side, how about the Bag 'n' Gag ('Our daily take-out lunch special served open face – Anything Dead on Bread')? Even dogs were catered for by way of the Possum Supreme Dog Food.

As for drinking at the Puke Pub, the Sale of Liquor Hours were strictly 'From Open to Close'. And should you feel like a jug or a mere swift half, just make sure you arrived sober, as 'pissed bastards won't be served'. Well, it's good to be upfront about these things. No point dallying politely around the bush.

Talking of bush, let's head into the Bushman's Museum – a darkened room filled with a few soporific possums, some eels the size of telegraph poles and, out past a sign warning: 'TALL MEN AND DUTCH GIRLS MIND HEAD' (Possum Pete was of the opinion that Dutch girls seem to have legs that go on for weeks, though Mrs Possum Pete said some people took unkindly to this and obviously had 'no sense of humour'), a large pig called Sir Ron Trotter. Back in the crepuscular museum and to the sound of a few possums scratching around half-heartedly in their pens, Gary and I sat down in an empty audience of chairs to watch a film on deer hunting which came with the warning: 'This video does contain a small amount of shooting. It may not be suitable for children or adults that come from Planet Bambi.'

Sounded good to me, so I continued sitting and this is what I learnt. Along with rabbits and possums and other vegetation-destroying animals, deer were first released in New Zealand in the middle of the nineteenth century for the pleasure of well-to-do hunters to shoot for sport. But things soon got out of hand with so many mammals running amok, killing and decimating native forests and bird life. By the 1930s professional deer cullers, centring on the West Coast, had headed into the mountains in an effort to remove large numbers of these feral animals that were destroying the fragile landscape. Over the next couple of decades or more, two million deer had been shot. But there were still a lot out there. During the 1950s feral deer were in demand for the start of a venison industry, which has since grown into the country having three million deer farms and a $260 million export market for venison.

But it was back in the sixties that capturing the deer was at its most exciting. Before the invention of a net gun, a Kiwi called Tim Wallace had the idea of having men jump out of low-flying

helicopters on to the backs of fleeing deer. There was film of this
and it looked like the most ridiculously dangerous pastime (but
most amusing to watch) you could imagine – a sort of chaotic deer
rodeo, only instead of leaping from steer back to steer back at
ground level, these cowboy-like men (one of whom used to be
Possum Pete) were dropping out of helicopters from a height of
thirty feet or more dressed in no more protective clothing than a
pair of old faded jeans and a checked logger's shirt. And it wasn't
exactly a soft landing. Many of these deer had antlers which,
judged wrong, must have felt like landing on a fence of spiked railings. Some of the deer were so terrified by the helicopter and
having a man landing on their back that they would go completely
berserk and charge straight over the edge of a precipice, sometimes taking the heli-hunters (as they were called) with them. Over
eighty men were killed in what became known as New Zealand's
Last Great Adventure.

Along with heli-hunting, one of the unusual things that had happened in New Zealand during its short Pakeha-inhabited history was
the itinerant life of the Puke Pub itself. It had started its days a mile
north of Pukekura at the Waitaha River ferry crossing. Then, at the
beginning of the twentieth century, someone had the bright idea of
relocating it by Lake Ianthe, about five miles away. I'm sure there are
easier things to relocate than pubs, but once Kiwis get one of their
ideas of great ingenuity they're like a bull with a dangling red rag in
their sights and charge headlong in to give it their all. So the pub
was scooped up and moved with great effort down the road as far as
Pukekura. In the flummoxing way that laws work, there was a bill, or
whatever the government had in those days, that said that pubs
could not be moved more than a mile a year. So in 1905 the pub was
plonked down in Pukekura. And there it stayed. Lake Ianthe was still
waiting for its pub a hundred years on.

From Pukekura I continued rolling up the coast through tall
forests and native bush, sandwiched all the time between the sea
and the Southern Alps and their various ranges like the Big Hill
Range, the Ragged Range and the Wild Man's Brother Range. At

the base of bush-clad Mount Greenland I met up with Gary in Ross, a tiny rural village that had sprung to fame in the gold-rush days because it lay on New Zealand's richest alluvial goldfield. It was here in 1907 that the Honourable Roddy was found, which at 99 oz was the largest gold nugget ever discovered in New Zealand. Named after the Minister of Mines, the Honourable Roddy ended up being given as a coronation gift to King George V, who melted it down to make royal tableware at Buckingham Palace.

A quick burst on the pedals took me to Hokitika, the first place of any size since Wanaka (some 450 km away) with the first bank and supermarket. It's another one of those towns that mushroomed overnight in the big gold rush of the 1860s, growing from a collection of forlorn rain-soaked canvas tents to a lively settlement of some 15,000 people (current population 3,500) and over a hundred hotels. The port here would have been one of the busiest in the country, with a score or more of ships arriving or leaving in a single day, mostly packed with Irish, Scots, Chinese, Australian and American immigrants. The quayside would have up to forty sailing ships mooring at any one time after running the treacherous sandbar at the entrance to the harbour. Spectators would line the shore to watch vessels negotiate this hazard by sailing broadside on to the seas. Between 1865 and 1867 a ship ran aground or was wrecked every ten days on average. At times the seafront had too many wrecks to count, and the flotsam sailed up the main street at high tide. More than forty ships were wrecked completely; the rest were raised by screwjacks and dragged across the bar to the river in an operation that became known as 'making the overland trip'.

Gary and I paid a visit to Jacquie Grant's Eco Centre to have a look at 'the biggest collection of giant eels in the world'. They resembled a large tangle of long logs and looked decidedly horrible, with squashy pug-nosed faces. And teeth. One of the female staff told us that they could live up to one hundred. That's a hundred years too long in my book. I said jokingly to the woman that I wouldn't want to find one of these at the bottom of my tent. She said, 'Well, it's quite possible! On their way from river to sea they cross land and people have found them in their tents before!' She also said they go all the way to Tonga to mate. Gary said, 'Much like a lot of tourists, then.'

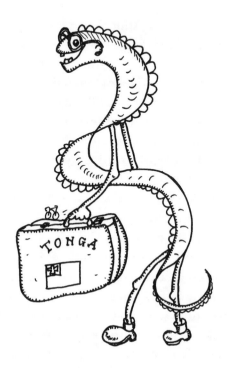

Over in the nocturnal house we peered at a fluffball of kiwis (which can live up to half the age of a giant eel), looking like a mixture between old men with metal detectors as they went rootling around in the leaf litter, and car mechanics dipsticking their long pointy nostril-mounted bills deep into the earth. Kiwis don't look like birds, more like large hamsters with beaks. They are tubby flightless things with defunct vestigial wings, Woody Allen eyesight, turkey legs and feathers that are more like soft downy hair. Apart from the precious few hours they spend at night poking about for worms, they pass the better part of their lives sleeping – up to twenty hours a day. Maybe all that egg-laying wears them out, for kiwis lay the largest eggs for their size of any bird: each egg weighs up to a third of the female's body weight. And they can lay up to a hundred in a lifetime. That could explain why, after all her hard work trying to prise the egg out, the female leaves the male to hatch it while she guards the burrow like a hawk.

Punakaiki, Westland, 30 August

Back on the bike I took off up the road passing the Coastpak factory – the 'Buyers and Processors of Quality Sphagnum Moss'. This moss grows in abundance around here and was used during the two world wars as sterile swabs. These days it is hoovered up by Japanese and Korean orchid growers for its spongily absorptive properties, though I think they should leave it where it is – looks much nicer out in the wilds.

The best part of the flat-to-undulating ride from Hokitika to Greymouth was the road–rail bridges, where trains share the same bridge with road traffic. I can imagine it leads to some exciting confrontations at times. The only drama I had while negotiating these accident-waiting-to-happen pinch-points was when a logging truck tried to overtake me (the bridges are one lane wide), which was not what I needed while concentrating hard on not getting my wheels caught in the wheel-swallowing grooves of the rail tracks.

Six months after my last wonky-ankled visit, I was back in the drabness of Greymouth. Gary and I picnicked beside the big rock breakwater wall built about ten years ago following two disastrous floods and now directing the force of the river currents against the sandbar at the river mouth. Like Hokitika's, this bar had been the cause of sinking too many ships in its time. A stone memorial was covered in plaques to commemorate some of the hundreds who had drowned on the bar. One of these engraved plaques conveyed the inevitable sadness of a death of a man, but also, in true Kiwi style, humour. 'In memory of Kenneth Rands,' it said, 'who tragically lost his life age 48 yrs on the Greymouth Bar with the capsize of the *FV CRAIG-EWEN*. August 2nd 1993. OFTEN LATE BUT LEFT TOO SOON.'

For once I seem to be in the right part of the country. Amazingly for such a notoriously wet coast, the sun has shone almost unbrokenly for the past ten days. Just across the mountains, Canterbury has been suffering with its snowiest month since 1988. Before that the snowiest was July 1939. Possum Pete told me that a good day on the West Coast was worth ten good days in Christchurch. He was right. It's been the best cycling coast I've had in a long chalk. And the wild and rocky stretch of bluffs and headlands with their white lacework of smashed sea north of Greymouth has been no exception. Gary and I camped at Punakaiki – a gorgeous gasp of deserted skimming-stone beach and the famous Pancake Rocks, strange outcrops of stratified limestone enclosing surging tunnels and spouting blowholes.

Collingwood, Nelson, 1 September

From Punakaiki I charged northwards past Seal Island and Woodpecker Bay and on through Charleston (another old gold-mining town with a population of 300, though it once had 12,000 souls and 80 grog shops and a direct sea link with Melbourne) to Cape Foulwind (named by Captain Cook, who hadn't taken kindly to the weather around here) and Westport, also once a prosperous gold-rushing place but now, despite its self-proclamation as the 'Adventure Capital of the Coast', an apparently uneventful place that a local man tried to make more eventful by telling us that Westport was the country's only successfully mined source of bituminous coal. Though this may sound riveting (to those with a keen interest in bituminous coal) and prompted Gary to get me to join him taking a turn around the local Coaltown Museum ('good flyball governors on the steam engine, Jose,'), it wasn't enough to make us linger for long so I gave chase to Gary up the Buller Gorge.

As we headed inland over the ranges the long unsullied skies finally gave way to an ominous cloudbank. Cold winds and sleet mixed up with bursts of sun and rain was the jumble of weather that threw itself at us through Murchison (scene of powerful 1929 quake), Tapawera ('party of plastic containers'), Motueka (slightly hippy wholesome hot-spot), Pupu Springs (the largest in the southern hemisphere), Takaka Hill (silly steep uphill hill – adorned at the top, at Caves Lookout, with the ubiquitous burnt-out boy-racer Subaru Legacy – but with glorious hairpin-bend 15 km descent) and the tiny 'township' of Collingwood, containing one store, one cafe, one pub, one petrol station, one (very small) museum dedicated to yet more gold-mining and one lugubrious seal practising a bit of half-hearted backstroke in the river beside our camp.

Auckland, 7 September

That seal was definitely taking to the waters in the calm before the storm. Collingwood sits bang on Golden Bay (originally called Murderer's Bay by Abel Tasman in 1642 when his clinker-built jolly-boat was rammed by a Maori canoe, killing four of his crew), which stretches in a long crescent, curving like a beckoning talon up to distant Farewell Spit – a long spit of sand beloved by godwits and dotterels.

On the night of our arrival in Collingwood, Farewell Spit was clearly visible from our camp spot, but by morning the scene had deteriorated into one of raging seas and sodden skies. The wind tore in from the west with such Tasman Sea strength that, not for the first time in New Zealand, it was impossible to stand, let alone cycle. Gary packed my bike into the van and we took off east along the same road I had cycled towards Picton. By the time we arrived in Havelock I was a fidgety van-induced heap of annoyance, so Gary, to gain some peace of mind, turfed me out so that I could cycle (for the second time) the scenically undulating Queen Charlotte Drive to Picton. The following morning the rain had stopped, so with time to spare before our afternoon ferry to Wellington, Gary joined me on his steed to cycle Queen Charlotte Drive again. We rode almost as far as Havelock, passing several FART (Fight Against Ridiculous Taxes) stickers stuck to homemade mailboxes, before turning round and riding back again.

Gary, who apart from when I've been cycling has been beside me for three months, has now gone – taken to the skies with boxed bike, twenty rolls of my film slides and four of my notebooks of notes. In a day and a half he'll be back at home in an autumnal-heading hemi-sphere and I'll still be here in Jacquie's flat, looking out of the window at the fast-flying clouds over Rangitoto and the flags snapping like lunatics from those strengthened flagpoles designed to withstand wind speeds of 170 km/h on Auckland Harbour Bridge.

Now that Gary has gone, Jacquie has moved back the mat around the foot of the toilet. She has a bit of a severe reaction to the thought of men standing up and spraying while they pee. Not to mention leaving the seat up. So from the outset of Gary's arrival back in June, Jacquie asked him if he could sit down while peeing. And that's what he had to do – lady pees, as he called them. When it comes down to it, none of us girls like spray or seats left up; it's just that some feel stronger about it than others. Take MAPSU – Mothers Against Peeing Standing Up – which seems to be an American (where else?) organisation, dedicated to 'transforming the way the world goes to the bathroom by 2010'. They have a web-site and they produce MAPSU T-shirts and print-out posters and the thesis that 'the longer the urine has to travel, the bigger the dissipation radius gets'. Apparently, peeing standing up destroys families. MAPSU urges that 'at some point you need to ask your-self, Is it worth it? What has peeing standing up cost me in my life?' But that's modern Western life for you. You didn't get dragged under by such hand-wringing soul-searching questions when it was all just a matter of course to go outside and water the soil.

Tauranga, Bay of Plenty, 3 October

After Gary left I went into mourning for twelve days. I never thought I'd miss him so much, but soon after he had walked through the departure gates for his 9.45 p.m. ANZ flight to LHR, I noticed immediately that empty rush of air that comes when a person you're accustomed to having around you is all at once gone.

During this time I took myself off on various ferries with bike and accompanying clobber to some of Auckland's outer islands, like Waiheke, which had houses called things like This'tle Doo. The west side of this island was fast becoming another Auckland suburb complete with boy-racing hoons, but the east side around the stony and corrugated dirt Man o' War Bay Road and Cowes was wild and empty and lovely.

I also sailed off to Tiritiri Matangi, a small scrubby island in the midst of the Hauraki Gulf Maritime Park. Tiritiri Matangi is a twitcher's paradise containing a veritable mêlée of endangered birds. As it is classified as an 'open sanctuary', a guide took me under his wing. He was a tall elderly chap called Ashley and he sported a wild tuffet of hair like a tomtit's tail that sprouted from the gap at the back of his baseball cap. With Ashley's aid, I spotted many fine-feathered oddities such as stitchbirds, saddlebacks, whiteheads (popokatea), shining cuckoos, little blue penguins (the Aussies call them fairy penguins), Caspian terns and the flightless and endangered takahe – stumpy birds, producing a short klowp and oomf alarm note, that were once thought to be extinct. There were also a fair few robins. Not scarlet-breasted, these ones, but ivory white. Oddly, outside the British Isles, robins are skulking and secretive birds, shy and infrequently seen. Only back home do they have this flamboyant trust in humans, ever happy to perch on a handle of a nearby spade.

Another scarcely seen bird I saw was the kokako, otherwise known as the wattled crow due to its big beady fleshy blue lobes hanging like fashion accessories off its throat. Ashley got very excited and told me that though he had been coming to this island for the past twenty years, he had never seen a kokako so close up or for so long. Which I can't say is a comment that many men have made to me in my time.

*

In Gary's last few hours in New Zealand we had taken the ferry to Half Moon Bay and then cycled down to Pakuranga to visit Frank and Jan Gardner. Frank had written to me a few years before, after reading my books, and invited me to visit him if I ever made it down this way. Straight away he was the sort of man that made you feel like you'd known him well for years, and Jan soon set to work feeding Gary with Danish pastries the size of UFOs while I was given a bunch of bananas and a pawpaw the size of a rugby ball. Frank, now retired, used to be an industrial chemist working with polyester resins. He also used to live in Manchester (his city of birth) and, like many Mancunians living on the doorstep of the Pennines, became a keen cyclist. So keen, in fact, that he would always ride so hard he would often get the bonk (that moment when a cyclist runs out of blood sugar and goes all wobbly and can't do sums), reducing him to collapsing flat out on the ground – sometimes even in the middle of a pavement in a town with people stepping around him a little perplexed.

The thick fog of smoggy pollution was so bad in Manchester as he was growing up that Frank decided he wanted to work in a city where the sun shone. So at the end of the sixties he moved to Sydney. 'But I never found Australia that interesting,' he said. 'The only interest is in the detail – the birds, the rocks, the plants. But on the surface, Australia is just dry and flat and hot.' Frank admitted he had never travelled as far as the middle of the country. 'Jan has though – and it flooded!'

Frank said about Australia. 'Ah, land of our convict ancestors! You've probably heard of the would-be settler being asked by immigration, "Do you have a criminal record?" "No," he answered, "I didn't realise that it's still compulsory."'

Since boyhood, Frank had always wanted to go to New Zealand. So one day not long after he moved to Australia, he came over here on holiday. 'And I've lived in Auckland ever since,' he said. The only trouble with New Zealand, according to Frank, was the country's lack of history. 'You won't find any building here much past 1840,' he said. 'And even that is considered pretty ancient.' Not so long ago Frank had been to a talk given by the Mayor of Devonport, who was interested in New Zealand's young history. 'He told us that one day he was standing with a friend on Mount Victoria when they started jumping up and down and realised the ground was moving. They investigated this earth-moving phenomenon and discovered an old filled-in gun emplacement. The mayor discovered the gun had been fired only once as a test and as it had broken every window in Devonport the authorities decided that the country had better not have a war after that.'

Frank asked if during my travels throughout the country I had ever come across references to No. 8 (fencing) wire. I had, but I'd never known exactly what people had been going on about apart from making something out of nothing. So Frank elaborated. 'Kiwis like to believe that they lead the world in ingenuity and can make or fix up anything with a bit of No. 8 wire and so you often hear of a No. 8 wire mentality. It probably harks back to the days when goods arrived infrequently after a long sea voyage and people meanwhile had to make do. Even as recently as the late sixties I was asked to bring in some aluminium foil from Sydney. Even that wasn't readily available.'

Frank had wanted to know whether I would be flying home with Gary. Ah, that old onion. And something I had been debating on and off with Gary over the past month. Gary had been surprisingly enthusiastic (I think he would like me to turn a bit more normal and not feel this need to cycle fifty miles a day all over the shop), but much as I would like to go home and start nesting procedures, I also fancy trying to travel right around the world by bike and boat. So that's my latest plan of action – to take a cargo ship to Australia and hope Gary might come out to meet me in Sydney for Christmas. And then I could cycle home from there, taking boats in between the watery bits. Shouldn't take too long if I push my legs into gear.

So, with Gary long gone, I'm now camping on the beach beside an edgy sea just south of Tauranga at Papamoa ('fatherly lawn-mowing services'). Back in Auckland I had gone wandering around the harbour and port trying to find a boat to take me to Australia with my bike. But, as I had discovered when I'd been in search of a ship to take me from home to New Zealand, things aren't like the good old days when you could just turn up at any port and work your passage. Unions, insurance, the ease at which people will sue, not to mention the fewer ships there are with the exponential increase of airlines, mean that it's a struggle now to find any captain who will gladly have you on board. Even if you're not fussy with your destination and don't mind which country you end up in, it's still not easy. For days I kept being greeted by lots of shaking heads and people rubbing their chins telling me that there was no way I would find a boat to take me to Australia any more – not when it's so cheap to fly and everyone now goes by plane.

Consistent pestering has its uses and after persistent talking and asking, someone gave me a number of someone they thought could help, and then that person gave me a number of someone else who they thought could help more than they could, and so on until finally I ended up here in Papamoa waiting to cycle up the road to the port in Tauranga where I'm supposed to be scooped up by the *Direct Kestrel*, a container ship to sail me to Melbourne.

Only trouble is the *Direct Kestrel* seems to be more like an *Indirect Kestrel*, as it was supposed to have picked me up about three weeks ago, but owing to a massive shortage of labour in ports up and down the west coast of America (Los Angeles, for instance, has taken on an extra 3,000 workers but that's still not enough to clear the backlog of cargo) my lift is now running well behind schedule. That, though, is the fun of travelling by boat. It's a hit and miss affair which only adds to the enjoyable uncertainty of it all. And if the *Direct Kestrel* had left Tauranga on time, I would never have seen the pod of five pilot whales heading south past my tent door this morning at dawn.

There again, if the *Direct Kestrel* had left on schedule I would now have a knee that works. As it is, I'm hobbling again. This is because the beach I'm camping on is an infinity of crisp and powder-crumb sand a good 20 km in length. While I've been waiting for the boat, never knowing whether it's going to be today or tomorrow or the day after, I've been walking about fifteen miles a day along it from the Maketu area in the east up to Mount Maunganui in the west. The trouble is people like walking their dogs on this beach. And the trouble with dogs is that they seem to be able to smell a bicycle on me a mile off even though my bike is nowhere to be seen. It was one of these dogs, a snarling brute the size of a small horse, that came charging towards me at full pelt bearing its fangs. So in order not to take the impact full frontal when it inevitably crashed into me, I swivelled at the hips to receive it broadside, but in doing so something went crack in my right knee and I've hardly been able to put any weight on it since.

That's the woeful news. On the happier side of things, I've got to be up at 5.30 tomorrow morning to pack up the tent and to cycle one-leggedly up to the port, as the *Indirect Kestrel* is on board for heading directly for Tauranga.

Somewhere in the middle of the Tasman Sea in a Force 10 gale, 7 October

New Zealand summertime began last Monday. Not that you would have known it. After days of camping on the beach in the sun, the morning that the clocks went forward an hour to recognise summer officially was the morning that a ferocious storm with tearing winds and torrential rain that caused flooding within moments threw itself upon Tauranga and my tussling attempts to dismantle my tent without being blown halfway across the Pacific. With a pain in my knee that felt as if a knife was being twisted deep under my kneecap, I rode through the storm to the port where I dodged among the container trucks and straddle-carriers rushing about the dockside like headless chickens.

The *Direct Kestrel* is a large 18,000 tonne lump of battleship-grey metal with a few incongruous primrose yellow bits for good measure. As with most container ships these days, the *Direct Kestrel* is a hotchpotch of nationalities. It was built in China at the end of the nineties, is registered in Monrovia, flies the flag of Liberia, is owned by the Germans and chartered by an English company based in Ipswich. Although the captain is called Norman, he answers to the name Ben, was born just north of Liverpool in Southport, but is of New Zealand nationality. He doesn't sound like a Kiwi, though. More like Eric Morecambe – and behaves like him too. A definite comedian. I keep imagining he's going to be caught on stage when the curtains close and grabbed from behind by an exasperated Ernie. He also has a whole vocabulary of words I've never heard before. Mutton birds, which are also known as salty shearwaters, he calls shit-hawks. Motor launches that many a Kiwi buzz around their shores on, he calls stinkpots or Tupperware fizz boats. As for yachties, he calls them WAFFIES – Wind Assisted Fuckwits.

The chief engineer, Arne Hinz, is from Germany, though he now lives in Nelson in the South Island. The rest of the twenty-one-strong crew is either Filipino or Kiribati with fantastic names like Bakoauea Timwemwe, Buenaventu Saluta, Nomeriano Liwag, Tiotaake Tiote and Toaitaake Tarakai.

There are four other passengers on board, all hovering some-where in the hinterland of their sixties. Angela, originally from Buckinghamshire (and she even lived in Guildford for a while), now lives in Australia with Ed. Ed, born in Shanghai, was interned in China during the war. When he was eleven he moved with his family to America. For twenty years he worked for the Bank of America in Hong Kong (where he met Angela). It gets a bit com-plicated but Ed's previous wife was Angela's best friend, but then she died and he married Angela. Ed doesn't have Australian citi-zenship so the maximum amount of time he can spend at their home in Newcastle, just north of Sydney, is three months. 'The rest of the year,' said Ed, 'we follow the sun around the world.' Ed's favoured ship wear seems to be an LL Bean sweatshirt, whereas Angela is wandering about in flip-flops and three-quarter-length trousers, pale blonde hair harnessed beneath a headscarf. They both joined the ship in Los Angeles after visiting family in California.

The other couple, David and Diana, are originally from London but have, as David puts it rather sinisterly, 'west-country connections'. David is a chemist ('not pharmacist,' he said very definitely) and he and Diana lived in Holland for ten years before moving to New Zealand, where they've lived mostly in Auckland for the past thirty years. And gone nowhere. 'That's because David hates travelling,' Diana told me. 'He never wants to go anywhere. But I would love to. I tell you, when I'm a widow, I'm off!' They now live out in the wilds of the wopwops in the north of the Coromandel Peninsula. Seems I cycled right past their door back in January. They're off to Australia for the first time ever to visit their son and his young children in Melbourne.

Despite having lived for so long in New Zealand, David still speaks like a rather well-to-do Englishman. He's a big talker with a no-messing attitude and a very dismissive opinion of Blighty. 'The British are lazy people,' he said. 'And dirty. And there are far too many Pakistanis, blacks and Welsh. In New Zealand I like the entrepreneurism – the "can-do" mentality of the place.'

Seems he doesn't have much to do with the Maoris either. One of his stories was about how he was once almost struck by lightning when out clipping the hedge at home on the Coromandel: the bolt threw him off the ladder and put out the water pump and phone, but not the computer. Diana said she heard a big bang and flash and as she couldn't see David when she looked out of the window she presumed he was dead, so went to her cupboard to get out her black funeral dress (which I told her I thought was a bit premature). David thought someone had taken a pot shot at him with a shotgun. 'There're a lot of marijuana fields around where we live,' he said by way of explanation, 'owned by Maoris. If you see one of "The Growers" crossing your land you turn your head and look the other way. If you ignore them, they ignore you. No, we don't mix with the Maori. If we pass them in town we say good morning or hello. But we don't socialise.'

David has a full set of charts of our intended route across the Tasman so he can do his own course plottings ('He likes to be in control,' Diana said to me on the quiet) and he strides about the bridge in jeans and deck shoes and a sort of Musto sailing jacket. 'We didn't know the sea existed until we got to Auckland,' he told me. Since then they have had their own motor launch and been part-time coastguard radio operators as well as being on the call-out team. One time they took their boat out to Waiheke Island to pick up a woman in labour and transport her to a hospital in Auckland. 'We hoped she wasn't going to give birth on board,' said Diana, 'but she held her breath.' They've been called out on all sorts of missions, from unmangling the hand of a child who had got his fingers caught in a winch, to helping comb stretches of sea searching for wreckage of a suspected plane crash.

'People will call up the coastguard for anything,' David told me. 'One time a man on a yacht just wanted to know what day it was. Another person rang up in a fraught state and said, "Someone's stolen our parrot!" They kept a parrot on their boat but whenever they reached an island they would release the parrot so it could get some exercise. It turned out someone on the island had spotted it and, thinking it lost, rescued it. Then there was the time we had a call from a man moored off Little Barrier Island who told us that the only creek where you could get fresh drinking water had a dead cow lying in it. So we spent five hours trying to contact the only farmer on the island (there were no telephones on the island) to tell him to remove his dead cow from the creek.'

The trouble with David is that, along with his interesting stories, he also launches into long-winded jokes or tales. Every mealtime so far all conversation has been put on hold for a good five to ten minutes while he rambles away on one of his stories. As soon as he starts on one, Captain Ben catches my eye and looks heavenwards (there's no hierarchy on this ship – we all mingle with the crew) and I say, 'Oh no – you're losing me already!' Last night's story revolved around a man falling off a balcony, angels, the pearly gates of hell and being found naked in a freezer. Apart from that I lost the gist. I did keep up with another of his stories, which was surprisingly short for David and went something like this: An old boy was lying in bed in hospital, a visitor sitting beside him in a chair, when a nurse came in to give the old boy two pills. The visitor asked what the two pills were for. 'The first pill is to help him sleep,' said the nurse, 'and the second pill is Viagra so he doesn't roll out of bed.'

Soon after I joined the ship my bike was swung on board by crane and I tethered it securely to the floor in my cabin. Just as well I did, as the weather from the start has not been promising. On my visit up to the bridge Captain Ben handed me the weather fax that showed we would have storms and winds against us all the way. He said the time of our arrival in Melbourne depended on how many 'pot holes' we fell into on the way. Captain Ben has been at sea since he was sixteen. During this time he has seen his fair share of storms. In one storm in the Atlantic he saw a man washed off the bow before being washed back on board further down the ship by another wave. 'He went straight out and bought a lottery ticket after that!' said Ben.

Things are not looking so good for us at the moment. After leaving Tauranga we plunged straight into a Force 9 storm. This felt bad enough with the ship slamming into the waves before sagging and staggering through the troughs. (Although I wasn't seasick once during the two-month voyage to New Zealand on the ex-Russian ice-breaker, I've been badly ill on board the *Kestrel* and have lost 4 kilos in as many days – this boat travel lark is a good diet if nothing else.) But now, out in the middle of the Tasman, one of the stormiest stretches of sea in the world, we're being hit by depression after depression and are currently in the middle of a Force 10 (classified on the Beaufort Scale as a 'whole gale') with winds of over 100 km/h. Thirty-foot waves are charging at the bow, though a few rogue ones are taking us from the sides. The ship is hogging over the crests, surfing down the watery slopes, sending masses of water boiling across the deck – which, among other things, has ripped the fire hoses from the side decks, never to be seen again. Even from the height of the bridge, the waves look alpine. Water is also reportedly getting into the holds. Bilges are working full pelt. The great patches of foam from the waves' long overhanging crests is being blown in dense white streaks along the direction of the wind, transforming the surface of the sea as far the eye can see (which is not far as visibility is severely affected) into an appearance of angrily frothy white. The tumbling of the sea is heavy and shock-locked. We are rolling and pitching violently. Everywhere there is the crash of falling objects.

I've heaved my way up the severely angled staircase to the bridge – not easy at the best of times, but painfully ridiculous with a knackered knee. The captain is up here with the chief officer and the chief engineer. None of them looks happy. The *Kestrel* has been slowed to its minimum manoeuvring speed (6½ knots) in an attempt to ease the ship's motion at the cost of delay. Tonight will be our fourth night of storms. Last night we were under attack from a vicious electrical tempest with forked lightning exploding all around. Outside the heavy bridge doors the wind is yowling like a million strangled cats, the rain pelting down like there was no tomorrow. Though I'm hoping there will be.

Captain Ben has told me it is what the wind does to the waves that is the worry. This reminds me of one of the books I read on the ship to New Zealand. I still have the bit that I copied into my diary from John Rousmaniere's *After the Storm* where he says:

> The sea itself usually shoots the fatal bullet, not the wind. 'The waves, not the wind,' sailors say of the worst risks. Because a cubic foot of seawater weighs sixty-four pounds, the power of even a moderate-sized ten-foot breaking wave flying at twenty knots is enormous. Waves are sledgehammers, and they are also sandbags. What they don't destroy, they fill and sink. As boats are pressed lower, they become less stable. Eventually they may capsize.

There is rumour that if this keeps up we could roll, which is a bit more excitement than I bargained for. I've long wanted to cross the Tasman Sea by ship, but I can't say I've ever been so keen that I've wanted to swim it.

Captain Ben, who is usually so jovial, is clinging to the rail (like we all are – the bridge is acting like a roller coaster) and staring out of the water-drenched windows at the walls of sea with a face deeply scored with anxiety and dread. It's not a good face to see on a captain. He tells me this is the worst storm he's ever seen. It seems we are being bombarded by two major depressions, and the back of one is behaving more like it should at the front. The thought that this is the worst storm the captain has ever seen in over forty years at sea has turned my stomach into a knot of mild fear. I want to hear some words of reassurance from the captain like, 'Oh, I've seen seas like this a hundred times. We'll get through this fine!' Instead he's muttering how unusual this storm is. When I joke by saying that at least he could treat the abnormality of it as an unusual maritime challenge, a faint trace of a smile lifts the corner of his mouth.

'That's one way of looking at it,' he says. 'But let's just say I'd rather not be here.'

And the knot in my stomach tightens another notch.

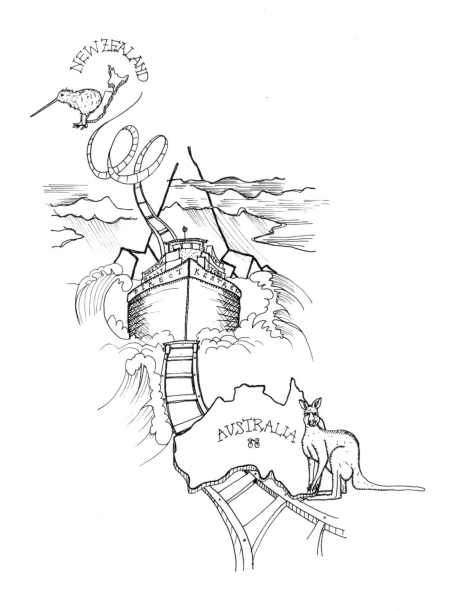

Appendix

Equipment Department

Bicycle

Frame	Custom-made 16" Roberts (Roughstuff) with custom Columbus Nivacrom tubing
Rims	Mavic D521 (36 H)
Hubs	Shimano Deore XT (36 H)
Spokes	DT double-butted stainless steel
Rim tape	Velox
Tyres	Continental Top Touring 26 × 1.75
Tubes	Specialized 26 × 1.5–2.2 (schrader)
Headset	Stronglight Headlight 1⅛
Stem	Alloy A-Head Uplift
Handlebars	Forma (TTT)
Handlebar tape	Cinelli cork with Marsas foam padding
Chainset	TA Zephyr 150 mm (with TA 6 mm self-extracting bolts)
Chainrings	TA 20/34/40
Chain	Sachs PC68
Bottom bracket	Shimano XT UN72
Front mech	Shimano RX100
Rear mech	Shimano XT
Cassette	Shimano XT (11-34)
Gear Levers	Shimano Dura Ace (downtube)
Brake Levers	Campagnolo Super Record (with Campag hoods)

Brakes	Shimano Deore XT Cantilever
Brake blocks	Shimano Deore XT
Pedals	TA Road Pedal
Seat post	Tranz X (alloy micro-adjust)
Saddle	Selle Italia trans am ldy
Racks	Tubus (seamless cromoly tubing). Front: Tara lowrider. Rear: Cargo
Water bottle cages	3 × Elite
Mudguards	SKS Chromo Plastics
Toe clips	Christophe, steel with leather toe protection
Toe Straps	Mt Christophe
Computer	Speedmaster 7000
Bike lights	Front: Busch & Muller Lumotec Plus dynamo Rear: Vistalite and Cateye (LED)
Bike stand	Esge Pletcher (double leg kick stand)
Mirrors	2 × Mirrycles (attach to top of brake hoods)

Panniers

Rear	Ortlieb Bike-Packer Plus (with additional outer pockets)
Front	Ortlieb Sport-Packer Plus (with additional outer pockets)
Handlebar bag	Ortlieb Ultimate 3 L Plus (with map case and inner pocket)
Rack packs	2 × Ortlieb roll-closure (size small) (All Ortlieb bags are completely waterproof but I still put most of pannier contents in plastic bags in plastic bags because I can't seem to grow out of the habit)

Sleeping Arrangements

Tent	The North Face Tadpole. (With Gary, used The North Face Nebula.) The Tadpole stood up to New Zealand's unreasonably unseasonable winds a treat, but is a very cold

and breezy tent in winter. Also, after several months continuous use in continuous rain, it started to leak in places, which I suppose is quite understandable considering the testing conditions

Pegs	The North Face Super Tent Peg plus a small aluminium sleeve (in case of pole breakage)
Groundsheet	The North Face Footprint
Bivi bag	Mountain Range Gore-tex. (On cold nights I slept in my inner sleeping bag in my sleeping bag in my bivi bag. And I was still cold)
Sleeping bag	The North Face Blue Igloo. (Multiple-feathered luxury)
Silk sleeping bag	Sea to Summit (Traveller)
Sleeping mat	Karrimor Karrimat Expedition, ¾-length

Kitchen Department

Stove: MSR Superfly (canister mount). (Very handy, very efficient)

Gas canister

Saucepan: MSR Alpine 2-litre pot with detachable handle. (Eat everything out of here whether cooked or uncooked)

Mixture of plastic containers

Mini chopping board

Plastic mug

Sharp knife, vegetable peeler, spoon

Lighter

Mini pot scourer and small square of tea towel

3 × water bottles to fit bicycle frame-mounted water cages

4-litre Ortlieb water bag

Plastic bags – lots

Food – have always got porridge oats, honey and raisins on board

Clothing

Specialized S1 bike helmet

Freestyle Gore-tex helmet cover (keeps head warmer)

The North Face Gore-tex jacket and overtrousers

The North Face windproof gillet
The North Face lightweight windproof jacket
North Cape Thermolite Plus padded sleeveless top
The North Face fleece
Two The North Face long-sleeved shirts
Two The North Face T-shirts
Two The North Face vests
Two pairs (wear one, wash one) Corinne Dennis non-lycra-
    looking cycling shorts
Pair of The North Face zip-off-to-shorts convertible trousers
Pair of ¾-length The North Face leggings
Pair of full-length thermal leggings
Pair of cycling mitts
Pair of The North Face Windstopper gloves
Pair of Extremities Gore-tex overmitts
Fleece hat
The North Face baseball cap
Pair of Eager Clothing Overshoes
Buff neck gaiter
Pair of The North Face hill-walking shoes (used for everything)
Pair of cheap flip-flops
Three pairs of knickers
Two sports bras
Three pairs of socks
Speedo swimming costume
Pair of Speedo swimming goggles

Washbag/First Aid and other essentially non-essential paraphernalia
Mini fast-drying travel towel
Lightweight washbag filled with toothbrush, toothpaste, dental
    floss, shampoo, soap, bodily ungents etc.
Mini flannel
Stash of toilet paper
Lipsalve
Sun-block lotion (which blocked the sun a little too effectively – I
    mostly saw rain)

Tiger Balm (good for aching muscles, sticking sandflies to and making your eyes water)

Arnica homeopathic pills and potion

Small bottle tea tree essential oil (good antiseptic)

Small bottle lavender oil (good for anything from burns and insect bites to soporific pillow aromas)

Pair of washable foam earplugs (good for those moments when you find yourself camping beneath a tree full of fighting and hissing possums)

Eyeshade (good for those moments when you find yourself camping beneath a streetlight or sleeping on the floor of a ferry)

Small selection of plasters, safety pins, needles and extra strong thread (good for sticking bits of clothes, tent and body back together again)

Mini Swiss Army tweezers (good for extracting sharp thorns and undesirable spiky objects out of tyres)

Mini mirror (good for starting fires and hoiking airborne insects out of eyes), mini nail clippers and clothes pegs

Office: pen, pencil, half a rubber, mini Pritt Stick, mini Sellotape, writing paper, envelopes, small notebook, Oxford Mini dictionary (good for reading when nothing else available and for reminding me how to spell)

Mini address book

Book(s) and maps. Best maps I used were the full set of New Zealand AA (Automobile Association) district maps scale 1:350 000. Best cycle touring guide books are the lightweight but information heavy *Pedallers' Paradise* by Nigel Rushton (very fun, very informative but detail a few too many mountainous contours for comfort)

Mini compass, mini thermometer

Leatherman Wave pocket knife with very useful pliers

Wallet, cash, credit card, debit card, American Express traveller's cheques, US dollars (the US dollars are good for using when I find myself in a country that I don't expect to be in)

Passport, driving licence, mobile phone, Dog Dazer (good for teaching bicycle-chasing dogs a lesson)

Petzl LED headtorch
Sunglasses
Mini Sony shortwave radio
Casio digital watch
Very old Cannon Sureshot camera
Even older Cannon AE1 Programme (SLR) camera with Tamron
    70-210 lens
Mini Minox tripod
20 × Fujichrome Sensia 200 ASA slide film (36 exps)
Leica 8 × 20 BCA mini binoculars
The North Face bumbag
The North Face backpack

Bicycle Tools and Bicycle Bits
Two spare inner tubes, plastic tyre levers, patches and glue
Spare spokes, brake and gear cables
Allen keys, lightweight pedal spanner, mini adjustable spanner,
    chainlink tool, Shimano cassette remover tool, spoke key, few
    spare nuts, allen bolts, washers, zip ties, webbing, pannier clips
Gaffer tape, insulating tape, short length 4 mm rock-climbing
    cord
Oil, rag
Topeak Road Morph bicycle pump
Bungees (or 'sriiitcheees' in local Kiwi lingo)
Cable lock and padlock
Cheap bike cover (good for hiding bike from bicycle-thieving
    eyes)
Reflective vest (good for life preservation)

*For the latest news about Josie's travels and
information on all her books,
please visit her website at:*

www.josiedew.co.uk